THE
ENGLISH WAY

Pierre Maillaud

THE
ENGLISH WAY

Humphrey Milford
OXFORD UNIVERSITY PRESS
London   New York   Toronto

OXFORD UNIVERSITY PRESS
AMEN HOUSE, E.C. 4
London Edinburgh Glasgow New York
Toronto Melbourne Capetown Bombay
Calcutta Madras

HUMPHREY MILFORD
Publisher to the University

First published July 1945
Reprinted October 1945

Printed in Great Britain
1544.6302

CONTENTS

VII. THE CHURCH

VIII. ENGLAND AT WAR

THIS is the book of a Frenchman who has lived in England for over fourteen years. When he came here he knew no English save such shreds as survive from school lessons in foreign languages. But this book—so deeply has he imbued himself in our language as well as in our ways—has been written by him in English. His Frenchness, I am glad to say, has not been attenuated, and a principal merit of his book is the characteristically French realism with which he faces problems that the English prefer to elude—the difficulty, for instance, of reconciling liberty with equality.

To his own countrymen he is known, under the *nom de guerre* of Pierre Bourdan, as one of the chief prophets of resistance. From the calamitous June of 1940 onwards he spoke five times a week on the French service of the B.B.C., commenting upon the news with a singular mixture of emotional fervour and intellectual integrity. Some day a book must be written, and a film produced, on the *Equipe de la B.B.C.*, the men who under the rubric *Les Français parlent aux Français* communicated their own confidence to all but a small minority of their compatriots. Their work, which sprang from a happy collaboration between Frenchmen of very various professions and opinions, is likely to rank as a classic of propaganda in the best sense of the word. All accounts I have received from France agree that these broadcasts were of superlative value in maintaining hope and resistance. With Jacques Duchesne at their head this little band of patriots performed a service that can hardly be exaggerated. Bombs canopied London in flame and smoke, the Germans reached the outskirts of Moscow, the frontiers of Egypt; and *les trois amis*—Duchesne, Jean Oberlé and the author of this book—continued each week to discuss the hideous situation with confidence and humour. Even those of us in England who listened found our spirits improved by their gaiety. It was like eavesdropping in a French *café*; and we guessed, rightly as it has proved, that behind the silence imposed by the Germans the French in France were maintaining the same hopefulness and spirit. Pierre Maillaud I place among the best broadcasters

I have heard, whether in these dialogues or in his commentaries. His voice is expressive, at moments profoundly moving, at others lethally mordant. (It was no surprise to learn that for a short time he headed a theatrical company of young enthusiasts who toured France playing medieval farces.) But it was the intellectual vigour of his broadcasts that always principally impressed me. They had no English equivalent. He was convincing to others, because he was himself convinced. And the act of faith in this country made by so realistic a Frenchman I take to be an extraordinary tribute to English character and institutions. He says that he believed in us, because he knew us. It is ironical that several of the Frenchmen who made a profession—I would even say a career—of knowing England were distinguished by their lack of belief. (To the names of Abel Hermant and Paul Morand must be added, most lamentably, that of André Maurois.) It may be argued in their excuse that these knew chiefly the England of MacDonald, Baldwin, and Chamberlain, an England feeble and irresolute alike in foreign and home affairs. How could an England that had watched with apathy the crippling of its productivity by mass unemployment and then the menace to its liberty so candidly announced in *Mein Kampf*, how could such an England be expected to stand alone against the overwhelming superiority of the Germans? I doubt if many of us even now realize how desperate was our situation in June 1940. To believe, against all evidence, in one's own country is not very difficult. To believe similarly in another country requires a prodigious act of faith. Pierre Maillaud was capable of this, because he knew not only Westminster, Mayfair and Fleet Street, but the suburbs, the provincial cities and the countryside. What he had learnt, what he has continued to learn, will be found in this book.

One point he makes which we English have usually preferred to overlook, with that distaste for facing uncomfortable facts which is a national characteristic. The feebleness of our foreign policy before the war was largely due to the necessity of gaining for it the agreement of the Dominions; and these Dominions knew little of Europe. It is significant that Field-Marshal Smuts recently spoke of France with open contempt, all the more significant because he is the representative of the Dominion in which racial inequality is openly applauded. No Englishman is likely to underrate the sacrifices made by the Dominions in the common cause; but many of us feel, though we rarely express, alarm at the possibility of England, once the war is won, being again drawn out of the European orbit by the gravitational force of the British Commonwealth.

The reasons for which Pierre Maillaud principally admires the English will be distasteful to the bigots alike of the Right and Left. He is distrustful of planning, and denounces the danger to the individual of 'anonymous power'. He sees Parliament controlled by the rival forces of organized capital and organized labour. He deplores the dwindling of the Liberal party, judging, I think rightly, that most Englishmen remain at heart Liberals, but he hardly allows enough for the English feeling that parliamentary government depends for its efficiency upon a two-party system. His analysis of the reasons for the weakness of our policy between the wars seems to me the clearest and most trenchant that has yet appeared.

Pierre Maillaud comes from old Protestant stock, which has helped him to his acute understanding of us islanders. French Protestants, like English Catholics, are particularly aware of Europe as a whole. But I fancy that he underrates the preoccupation of Catholics with political and social problems. When for instance he teases Anglican prelates for their concern with banking, he seems to forget the signal importance attached by Catholic theologians and casuists to the sin of usury. I have been surprised moreover to find so little in his book about the intellectual life of England, for unlike many writers on politics he is a profoundly cultivated man. (When writing a study of Mallarmé I found his advice invaluable.) But the sad truth is that the influence of intellectuals has been smaller in England during the last twenty-five years than ever before in our history.

If the values of Western Europe are to survive, the closest friendship between England and France is necessary. Pierre Maillaud justly emphasizes the demographic situation of the two countries. In population even when we include the Dominions we cannot compare with the Germans, much less with our gallant Allies, the U.S.A. and the U.S.S.R., whose traditions and history are so different from our own. Unless England and France can join hands and then gain the sympathy of their even smaller neighbours in Scandinavia and the Low Countries, each will dwindle into a satellite upon one of the more multitudinous powers. Like M. Maillaud I believe the difference between the English and the French to be much more superficial than their similarities. I hope for a great increase in interchanges between our two peoples, because I have noticed that deeper reciprocal knowledge between them almost always makes for warmer liking. Some of us English who enjoyed the privilege of knowing France well have never ceased to express our confidence in her revival. And this book is similarly the fruit of a liking based upon knowledge. I cannot too vehemently recommend it to readers on both sides of the Channel.

RAYMOND MORTIMER

1944

I. A PILGRIM'S PROGRESS

CHAPTER I

ON ENGLISH ROADS

LOOKING back on the years which I have spent in England I find that my first friends were the roads. On them and through them I learned much about this country, perhaps because I learned it fondly. To-day, were I asked to single out one feature of this island as most suggestive of its mood and atmosphere, I would, I believe, choose its roads rather than its seaports, its industrial cities, its pageants or its laws.

Roads in an island are not connecting links with the outside world. They have a purely national purpose and can therefore truly express local inclinations and ways of life. And England is one of the last countries of Western Europe where they show some regard for the permanent values of the land.

English roads seldom attempt to coerce nature but prefer to follow its pattern. They do not mean, it seems, to carry the wayfarer from one point to another without allowing for his fancy and his sense of leisure in a world of speed-worship. Occasionally they slow down his pace and compel him to linger or pause altogether. Confronted with the Gordian knot of a town, they do not cut it but either submit to its caprices or else by-pass it. The busy traveller can swerve by the city; others may accept its invitation and linger through streets and market place. They may well evoke with G. K. Chesterton's Dorian Wimpole the early history of English roads:

> Before the Roman came to Rye or out to Severn strode,
> The rolling English drunkard made the rolling English road.
> A reeling road, a rolling road, that rambles round the shire,
> And after him the parson ran, the sexton and the squire;
> A merry road, a mazy road, and such as we did tread
> The night we went to Birmingham by way of Beachy Head.

Positive minds will no doubt explain in some practical way the singular quality of English roads. They will say that roads have to wind round because they cannot run across private grounds and estates, that their width and character vary with each parish or borough, because they are by tradition a local and not a national responsibility; and that by-passes have been built for want of more sweeping reforms in English topography. As against Wimpole's romantic version they would set Mr. Pump's prosaic reminder that:

> *The road turned first towards the left*
> *Where Pinker's quarry made the cleft;*
> *The path turned next towards the right,*
> *Because the mastiff used to bite.*

Yet even this further bears out my contention that English roads have much to teach: for it shows a tendency to tolerate local dispositions rather than impose uniformity, to correct rather than revolutionize, to offer alternative means rather than to dictate a single solution.

Whether or not more drastic methods would serve the general economy better, is beside the point. I, for one, would watch with sorrow the spreading over this country of a perfect net-work of straight highways crossing each other at right angles, cutting across hill, dale, plain, and city, from east to west and from north to south, where discreet lanes once followed the varying pleasure of the land, revealed an unexpected village, shared in the fragrance of a wood, unfolded a broad horizon.

Before the present war it was still possible, with a good map of roads, lanes, and bridle paths to travel on horseback through parts of England and find daily accommodation for rider and mount. In the summer of 1938 I spent a fortnight visiting in that way, after I had tried many others, Surrey, Sussex and Hampshire; for a long time to come there would be little chance of renewing the experience; and it was indeed well worth the attempt.

Although the great advantage of that sort of journey is that one can vary one's pace and thus break the monotony inherent in a journey on foot, one sees as much as the pedestrian tourist and more. Besides, each way of travelling shows things and people from a different angle, discloses a different aspect of the world. The train passenger, the motorist, the walker, all have a vision of men and country to some extent governed by their means of transport, and their range of experience contrasts accordingly. A motor trip displays an England of filling-stations, main roads, parking places, road-houses, mechanics, garage hands, modern or modernized hotels, American bars and police-men. A riding tour offers an England of bridlepaths, under-wood alleys, stone troughs, farms, stable inns, cobbled yards and village blacksmiths. It is, in a way, a retrospect. It is also a larger and more detailed spectacle, one seen in 'close up' and 'slow motion'.

The ideal approach to any modern nation should probably be the very opposite of that usually adopted by the visitor: instead of beginning with the capital and leaving the country to be explored later, he should retrace the progress of history and advance by stages from the hamlet to the city. London, the outcome of a long evolution, would thus become far more intel-ligible than it is at first sight without its English context.

Short of such an approach which is barely possible, a leisurely journey on foot or on horseback is a pleasant complement to one's previous and inevitably scattered acquaintance with a country. It seems to add a few links, if only emotional ones, to the chain. In 1938 I had already trodden more English roads than I could remember. I was following a familiar trail. Yet there was this time, everywhere, a new and a far greater sense of intimacy with my surroundings than I had ever known and one which seemed to spread from them to all that was left behind or lived beyond.

In spite of tar and traffic, the roads to which I took when there was no practicable track across country had gained a depth and richness which completely renewed them. A house, a hamlet which before had been hastily glimpsed on a fleeting scene were brought into relief with a meaning of their own. Fast travel destroys the reality of things. Distance is a sentimental notion and it is a matter of time rather than mileage. The village of which we catch a glance after an hour's drive from London can only be as lifeless as a film reel. It is too near in thought to be a little realm of its own. After two days' riding the same village resumes its true significance, atmosphere and destiny.

There were, I found, more years than miles between London and any town that I discovered in that way although the dwellers in both might enjoy the common privilege of an easy access to the same make of car, safety razor or wireless set. It was

a far call from a London foreman to the blacksmith at Wisbor-
ough Green who worked for an hour on a second-hand horseshoe
to save me the purchase of a new one and sacrificed a good personal profit into the bargain. Yet town and capital, village
artisan and factory foreman were parts of a whole scheme of
things, variations in time and space on the same English theme.
The slow pulse of a cluster of houses gave a more precise meaning to the vast murmur of London, the blacksmith's hammer to
the machine-tool controlled by the foreman.

The road that led to London might well be swerving and
crooked: it was truer to life thus than an *autostrada*. For thus it
authentically reflected the human pilgrimage. From a mere
track it had grown to a highway but still one which retained,
as England does, as London itself does, the memories of its
successive transformations, the marks of its history.

Perhaps because of threatening events I appreciated during
that trip more than ever before that quality which I have found
elsewhere only in France and Northern Italy, irrespective of
climate and colours, a *douceur de vivre* which is the patient
product of a temperate land polished by a temperate civilization. And, perhaps also for the same reason, I often evoked by
contrast my first impressions of this country which must have
been those of many fellowcountrymen before and after me in
the days that follow their landing.

Two images stood out in my memory: the cliffs of Dover and
London—the former with their stately melancholy rise from the
sea like a symbol of exile to the immigrant, the latter at first
disconcerting and depressing. In between, there had been the
business of landing, the series of examinations from which the
timid stranger emerges in the frame of mind of a pupil whose
admission to the school is due to the leniency of the master, and
then the train journey through fields of wintry greenness.

I know of no city where one at once feels more marooned
than in London, without guidance in any very precise direction. At its best London is like the magician's bowl of enchanted
water where the eye perceives nothing for a while and then discovers shapes, meanings, figures and sense. He who has never
been there and remembers other European capitals looks for the
attributes of history which do not conspicuously assert themselves in London. Lost in a maze of darkened brick and stone,
of roads which run like capricious streams and often wind into

whirlpools without apparent outlet, he wonders all the time whether he is being driven along a side-street or a main artery, covers miles without feeling that he has crossed the centre of a city which has none, or located its heart. He vaguely expects the places of renown of which he has heard to be ushered into view by broad avenues or set by the architect in a favourable perspective. Lost in what strikes him as uniform greyness he experiences a type of nostalgia which is rather akin to sulkiness. The secrecy of London, the rewards which it offers to the strol-ler, these are as yet parts of a riddle which baffles his efforts at orientation, shocks his traditional conception of town plan-ning and adds to his sensation of solitude one of growing meaninglessness.

Such at least were my first impressions in February 1932. I saw a huge city without a distinct shape, almost ostenta-tiously unplanned, which would have to be painfully deciphered, streets with mysterious currents of traffic and above all kerbs on which nobody seemed to loiter as do those who enjoy their capital for its own sake when neither work nor other obligation gives a definite purpose to their steps.

Occasionally I may have been impressed by signs of imperial power and far-flung interests which arrest the attention and carry the visitor without transition from province to empire. Yet those merely made London more difficult to grasp as an individual city, underlined its dispersion and looseness. Elsewhere the traveller often feels overcrowded with novelty, oppressed under an unduly heavy atmosphere. I experienced here an opposite phenomenon: an excess of independence, of elbow-room, of no-man's-land. Contact with things and people, communication with the new milieu, retain for some time a somewhat eerie character. Then to try and force the pace is futile as well as imprudent. The over-earnest novice arouses in most quarters a sentiment rather like that of a hostess who fears for the safety of her silver.

For weeks and probably months my feelings remained those of a spectator, indifferent at first and then more and more attentive. London specializes in hiding the best of itself. It may discourage the sightseeing tourist who carries a 6 x 20 film in his pocket instead of a retina in his eye, for those who like it do not like it skin-deep. They become fond of it because its con-quest is a love's labour, because its stones, too well 'besmeared with sluttish time', have begun to whisper what sounds to the listener like a personal message or else is never heard. One day I simply ceased to wonder whether London was beautiful or not as a whole. It held me by so many singular qualities and by such endearing details that I gave up all orthodox views of a capital as an orderly synthesis of architectural genius.

In each of London's districts, or rather little towns joined together haphazard, different in habits, ways of living, rhythm, colour, stones, I found inviting the loiterer or the star gazer, a retreat for an individualism menaced the world over by urban as well as moral uniformity. A square, a churchyard, an inn, the line of a tree in a backyard, the sweep of a side-street discovered by chance, all these are still valued for themselves in London. They may not embrace many of the accepted prides of a great city but they tell how men have grown with their town, how it has come to be what it is now. If ever London should be strewn with Dorchester Hotels, it would not acquire the architectural cohesion that it lacks, but lose its true originality which lies in its unexpectedness, in its tolerance, in its indulgence towards little things and little privacies.

It is those that make London grow on the stranger. By a paradox of its own the same capital which strikes the newcomer as uninviting, unseizable, and, so to speak, unlived in, later endears itself to him by its intimacy, by its appeal to his fancy; intimacy and not promiscuity. London is the least promiscuous of all European capitals. It even lacks characteristic scents and smells, and has shades rather than colours. Those who can only respond to an atmosphere which challenges or stimulates the senses will never see London smile. It will remain an alien city.

London's company is discreet. Its contact is one of mood and almost imperceptible feelings. One day it becomes a friendly presence and that is all. It might happen, as was the case with me, in the Inner Temple which deserved more than aesthetic praise, or it might be elsewhere; but from that day onwards the spell is cast. The freedom of the city has been granted.

It is strange that one's fancy could wander in London for a long while without being immediately arrested by its river. Paradoxical though this may sound to an Englishman, the Thames which plays such a great part in the nation's life plays a far smaller one in the everyday life of the Londoner. The river may well be one of his prides, but it is not his intimate friend or his playmate as the Seine is to the Parisian. It is a river for specialists: it is a highway, a workshop, a trade, a power wielded by swarms of toiling Englishmen. It even is, sometimes, as in the lovely stretch of Chiswick Mall recalling A. P. Herbert's *Water Gypsies*, the cradle of a community of its own far remote from the capital in time and atmosphere. But most of its approaches are not truly lived in. Few Londoners cross their river, save by underground. Many of them can spend years without leaning over its parapets. It still is a world apart much as it was two hundred years ago when marshes lay along its southern bank. It still remains enough of an enigma to provide writers of detective stories in the Edgar Wallace vein with an ideal setting for nightly man-hunts and adventures in the convenient shadow of the Tower. Like London itself, the river is not one save geographically; it is multifarious; and each of its aspects must be discovered in turn.

However comprehensive one's knowledge of London may be, there is something which the capital alone will never give unless one has first discovered it in the country: a pleasant and mellow quality to be found in a polished, perhaps over-polished, way in the home counties and farther afield in its genuine expression.

Continental notions of England, apart from its capital, are usually of the vaguest, and amount to little more than names of manufacturing towns, harbours, royal castles and a few places the fame of which dates back to the Wars of the Roses. To this may be added a favourable opinion of English scenery borrowed from romantic Victorian literature. At the time of my arrival my own ignorance was, if anything, well above the Continental average. And my curiosity, which largely made up for it, ran a serious risk of being nipped in the bud when my first trip out of London after two months of residence happened to take me to Birmingham. When I told the Cockney porter of my small hotel to call me early in the morning as I had a train to catch for Birmingham, he looked up and said: 'Birmingham? Eh? Business?'—'No, pleasure,' I answered truthfully. Whereupon he laughed himself out of my room and reminded me a long time afterwards of the day 'when I had cracked my first good joke in English'.

However, this citadel of the Chamberlains did not discourage me from further attempts, but merely postponed by a few years any serious renewal of acquaintance with great industrial centres. Most foreigners and especially Frenchmen have a pre-conceived vision of England as the land of mechanical power, blast furnaces, cotton mills, foundries, steelworks and the like, with somewhere in between a few pictures of a lovely and minute conservative countryside. Once in this country, they unenter-prisingly try to reconcile these two contrasting conceptions and first turn to those towns which are symbols of industrial might, but finding casualness and daily routine where they had anti-cipated a modern inferno of iron and fire, they relinquish further investigation, falling back on Richmond Park and its deer in order to gratify at least one of their conventional expectations.

There is in England, again as in France and nowhere else in the same way, a contentment with life, a quiet humour, which escapes the casual visitor. It emanates from the land and has to be discovered by contact with it. London alone does not reveal it, nor does its immediate neighbourhood. There is an exquisite grace in Hampton Court but it is full of melancholy. What is joyful and bountiful here, although it may run in the veins of townsman and factory worker, can only be communi-cated to the stranger deep in the country and not even, as the tourist believes, on the waterfront of those seaside resorts which are the least English achievement of an insular nation. That there is truer gaiety in a day's punting on the Avon than on any English beach is, perhaps, the greatest surprise which awaits the foreigner. The explanation of British international behaviour may well be the sea which circles about the cliffs of the island. The nation's true self is well inland. If I had any advice to give to a student of this country, one who comes here, as I did, with more than the average idler's interest in it, I should probably say: 'Take to the roads, the lanes, the paths and make no more plans than you strictly need. Feel first and learn afterwards, when you are cured of your prejudices. Fumble your way into England until you like it, for if you do not, you will never under-stand although you may be tempted to judge. Forget for a time that it is a maritime nation until you rediscover this for yourself.'

Here is another characteristic that makes England undeci-pherable to the superficial visitor: she is markedly regionalist and sentimentally decentralized, in the same way as London is decentralized within itself as a capital. 'There is one thing you must always bear in mind if you go to England, although it seems so obvious, one is told on the continent, 'namely that it is an island.' I think this recommendation may be unwise unless it is strongly qualified and elaborated. For it will lead the foreign student to look for her in her seaports, to understand her destiny rather than her tastes, her outward determination rather than her individual nature. He may realize why her sailors, her fishermen, her aristocracy of empire builders, her Indian or African cadres, her body of administrators and diplomatists have been trained to cast their destinies, nets, or thoughts, across the seas, but he will not guess why they invariably return to their mist, their winds, their gardens and their moors, nor why, behind her shores, a far larger population leaves these worldwide pursuits to a handful of men, lives contented within its limited horizon and takes more pride in winning the Cup Final at Wembley than in beating Italy in an international championship. It is that inward trend of English insularity, which coasts and harbours cannot account for, which stamps England as a Western European nation as well as a sea-conscious power, and the traveller only becomes sensible of this if he accepts the capricious invitation of the roads.

From them he must not expect more, of course, than a method of approach. There is no magic key to a country; nor does it lend itself to any single comprehensive explanation. But it can be sensed; and I believe that it can best be sensed from inside, from what are its earliest, most genuine and least evolved features. To find on the hills of Gloucestershire or in the fields of Lincolnshire what Blake called 'the lineaments of gratified desire' may suggest why imperialism in England even at its height, has never grown into a mass psychosis. The paradox of a nation which produces Leeds or Halifax and at the same time educates its scholars in medieval palaces surrounded by silent lawns, is not accounted for by its maritime adventures but perhaps, if at all, by its most parochial attachments and the aptitude of its earth to renew men and retain traditions. So that it may well be less interesting to discover the self-evident reasons why Englishmen have to sail to China or fight in the Sea of Timor than why most of them prefer the roses of their gardens to the map of the world.

I have always known why the French love their land: it is

their work, their sweat and their blood. I have often thought when I drove or walked or rode through England, always aimlessly, that to the English it is their pleasure, their pride, their art, sometimes their philosophy, and all in life that is not part of the daily burden. It is the escape from the factory, the shop and the bank, the return of the yeoman into his own. Without it neither Birmingham nor perhaps Liverpool or Newcastle could indefinitely survive. Because it is an object of constant and fond care as well as a natural gift, that land conveys an impression of civilization.

The German earth, where it is most moving, is haunted by legends. The splendour of Italy is out of time and Spain holds out a threat in its very fascination. In two different ways I felt that the English and the French lands had both kept pace with men: they are ancient and yet they are as alive to-day as they were a thousand years ago. They are friends of the new generations and not ghosts from the past or magnificent illuminations of ancient times. And the best way towards men, which is also the most amiable, seems to lie across the land.

I have recalled a ride through the southern counties in 1938 not merely as a pleasant memory but because there was then in Europe a sense of impending danger which added to it some of the grave charm of a pilgrimage. In fact, although another year elapsed before the omens were fulfilled, it was the last chance I had of loitering, if not of travelling, in England. The country I saw might never be the same again. Familiar as it had then become to me, it invited recollections of days when its people, as well as its aspect, were still a closed book to a newcomer.

CHAPTER 2

MEN AND PREJUDICES

THE Continent in general knows little more of the English than of England although there are more popular fallacies about the people than the land. The picture conjured up by the fairly well educated Continental would present the English as sporting, practical, sparing of words, businesslike, conservative, disciplined, either puritanical or oddly eccentric and melancholy. Such, I think, is or was the sum total of impressions left by a few English tourists and fewer English novels upon most minds. Where there was less tourism and more reading, a poetical or lyrical gift may have been added to this portrait.

From travellers to England who had made a short stay there, one would gather cursory observations like snapshots, varying according to the experiences of the visitor and his circumstances, from boarding-houses, the nightmare of the Continental in England, 'where they give you fish for dessert', to country houses 'which the English alone know how to build'. There were of course the usual references to the cost of living, the quality of English tailoring, the solecisms of English cooking, the exhilaration of fox-hunting, and the 'Greek atmosphere' of Oxford and Cambridge. It is a remarkable thing that a few years ago, with London within two hours of Paris, Brussels or Amsterdam, the well-travelled man on the Continent still spoke of England as Marco Polo did of China at the beginning of the fourteenth century. Indeed, even among the better educated, English culture was making less impression than it had in previous centuries.

To the conventional and current notions was sometimes added the spice of bizarre fancies. One of them was that the Englishman is more prone than anybody else to commit suicide, out of sulkiness or for a whim and not necessarily because of personal disasters. I remember to this day a paragraph that appeared in a newspaper diary some eighteen years ago, reporting that a wealthy Englishman had blown his brains out in an hotel suite and left behind this laconic note: 'Too many buttons

to do and to undo in this life. Let's clear out.' Whether that was
an actual happening or a joke, that queer incident long remained part of my mental equipment on England until I
realized that Englishmen buttoned their coats with rather more
care than other people and that self-immolation was far less
cultivated in this country than such arts of living as racing,
cricket or shove ha'penny. Trite or odd prejudices will cross the
Channel with the novice, whether he believes with the Pro-
vençal navvy that 'the English are all raw steak and check
plus-fours' or romantically expects to find a Chatterton in his
compartment on the boat-train from Dover to London.

I suppose that the most flattering beginning, when recording
first impressions to a people at home, should be some such sentence as: 'What struck me at once about them was the fact
that . . .': but the truth is that nothing struck me at all except
my utter inability to make myself understood in a language
with which I had some previous, albeit superficial, acquaintance.

The nation prides itself on being unostentatious in appearance, habits, and speech, and the claim is amply justified. The
visitor, to be sure, may well spend a long time in England without detecting any strong characteristic and even carry about
his own arsenal of prejudices without running across anything
that clashes with them or anybody ready to disprove them. He
soon registers on the other hand the existence of English counter-
prejudices at his own expense and makes, *inter alia*, the sad
reflection that in an insular country foreigners' bills are presented for payment a little more promptly than those of other
customers.

In fact English prejudices, favourable or otherwise, about
strangers and Continental peoples in general, often remain for
a while the visitor's main subjects of observation for, in an
island which is not conspicuously self-assertive, they are one of
the few comparatively obvious or noticeable features.

It is primarily on matters of codes, gastronomic, sporting or
social, that a foreigner is likely to break the first lances with his
hosts. In particular the French or Belgians who arrive here with
a deeply-rooted sense of superiority on all questions of food and
with their colours nailed to the mast, discover with the horror
of true Faith before Heresy that their supremacy is contested
and even occasionally derided. That a sauce made of eggs, milk

and flour should be described as heavy while a wholly chemical
ketchup is reputed 'nice and stimulating'; that a glass of wine
at 20 degrees of alcohol should be scorned as 'livery' while
whisky at some 42 is 'healthy and clean'; or that an elaborate
French pastry should be dismissed as 'too rich' while a trans-
parent jelly quivering from the conflict among its formidable in-
gredients should be greeted as 'light and wholesome': all these
blasphemies seldom fail to arouse Continental crusading
instincts.

Milder controversies may arise on sporting tenets, for the
English appear to have established once and for all an arbitrary
hierarchy of animals ranging from those which it is honourable
to those which it is anathema to destroy; and they have
unerringly assessed the fair proportion of chances left to each
quarry by true sportsmanship. Whenever I dared to suggest
that infringements of humane principles were occasionally committed in England, I was sternly reminded that it was unquestionably fair to run a fox down because the fox rather enjoyed
the pursuit, and to use goats as baits for the panther in India
because it is well established that goats hardly ever suffer (unless
they do it for spite). Those practices could not be compared
with the Continental's vile habit of shooting at anything that
flew including sweet song birds.

Deeper prejudices such as those of a social order do not
directly affect the foreigner for the simple reason that he has
no place in the subtle English hierarchy of values instituted by
tradition. He soon notices that, socially, he is not quite a real
person and enjoys the privilege of remaining courteously
unclassified. Should his hosts' references to his own country
denote prejudice, it is usually mitigated with indulgence:
there is an implicit admission that the severity of English
standards must relax or be qualified where strange nations are
concerned.

Shall I say that I never seriously resented English prejudices?
Each nation must have its peculiar form of self-complacency.
To the onlooker it may, now and then, cause irritation. Yet if
good-humoured acceptance of one's national lot be inseparable
from self-satisfaction, by all means let self-satisfaction survive.
There is less danger in the Englishman's contentment with his
island, even if it must entail that a foreigner can never achieve
the status of a gentleman, than in the unbiased but covetous

interest of the German in everything that breathes beyond his own frontiers.

The self-conscious newcomer is primarily occupied, I think, with English reactions to himself or his own people in general—and sometimes, more sadly, with the absence of English reactions to both. Next to those, his impressions of the country naturally consist of details which contrast with his national habits, visual or otherwise. He compares rather than observes.

I have always admired the ubiquitous traveller-writer who can spend two months in China and come back with the philosophy of Lao-Tsu brought up to date, having covered centuries and provinces at the mental speed of a shooting-star. I must confess that, for weeks, my own observations were confined to those things which most differed from France and the Continent or which destroyed a few preconceptions of England. Thus I judged at first that the English were gregarious because their children wore 'uniforms' at school and men often liked to recall earlier associations with college, club or other groups by wearing special badges or ties: had I come from Heidelberg instead of Paris, I should probably have ranked them as hopeless individualists because they took a stroll in the park without parading four abreast and singing marching songs. Then again I was surprised to find that in a country of so-called shopkeepers many salesmen and shop assistants often looked upon would-be purchasers as trespassers upon their peace of mind.

Broadly speaking I found everywhere a far more leisurely attitude towards the business of money-making than I had anticipated. Although the subject itself was mentioned with more openness than elsewhere, the acquisition of money in a small or in a big way seemed to arouse much less eagerness and tension than I had anticipated. That a taxi-driver should prefer his cup of tea to a profitable fare and a broker a long week-end to an alluring speculation, did not in the least tally with conventional portraits. English people were more easy-going, more casual in business, less tense in their work and more detached in most pursuits than was commonly imagined abroad.

Another national trait which belied their reputation for practical-mindedness was their apparent indifference to all that lay or took place in districts, towns or counties other than their own. More generally inquiries on most things—places, ways and means of travelling or of reaching a particular destination—

would surprise and even sadden those who were not specialists in guidance and information. I usually found myself caught between two kinds of abstentionists: the 'stranger in these parts' whom you invariably meet when you try to locate a building within fifty yards of the place where you are standing or, alternatively, the man who 'would not know' as far as that, if you venture to travel more than half a mile from your base. Conversely I felt that the most conspicuous foreigner was expected by everybody to know his bearings and direction without asking. 'Train for Y? No. 3 platform? AS usual.' 'Bus for X? Well, of course, number 945. Don't you know it?' To which the unkind traveller is peevish enough to reply, 'Obviously not,' sometimes to be pleased by the discovery that platform No. 3 and bus 945 were the wrong ones after all. As, nevertheless, the system works to the minute on both rail and road, there often grows in his heart a secret resentment that the laws of logic should be trampled with impunity and that airy stationmasters should run aggressively punctual trains.

Indeed it is the earnestness or the punctiliousness of the visitor, be he German, French, Latin, which is baffled at every turn in his first association with the English world. He sees things done without that emphatic application, without that manifest eagerness which he instinctively identifies with the successful performance of all tasks. He believes that institutions must function better if men are passionately serious, or at least sternly precise in their operation; and he realizes that they work in England even if the charabanc conductor collects his milk for the family on the way. He is used to pursue an argument to the last ditch and meets people who concede the point rather than follow it up and yet retain their conviction. He has been prepared for a grave, methodical, calmly pugnacious community, almost an anthill; and because English people are not demonstrative either in toil or leisure he may go on believing for some time in their constant singleness of purpose; and then he learns gradually that pauses, respites, fancies, and even touches of moderate Bohemia strew that apparently ticketed and docketed community. Either in words or deeds he feels an uncanny elasticity in a world which he had pictured as rigid and planned to the last dot. He senses, without fathoming it, what Clive Bell describes as 'the frivolity' of the English, a disinclination to over-stress, to strain things, activities, pastimes or human beings to the utmost. It may take a long time yet before he understands that this seemingly negative quality is a great preserver of the strength of the nation.

The absence of high relief and the elusiveness of London as a capital which, to me, had made it uninviting at first also characterized people in my early intercourse with them. There was little which stood out conspicuously. Contacts were easier in many ways and more pleasant than in many other countries, but surface-deep. It is true that Continental years of café metaphysics and exhaustive arguments on subjects ranging from Lenin's Memoirs to Saint-Granier's last song oddly clashed with the whispers of an English club or the discreet oscillations of a drawing-room conversation. How usurped in a way was the French reputation for lightness, how underlined our most insignificant pastimes, in comparison with an English setting where social relations would be sketched out with sparse, understated touches, unsubstantial perhaps to a French eye; an eye accustomed to colour might at first register but a greyish background. Where chats were full of trifles and discussions were left with straggling loose ends or went off at a tangent, I found that elaborate arguments often provoked unforeseen responses, like the keys of a piano connected with unexpected strings. There was a constant sensation of demanding too much from a conversation or exacting too heavy a tribute from acquaintanceship. An alarming feeling of behaving in London much as a German professor would in Paris must, I fear, have been the common lot of many of my fellowcountrymen who brought to England that native curiosity which is their only stimulus to travelling. (Who said that the English travelled abroad not to see people but to see fewer Englishmen with the result that they travelled rather more than the French who travel, when they do, to meet different people?)

I had to learn, after many others, that in a country as rich as any in the attainments of the mind, the intellectual approach is perhaps the least rewarding of all. On superficial problems and fashions the newcomer's apprenticeship is somewhat longer in England than in most countries: he has to learn what to avoid rather than what to mention. English people will derive enjoyment from many little things, unfinished conversations, half-way jokes, small oddities in situations or happenings, slight suggestions, simple encounters, and begin to tire at the very point where the foreigner begins to settle into his proper stride. The undiluted intellectual who cannot dispense with a daily discussion in three points as a mental constitutional will probably leave these islands, after he has exhausted the substance of most of the galleries and public libraries, wondering how books have come to be written and canvases to be painted. The plight of the hundred-per-cent sportsman is hardly more enviable for he will show the same thoroughness in his own muscular realm and outbore the most inveterate club-bore. Little by little both must study the art of inconstancy. Perhaps before that changing scene, in this mutable human atmosphere, they may discover a restful, agreeable quality. Communication by words which is not a specifically English talent will somehow, some time, become easier. Alternatively, they may choose to be quietly ostracized.

There is nothing in England which *persuades* the visitor to stay. Relations with people and contacts with the country remain to the stranger, as it were, in an undertone. English life does not stimulate nor do English people captivate. There is even a suggestion of 'take it or leave it' smoothed by a smile. The charm, to which one may or may not respond, lies precisely in that which at first is most disconcerting: an extreme freedom of movement and thought, unimpaired by the weight of the community which, in some nations, bears rather heavily on the individual, irrespective of laws and régime. There are more restrictions in England than elsewhere on the exercise of the daily freedoms, in the shape of licensing regulations, speed limits, hours of sales, and the like, only tolerated because of their very oddity and, in many cases, irrelevance: more logical regulations would probably be looked upon as deliberate encroachments on freedom. Yet there is at the same time an almost unrivalled sense of personal independence because the plain human relationship between people is uncommonly flexible, because acquaintanceship, friendship or even kinship places neither burdens nor fetters on the individual; nor do they trespass on his privacy.

That is a species of freedom that charters and codes cannot establish. It is one indeed which to some Continentals makes a stay in England depressing in the long run, as though the atmosphere were too light after the closeness and emphasis of social intercourse in other countries. This sense of freedom, or more precisely of independence (words which I do not use in their political acceptation), is, I think, one of the earliest of those impressions that I formed which were to count and to endure. It did not altogether destroy that of a certain English gregariousness manifest in the enjoyment of collective pursuits, games, entertainments, but it showed that tendency to be very superficial. It also pointed the way to the original nature of English individualism.

In recording some of my first reactions to the English milieu, a discussion of English individualism would be premature. This much however I would venture to say: that to the Frenchman or to the Latin the first *real* contact with England dates from the day when he has discovered here truly individual characteristics and shaken off the fairly wide spread fallacy that the English exist chiefly as a nation and very little as individuals, a prejudice of the sort to be found not in the 'man in the street' but rather among intellectuals in various countries. He may or he may not realize it. English understatement, reluctance to display intellectual or moral features may wear out his attention. For my own part I came, after many experiences and encounters to take the opposite view and consider the English as very 'individualized' although this is not necessarily revealed in words and speech, though this individualism, here as elsewhere, is threatened by a certain political and social evolution.

For a Continental it is that acknowledgement, conscious or not, which forges the first link, lends to the English people a reality beyond its place on the map, its political history, its power or its various amenities. In spite of history, traditions, fashions, I soon felt that it firmly set England in the Western Europe where I belonged and with which she had not really parted company.

CHAPTER 3

AN ENGLISH NEWS-REEL

ENGLAND seemed, indeed, to move away from Europe when I first landed here. In most ways, she was more English and less European in 1932 than at any other time between the two world wars. The tide that had carried her upon the Continent during the first conflict had ebbed. Her great concern was to redeem the mortgage and return to ocean breezes and imperial pursuits; to achieve a new birth by cutting the umbilical cord which held her to the womb of Europe. The cord resisted. To dispose of the financial burden by solving the reparations problem once and for all, the military burden by an agreement at the Disarmament Conference: those were the tasks to be performed in order to sever the ties with the Continent. Meanwhile all eyes were turned towards the future, the forthcoming Ottawa Conference and the promises which it held. In Europe, the true watchword was disentanglement; in Canada, imperial moorings.

The statesmen's vocabulary, to be sure, was still very European and even universal. Never had so much been said about the promotion of world peace and world happiness. International solidarity was on all lips. Nothing was too worldwide in dialectics. But words had seldom been emptier. Whilst the 'rump' of an old Labour majority was left to wear out the catchwords left over from the immediate post-war years, the real business in hand was entrusted to Conservative statesmen less vocal but strongly entrenched. As fate would have it, in seven swift years, England was drawn back to Europe and the impact nearly destroyed her. But there were no forebodings of such a future in England in the early months of 1932.

Tariffs had been introduced for the first time in seventy-six years. Imperial protection was contemplated, Isolation dreamt of, Non-entanglement whispered on every side. It was the nadir of English European-mindedness, the turning point between two eras, one of gradual dissociation from the Continent, one of progressive and compulsory return towards its shores.

Twelve years have elapsed since my early London days, a far longer term than I had originally bargained for, but a brief space for a great city. Yet, by contrast, the impression which it left upon my mind and which has endured, as all first visions do, now seems to belong to a collection of old engravings. Images of the capital together with memories of events which rippled its surface or trifles which coloured its atmosphere, all have the still-life quality of things which have no replica in the England of to-day locked with Europe in her struggle. The nation's thoughts were then far away from the mainland.

The country slowly emerged from the financial crisis which nearly shattered her credit and which had brought the National Government to power. Huge 'Buy British' posters heralded an attempt at Imperial Economy. The slogan was 'Spend More', not 'Save More'. In West End cinemas a merchant seaman would declaim on the stage a patriotic poem to the glory of British Overseas Trade before Frederic March thrilled the audience in 'Dr. Jekyll and Mr. Hyde'. In the wake of this campaign English dressmakers tried to wrest the sceptre of fashion from Parisian hands and advertised: 'Why Paris and not London?' Meanwhile old Manchester clenched its fist at its cheap rival, Yokohama. Rulers of Indian States who had come for the Round Table Conference quietly drove through London. The Disarmament Conference was in full swing at Geneva and Londoners discussed the chances of a reduction in French military forces. 'Why not give Germany a chance?' However, the rise of De Valera in Ireland was a more popular topic and Cabinet meetings on the Irish Question drew large crowds to Downing Street where vocal visitors from Dublin and Prince Monolulu back from Newmarket made rival claims upon the public attention. With an escort of police keeping in step, the first hunger marchers paraded through London to claim the abolition of the Means Test and some of them wrote at the bottom of 'Buy British' posters: 'With what? The dole?' The City man opened his paper to watch the slow rise of 'gilt-edged' and the Cockney the result of the football pool or the sweepstake. True to a self-established tradition, a group of elderly ladies were knitting garments to be presented to Ramsay MacDonald upon his birthday.

Local, not outlandish, interests, were the order of the day:

there was talk of a forthcoming revolution in motor-car gears, of a dashing American tennis player by the name of Vines who might win the English championship at Wimbledon in July, of a murderer called Furnace who was sought at all railway stations, of shares in African mines and of English daffodils which had been late in the parks that year, and of the bad weather prospects for the summer. London and England were self-centred, occupied with themselves, their trade, their work, their life, their toys, their shows, their flowers and their sky.

There was no cosmopolitan touch about the capital. It was more English than Paris was French, or Vienna, Austrian. Foreign settlements were still well defined in limited areas. A few transients from across the North Sea or the Channel, Dutch business men or German 'students', and a sprinkling of French tourists represented London's foreign contacts. The Germans scattered over a score of quiet boarding-houses were already testing the average Englishman's response to a tea-time course on the iniquities of Versailles. The French allured by an improved rate of exchange quickened the pulse of a few West End restaurants. A broken accent still caused the solitary English diner to raise an eyelid over his paper.

Nor did the physical aspect of London bear, as yet, many marks of extraneous influences. Flat life was just dawning and fiercely caricatured by Mr. Punch. Blocks of them had begun to intrude among Edwardian, Victorian, Georgian or nondescript mansions, but the Royal Commission still wielded a stern wand in warning to those who threatened a moderate capital with newfangled structures imported from New York or Frankfort. Berkeley Square was almost unscathed and the Adelphi breathed quietly. Most of the blocks which have since stirred Osbert Lancaster to his wittiest crusade had an air of being kept in quarantine out of the stroller's traditional hunting grounds. Over the full course of the Lord Mayor's procession only the *Daily Express* building and Shell Mex House would shock the eye of that dignitary and his aldermen.

Horsedrawn traffic lingered on, enjoying its swan song by encumbering South London, the City and part of the West End, cursed from Westminster to London Bridge by streams of rampant motorists. Mr. Hore-Belisha had not yet achieved fame by adding his beacons to their many trials, nor Mr. Morrison by pulling down Waterloo Bridge. Road congestion was the serious problem which confronted eight million Londoners. The pound sterling at twelve and six and the forthcoming budget were the great political preoccupation of forty-five million Englishmen. Statesmen may have had worries in Europe, or hopes in the Empire, but their hearts, I think, were well within the cliffs of England.

At first I had no interests in common with these people who went by me, who talked of remote ventures or of local events, discussed games which were not played beyond their shores, were unruffled by great Continental events, yet aroused by the hieroglyphics of cricket scores or market quotations in the stop press of an evening paper and who in matters not specifically English were more attracted by the antipodes than by their neighbours across the Channel.

It took me weeks to decipher those mysterious yells which I heard in the afternoon, to discover that newspaper editions were often called in terms of racing results, and to avoid being knocked down by packs of newsboys merely because 'Elsa the Second' had won by a short neck. I derived little stimulus from a headline recording the fact that the King's Wiltshire bullock had been awarded first prize at the cattle show when I naïvely looked in the same column for the speech of the French delegate at Geneva.

Rumours from continental Europe seemed to reach England in muffled echoes. Even in the House of Commons where world problems were thrashed out, there was an air of unreality when such faraway topics as foreign wars were on the Order Paper. The low price of Argentine meat seemed to cause more pangs than the high spirits of two belligerent states in the same hemisphere. The sessions of the Commons themselves looked like family affairs with little solemnity, an unostentatious and outwardly irrelevant ritual, discussions in the tone of voice of two persons in a conversation-piece and debates which ended, not because a conclusion had been reached but because the subject had to be dropped sooner or later anyhow.

The English scene for a long time had barely more significance for me than a newsreel. It was not three dimensional. It was instructive in the same way as illustrations are to a child in a book which he cannot yet read. In other capitals there was a cosmopolitan polish which smoothed the first contact, which served as a transition between two countries. The foreigner had a little part of the treat at once. Not so in the largest capital in the world.

England made no allowances. She had to be accepted without qualifications. Her language would remain meaningless unless I shared her own interests, her own preoccupations and even her own vision of things. I began to find how very difficult it is to live here in normal times without either becoming de-nationalized or else perpetually feeling that one is playing a game of pretence (or alternatively turning into the stereotype of a disgruntled exile). By another paradox the country which makes the least demands and claims upon the stranger's atten-tion turns out to be the most exacting if he wishes not only to understand it but to enjoy it at all.

If one looks through field glasses in reverse the objects one sees are just as clear, but increasingly smaller. That is the kind of vision of Europe which I then attributed to most English eyes. And one of the most difficult achievements for a Continental who intends to retain his own national scale of values is to resist the insensible process of adaptation to the insular focus. For it often happens that when English life begins to make sense and English events to become comfortably fami-liar the outside world begins to dwindle. That means that Alice has followed the rabbit a little too far, which I hope, I have not, or else this book would bring very little to the English reader.

Acclimatization to the English Order of Things and its rela-tive values, political and otherwise, somehow always resembles a progress through Wonderland, until one discovers much later that its reality is very much nearer to one's own than its surface. To my untrained eyes and ears, Wonderland appeared at its height in 1932. What most mattered to me was of third-rate importance here; what would have been dismissed as a trifle on the other side of the Channel was of the greatest moment to this country. There was solemnity in local pageants which else-where would have been pretexts for fun, but apparent casual-ness in state deliberations. Germany was beginning to stir, and the *Morning Post* wrote an exquisite leader on the flower show. British ministers returned from the Continent unnoticed, but cricketers were mobbed at railway stations. The grin of the Cheshire Cat was not 'the funniest thing in the world' but a commonplace.

What is true of England in general is also true of English poli-

c

tical or international life: its striking historic manifestations may be gauged and perhaps foreseen from outside. Its motives and mainsprings can only be understood and clearly appreciated from inside. It is not to be learned from books, not even English books, for they are seldom deliberately introspective. They offer the product of creation but remain silent on its process. This may no more be judged from the result, than a Manchester weaving mill can be imagined from a piece of cloth. And it is almost impossible to see England in a detached and quite dispassionate way because to understand, here more than anywhere else, means to partake.

Even after many years of partaking, who could pretend to have a comprehensive picture of an old and diverse nation whose roots go deep into history, whose motives may vary from county to county and whose share of hazards and uncertainties is increased by its far-flung ventures? An old and sceptical friend of mine would sometimes say: 'You ask me what this country will do in such and such circumstances? Tell me first whether the then Prime Minister will come from Exeter or Glasgow, whether the Canadian wheat crop will show a surplus, whether British investments in South America will be safe, and whether the Fleet will be lying in the Mediterranean or cruising in the North Sea. Then, perhaps I might make a guess: probably a wrong one.'

Although things look clearer in retrospect, or at least more accountable, there remain an infinite number of unknown quantities. Since the days of those first impressions which I have evoked, I have watched this country not through a looking-glass but with the naked eye and almost continuously with sympathy. In whatever I understood, I have found nothing truly *alien* to me or to my nation in all that really makes and maintains a civilization, and it is not because I have become assimilated: the French, I fear, are even more insular than the English in that respect. It is because behind fashions and ways of living which differ at every turn, I have found individual motives and fundamental pursuits to be very similar. It is, no doubt, to be deplored that History is not written on these similarities; but then History is less real than Life.

Having done with these early reminiscences, I must now face the harder task of judging—harder since I can no more claim the prerogatives of a newcomer.

CHAPTER 4

THE SOCIAL GAME: CONFORMITY AND TRANSGRESSION

Children, behave yourselves

THE Englishman of every class, as compared to his opposite number on the Continent, strikes the outside observer as a social conformist. He is not only law-abiding but respectful of social conventions. Yet this disposition has nothing in common with the political discipline of the German which is indiscriminate and akin to the herd instinct, nor does it exclude a deep individualism.

Some time before the war I was spending a few weeks on a farm in Dorset. The old 'Master' was one of those genuine anti-Papists who love a lively controversy across the Sunday joint. In good-humoured vehemence he would, at times, brandish the carving knife against the Church of Rome. Yet he freely criticized his own persuasion and often spent part of his meal-time deprecating points of Anglican dogma, the sermon we had heard, the parson and the village church. One day I could not refrain from tackling him:

'Since you disapprove of everything in your own parish, let alone others,' I said, 'why do you go to church at all?' He paused for a while, then chuckled and eventually replied: 'Well, that's a queer question, to be sure. Not but I'll tell you. I like the idea of all the folk in the village, or as many as may be, doing the same good thing on the same good day. That I do. It keeps them like that [he interlocked the fingers of both hands] and they are the better for it.' Then he winked at me and added: 'And, mark you, they don't *have* to. No Inquisition in these parts.' And he chuckled again for a solid minute while his wife looked at him reproachfully for his daring. The Great Inquisition was his historic bogey, although I had, by then, succeeded in convincing him that the Black Hood had not been donned in my own land for many a century.

His answer, all the same, had been as satisfactory as I could have bargained for. He was not one of those men, of whom I have met a few in the West Country, who would even in these days go to the stake for Faith and, perhaps, Constitution; but he liked the footprints on his way to church to be clear, deepset, and orderly. He knew the men of his own village. He had seen them in the raw. Individually they might at times be rough and unruly. Yet they formed a well-regulated community. For generations they had freely respected a number of rules evolved by common consent. They kept these alive, not as tenets of unquestionable perfection, but as active links between man and man. In my old farmer's mind churchgoing was one of the rules which turned a crowd into a society. A Latin peasant would have spoken of the intrinsic truth that lay in his persuasion, but this man was more concerned with its operative value, its moral and social function.

This practical conception of ethical problems or, to speak more accurately, this application of practical sense to issues which other nations might consider solely on their spiritual merits, is certainly characteristic of the English and it largely accounts for a high degree of social civilization.

It is sometimes assumed abroad that social culture in this country is the effortless achievement of a moderate and easily disciplined nation. This is an opinion of England formed in West End restaurants; but it is in fact the patient conquest of a people over its own natural temperament, which is by no means forbearing and acquiescent. Religion, education and all the moral forces which elsewhere tend to expend themselves on the individual or the family, have in England fostered the sense of social responsibility and helped to create the moral power of Society. Constantly strengthened by new conventions this power is considerable. The French are inclined to leave the settlement of moral problems either to their own conscience or the Church if they affect the individual, or to the Law if they affect the community. The English more readily submit them to the tribunal of public opinion which, acting in constant self-defence, is often more exacting than the High Court or the Assizes.

It is often said that English education lays emphasis on character rather than on intellect. But men's characters can be judged by society only according to their behaviour, not their motives. The effect of English education in a nation where extensive moral authority is vested in society is therefore to stress the importance of behaviour, and, above all, of social conduct and social codes. The uncharted legislation of English society piled up by tradition tends to infinity. Few countries have evolved a more comprehensive etiquette of human intercourse. It is not burdensome. It is light and invisible but ever present and effective. It is by no means confined to the upper classes; there was hardly an Englishman at the time of the abdication of Edward VIII who did not discuss the problem on grounds of moral and social conventions; and, as I found, it was among the humbler people that the most rigid standards of judgement were applied to the question. Everywhere in England there is a strong sense of what is 'done' and 'not done', 'proper', and 'improper', and, above all, 'right' and 'not right' both as regards trifling matters and issues of great moment.

That such a firm upholding of codes has produced an orderly and responsible society is beyond question. Despite inevitable relaxation, social ethics have survived even the shattering impact of war; I had proof of this in foreign lands where British troops were stationed and where, as armies go, their behaviour was remarkably good.[1]

On the other hand one might question whether the extensive rights granted to Society do not press unduly on the individual, whether, in other words, they do not impair the 'art of living', which Continentals are inclined to associate with greater social freedom and *laisser-faire*. This point may perhaps be best approached by a detour.

In a lecture on Leadership in War, Field-Marshal Viscount Wavell raised one of the oldest and most controversial questions set to military thinkers: Is warfare an art or a science? The French would be inclined to regard it as an art, the Germans as a science. Lord Wavell's reply was characteristic and instructive. Warfare might be both but, in his opinion, it was most aptly compared to a game, for both demanded the same sort of qualities: full knowledge of the rules and flexibility in their application; readiness to seize opportunities and act on them; swift perception of the opponent's weak points; good-humoured endurance and self-control in adversity; proper adaptation to teamwork, and respect of one's obligations to others.

Although the effect of war is destruction, whereas that of life is the exact opposite, Lord Wavell's comparison may well throw

[1] In itself, if not always as a contribution to an effort towards a better understanding of local problems and peoples.

some light on the difference between the French and the English ways of living. In order to cultivate an art the means to be applied are those which serve to bring it to its highest point of perfection; the only limiting rules are those necessary to prevent the community from suffering by its pursuit. In a game, on the other hand, the rules really form part of the pleasure derived from its practice. Without base-lines, side-lines, service-lines, net and penalties for faults, lawn tennis would be futile. There is enjoyment in the skilful observance of the rules as well as in the physical exercise and should the game become too erratic, it would lose its interest.

I often fancy that English life is partly imbued with the same underlying belief in the values of rules in themselves, and that their observance forms an integral part of the 'art of living'. To make a last comparison with sport, even the restrictions which regulations impose upon the individual are not dissimilar from the placing of hazards on a golf course, where they are at once an obstacle and a stimulus to the players. In other words, the rewards of social conformity often lie in its very exactions.

As in all communities, English society also has its drawbacks, which are the reverse of the medal. The most obvious in England are social prejudice and social consciousness which, independent of class feeling, are alive everywhere, save perhaps among the nobility whose very status keeps them immune from it. From the very superficial classification made immediately according to accent (and from which there was no appeal) to subtle distinctions amid which the uninitiated lost the scent, there were almost as many social degrees in pre-war England as in the hierarchy of an Indian state, except that the English order was preserved by human respect and discretion.

Up to the outbreak of the war, social snobbery, assailed though it was from many quarters, still remained a widespread English disease. It is the natural offspring of social conformity. Aldous Huxley once remarked that England was the only place where such a newspaper headline as, 'Peer's cousin in motor-car accident' was conceivable. It was almost impossible before the war to meet anyone in any class who had not 'been in better circumstances' or who did not 'accidentally' remind you that he knew people whose acquaintance was calculated to enhance his social status. For social status, not intellectual or financial distinction, is the English snob's quarry or ambition. In some countries snobbery is intellectual. In others, where 'social climbing' is possible within a lifetime, snobbery is social but ostentatious and coarse: there is a touch of 'go and get it' about it. In traditional England, where the ascent might take generations to achieve, it often turned into an art. Certainly it was no sinecure. In France, it might impose upon its adepts a tremendous intellectual strain, long vigils over the deciphering of an *avant-garde* poem, and much shuffling of feet in baffling art galleries. In England, it requires (or required) Napoleonic attention to details, such as the tone of the voice, the practice of a cordial detachment, the suitable dose of affability, and perhaps the proper variations of address to animals, from hunter to Pekinese.

Distinctions of a purely social kind were not the only ones to be sensed, although they were the most immediately conspicuous. To this day, ancient divisions cast their reflection upon the English community. Irrespective of social status and circumstances, one can feel even now a definite contrast between a Cavalier and a Roundhead attitude to the problems of life.

The Cavaliers will more readily forgive a moral than an aesthetic lapse, a breach of promise than a *faute de goût*, a weakness than an absurdity, a cynic than a bore, a rogue than a coward. The Roundheads prefer intellectual conformity to talent, dullness to flippancy, pious pretence to unpleasant realities, modest stammering to brilliance. The former may grumble when they notice greasy paper in the parks; the latter will resent an arm round a waist. It is Cavalier to pronounce the social death of a man who has been warned by the Stewards of the Jockey Club, because that presupposes a grave breach of social behaviour. But a Roundhead is more likely to ostracize an illegitimate child.

Apart from social status, it is usually the Cavalier type and not the Roundhead which serves as a pattern to the snob. He it is who sets the standards. However, as a slight stammer and slightly baggy trousers are not always in themselves sufficient evidence of gentility, the task of the conscientious snob, either in discovering or in imitating his models, is most unenviable. Several writers of fiction and film producers have supplied the masses with a standard type of landed aristocrat which might have eased the way, were it not for the fact that the waxwork

figure which they have fashioned would hardly deceive the
most uncouth newcomer to this country. I remember in this
connexion a film in which a very good actor playing the part
of a ruined aristocrat had to speak the following lines, lines
which Evelyn Waugh might well use in a pastiche: 'What, am
I now to ask her to share my fate? A poor country gentleman
galloping on his last hunter into a bankruptcy court?' Small
wonder that there was some sniffing and hard swallowing
amongst an emotional audience!

Social conformity as applied to behaviour produces snobbery.
Social conformity as applied to character produces hypocrisy.
The former is a by-product of social hierarchy and of the Cavalier spirit; the latter a by-product of social-moral discipline and
of the Roundhead attitude to life. The snob tries to cheat
superficially; the hypocrite is a transgressor at heart, in a way,
a moral snob, a Roundhead snob. Both are liabilities of a
conformist society.

Social hypocrisy is by no means as general in England as the
English themselves are often ready to admit. Nevertheless it cannot but play its part in a nation which sets itself high moral
standards, where both religion and society lay emphasis on behaviour, where they are less inclined to scrutinize individual
consciences and individual motives than to keep order within
the community and prevent the individual from impairing its
balance. The greater the importance attached to order and
average morality, the more it will be held that the fault lies in
the scandal rather than in the commission of the act. To that
extent, social hypocrisy has the advantage of preventing un-
healthy proselytism. Perhaps the optimist will even invoke Max
Beerbohm's *Happy Hypocrite* to prove that true beauty can be
achieved by the mere process of hiding one's face.

What England does not produce in any great numbers is the
open transgressor of the social code. Whoever is not a conformist, sincere or not, is an 'outsider' rather than a rebel. A distinctive feature of English society is its ability to produce
individuals who do not challenge the social order but choose
to break away from conformity by singular pursuits and harmless oddities. I mean primarily the eccentrics. Like social
hypocrites, although for different reasons, eccentrics in England
are on the decline. A world craving for uniformity is against
them. I fear that one day they may all have been rolled, rubbed

and polished into those human pebbles which seem to be the models of modern legislators. And that will be a great loss, for they are the last knights of that moderate, innocuous anarchy without which civilized life soon becomes overpowering.

By eccentrics, I do not mean the specimens familiarized by the music halls or in cheap fiction such as Jules Verne's American who claimed admittance to London's Eccentric Club on the ground that he had walked around the Red Sea backwards but was rejected because he had used both legs; or the drawing-room 'lion' whose only accomplishment was that he could go round a boudoir without touching the ground—by jumping from each piece of furniture to the next. Those were merely the fictitious forerunners of modern record-hunters in jitter-bug-ging, spinning or even dishwashing.

The true English eccentric has two great merits which raise him above his foreign competitors: his eccentricity does not depend upon his wallet; and he is not an exhibitionist. He does not demand any audience but himself. Sometimes he even hides, not out of fear, but to enjoy his hobby all the more. He is an example not only of sheer harmless individualism but of the contentment that life can offer to the wise if it is crossed on a few selected and original stones instead of by the communal bridge. There is usually a distinct touch of the quixotic about him and his enterprises. The genuine eccentric does not attempt to defy society and its laws. He pays the unavoidable tribute to social order and then finds refuge and consolation in doing what the law and even the world permits, but in a way and according to rites of his own. There is nothing calculated in this. It springs from inspiration. The eccentrics were a great English asset and a country that breeds eccentrics is immune from 'caporaliza-tion'. Who ever heard of an eccentric Prussian?

Fortunately, besides acknowledged eccentrics, the English social scene presents an uncommonly wide range of characters, almost unknown elsewhere, who distinguish themselves not by their inborn singularity but by the peculiarity of their individual pursuits.

On the whole, the scope of a Frenchman's interests is probably wider than an Englishman's. There is in every Frenchman a yearning for some sort of intellectual universality. Interests in England vary more from individual to individual, whether they be in the nature of professions or hobbies. Consequently, there is practically no pursuit from the highest and most serious to the most trifling and unexpected which is not followed, and thoroughly so, by someone somewhere. The singularity of a hobby is a greater stimulus than its practical value. England seems to produce, in the self-same spirit, missionaries and bird-watchers, poodle-combers and kingdom-repairers. There is no branch of human activity, however remote and minute, whether useful or altogether odd, which does not turn out to have been explored by some Englishman. A controversy on the French ejaculation 'Zut' which raged a few years ago in the columns of *The Times* unloosed a torrent of learning which would have swept a Paris philologist off his feet, and I have no doubt that at a moment's notice an advertisement in that paper would instantly produce a recipe for turning aspidistras into eatables or a fully qualified Messiah for the last Hottentot tribes.

The originality of those pursuits and the breadth of their range proves that, despite its minute regulations, English society leaves ample elbow-room to the individual; they also point to the nature of his individualism, which does not defy the existing state of things, but on the contrary remains superficially conformist. While, in politics and in religion, parties or groups as such make an ample display of dissent, there is far less individual non-conformity with the agreed way of living in England than in France, Belgium, Spain or Italy in normal times. English individualism expresses itself in by-ways. Perhaps it is that particular feature which gives the English community the smoothness which elsewhere might only be purchased by the sacrifice of individual personality. Behind English conformity, which is not passive but deliberate, will be found private worlds and human recesses where life is cultivated gently and richly.

Even among those who infringe the rules of the social game, the value of tradition and order is implicitly acknowledged. I have had the occasional privilege of meeting a few crooks in England. What impressed me was their respect for all the conventions which their calling did not absolutely compel them to violate. They reminded me of the gangster in *The Petrified Forest* who was ready to slaughter a whole family but deeply resented the rude behaviour of the girl towards her grandfather. It may be because the scope of law-breakers is limited that they lack versatility in their trade. Yet in other countries these law-breakers often try to find their justification in social injustice or national shortcomings. Not so in England. The outlaw is a conformist. He takes advantage of society but respects its principles. He is an outsider *par force*, but not an ethical rebel. Perhaps there is some comfort in being robbed in a purely technical rather than in a malicious manner.

Finally, the strength of the social bond in England is illustrated by the procedure of English justice: justice here is, to a far greater extent than elsewhere, the defender of common ethics. Like society it passes sentence on facts and results rather than motives and impulses. The community seldom takes motives into account. It does not accept the dictum that 'to understand all is to forgive all'; for it strikes the offender in order to warn off would-be offenders, in order to protect itself, not according to varying degrees of basic wickedness. A French jury may deliver its verdict against a murderer and then find extenuating circumstances. An English jury will probably hesitate to deliver its verdict on the same evidence, but, once it has done so, justice will strike harder and with more finality. French justice is the servant of the statute book which is almost an abstraction, and then it mitigates its sanction on purely individual human grounds. English justice is broader-minded and less systematic in its examination of a case, but, once the case is closed, it acts as the trustee of society and strikes more sternly at the social offender. In other words, it shows its regard for the individual by ensuring his protection within the social order. The French achieve this result by making exceptions to the enforcement of the law in favour of individual cases.

There is in the French an underlying disposition to forgive individual rebellion against the existing order, an implicit acknowledgement that the individual may suffer from the pressure of society, laws and conventions. In England, on the contrary, there is a general assumption that, since the existing order is accepted by the majority, it must therefore be bearable to most individuals. Consequently, the defence of the individual is best ensured through defence of the codes of conduct on which society has agreed.

What is not always realized is that English social conformity, often criticized as conservatism, largely accounts for that tolerance which is still one of the greatest English assets. By tolerance,

Continental nations often mean the understanding of people's motives, or the ability of one person to excuse the actions of another. This is by no means the sum total of tolerance. The English by tolerance mean non-interference with the lives or pursuits of other people. Contrary to one of their favourite claims, I do not believe that Englishmen are more capable than others of 'understanding the other man's point of view'. What is certain is that they do take it into account more readily than other people. This is not the same, but the reason for it is to be sought in other characteristics. One of these, the love of fair play, is the product of education, while the other is innate. This is a certain nonchalance in human relationships which makes the Englishman very reluctant to bring pressure to bear on anybody else, either to satisfy curiosity, or for personal interest, or for self-advancement. Both, I believe, are responsible for several traits regarded as 'English' which may often appear incompatible: the readiness to accept things as they are, to tolerate social inequality and to abide by conventions (and, conversely, a disinclination to take advantage of either); a natural gift for contractual agreements; a spontaneous, unstrained discipline; and, in general, a talent for easy human relationships which is not an art, but which, though it often proceeds from mental laziness, is nevertheless a cultural accomplishment.

Irrespective of its political shortcomings, English society has hitherto struck a sound balance between the two extremes of which we have recently witnessed the dangers: boundless individualism which borders on anarchy, and a uniformity which holds an even greater threat. This quality has so far remained independent of the political context in which it is set at present. It does not follow that it is immutable and cannot be lost by political upheavals. On that subject the free individual as well as the socially-conscious person has his word to say.

CHAPTER 5

ENGLISHMEN AND LIFE

There is nothing, Sir, too little for such a creature as Man. It is by studying little things that we attain the great art of having as little misery and as much happiness as possible. . . .

DR. JOHNSON (quoted by Boswell)

IF Dr. Johnson were to reappear among us, he would realize what force his epigram has gained and what torments our world has suffered through its contempt for little things. 'It's the little things that are most important,' an old French mechanic would keep repeating. They are important indeed because they are real and therefore serious. A politician can trick millions of men into believing in Utopian worlds, but my old mechanic could not trick a plain sparking plug into firing unless he had, honestly, cleaned it. If a nation cannot perform its little tasks with care and good temper and find entertainment as well as truth in them, no sense of greatness that it may possess will prevent it from being both a failure and a curse.

To say that a people finds satisfaction in little things is not to minimize it. For it is through the cultivation of such things that men keep their contact with the world, with nature, and finally with themselves; it is also in them that a nation finds a safeguard against the various kinds of excesses which the Greeks described as *Hubris*. The faculty for making much, occasionally too much, out of little things is an outstanding English gift, the gift of a nation whose national pursuits are paradoxically great and far-flung. Such a contrast is normal in modern life. The English miner who gives strength to his country by building up its coal output and economic power will, when his day is done, turn towards life at very close range and on a small scale: a good joke at the local pub, a good shot on the local football ground.

The cultivation of life in a world of mechanization and mass labour turns partly into a form of escapism. The individual looks for a refuge from work and heavy routine. This tendency is more definite in England than elsewhere; the contrast between the two poles of modern existence, work, and leisure, are

more distinctly, almost exaggerately, underlined. History itself
easily explains this.

A robust, rural community with its feet firmly set on the
earth, with bracing air in its lungs, with harbours and fishing
coves notching its girdle of cliffs guarded by hardy seamen, has
turned in less than a century into a nation of which four-fifths
is clustered around its foundries, mines, workshops, factories,
banks and shops. It has retained its attachment to green pas-
tures, to trees and to fresh air, as a tradition, as a memory, as
a yearning. Circumstances, indeed, have probably increased
this attachment by contrast. Only an industrialized country
could evolve such an institution as the week-end to give the
townsman a chance to see a spot of green, were it merely in one
of those parks where some memory of nature manages to survive the smoke of blast furnaces and the petrol fumes of an
enveloping traffic. Thus the escape is often an instinctive
attempt to recover a normal balance. It is an unconscious return
towards nature, whether nature be represented by a bed
of sickly flowers, a playground, or the swarming beaches on
Southend.

There is little left now of what was known as Merrie England.
Gone are the days of the 'Jolly Farmer', of the beef-and-beer and
the puritan types alike, for whom toil and leisure were all one,
save on the Sabbath. The *Rural Rides* of William Cobbett, their
last spokesman, evoke an England as lost and legendary as that
of the early ballads. That stout, truculent, pungent breed of
men has almost become extinct. But so has in its turn that first
product of a swift economic revolution, the blasé, melancholy
Englishman who sought diversion from factory, bank, or idle
estate in extravagant or paradoxical pursuits, while gentlemen
adventurers and morose conquerors went out to build empires
and came back without a smile. The notorious English boredom
which supplied not only the continental stage but also Shaw's
early plays with a rich stock-in-trade has ceased to be a feature
of English life. It was no more, perhaps, than the teething
trouble of a rapidly industrialized England.

After a time-lag, the nation adapted herself emotionally to
her economic transformation without changing fundamentally
in her own self, just as her book-keepers accustomed themselves to larger figures without altering their methods of
computation. Games were developed as a substitute for nature;

leisure as some mitigation for mass labour. So that the recoil from life in its compulsory aspects produced a comprehensive system for the cultivation of the boons of life. Englishmen may have forgotten the essential pursuits of their forebears and before the present war they teased their land rather than tilled it, but they wanted it to be there to reassure them by its companionship.

Industrialization could not, of course, fail to leave its stamp. A nation of peasants is a nation of realists because reality can be faced at all times without soul-weariness. An industrial nation engenders escapism because its daily toil is monotonous. Yet what matters is the quality of that escapism: the German way of escape in the last seventy-five years has often been wanderlust, restlessness, collective hysteria. The English way is individualistic, not gregarious; natural, not morbid. Some time ago I listened with a few English friends to a discussion on 'English Culture' by the B.B.C. Brains Trust. Towards the end one of the debaters rather gruffly declared that 'he did not see why the English should even question the value of their cultural achievements: apart from art and books, was not a game of cricket as fine an assertion of culture as any accomplishment?' In our own circle of listeners I was the only one not to burst out laughing. That reserve was not due to good manners. I was thinking of many a village green or town playing-field where I had witnessed good comradeship, simple enjoyment of air, sun and even rain; of a precious aptitude of men to live together without bitterness; of games which uphold the tradition of things well done, from a batsman's fine stroke to a work of art, which allow for little human prides and give scope to natural gifts, which remind men that life is still there and within their reach. Thus, after all, did the Greeks develop their sense of measure which is also the basis of good citizenship. I considered this also to be culture, at an elementary yet vital stage.

Thus the Englishman's reaction to the daily pressure of circumstances, work, routine, overcrowding, is not negative and destructive but positive and constructive. He goes in search of personal compensations in the cultivation of a taste, a pursuit, a hobby. It is not in him, whether he be stockbroker, foreman, bank clerk or ticket collector, to brood over the misery of his plight or the dullness of his work and to find an eventual outlet in mass hysteria. The English workman's fancy may wander

towards a pint of beer and a game of darts. He may build
castles in the air on the prospective return of a lucky bet with
the next bookie or of a lucky guess in the football pool. But
neither the mill nor the mine have produced in any numbers a
class of disgruntled, splenetic men. The English are not a
nation of grumblers. They will show roughness around the party
platform and they will fight hard for better conditions, for more
bread and butter. That is in a different sphere. In daily affairs,
they have retained, even in their changed way of living, the
solid aptitude for individual happiness, for individual contact
with the good things of life which their rural forefathers
possessed.

They share with the French, the Belgian, the Dutch, the
Italians and in general with the nations born of Western and
Mediterranean civilization, the art of understanding life as it
is, or, as a French writer put it 'of living on good terms with life'.
I have even found it where one would least expect it: in the cage
going down the shafts of those Northumberland pits, the surface
works of which rank among the most sullen and unsmiling
spectacles in Europe. Even in such places one may suddenly
discover that a plain coarse jest does sometimes bear witness to
the existence of the soul, or that a 'little thing' assumes a deep
significance.

For the English, the appreciation of 'little things' is the main
basis of contact between people; social intercourse here does not
thrive on the consideration of essential problems which may
strain it, but rather on the cultivation of common tastes and
pleasant interests. There still lingers abroad the legend that 'the
English are not particularly sociable'. It is still kept alive by the
tourists who, in all nations, share an uncanny aptitude for
making their own country more unpopular in a few days than
would three unprovoked aggressions within a lifetime. The
English are eminently sociable. One of the first observations
which I made when travelling in this country was the 'openness'
of English houses. Front door, garden, or estate, all open or
spread towards the highway, the outside world, the visitors.
There are far fewer walls in England than in France or in
Italy. There is no secrecy, even less privacy than elsewhere, in
the household itself. It is a part of society as much as a family
cell. The average Englishman, indeed, the poor Englishman, is
much more sociable than his 'opposite number' in almost any

other nation. He naturally 'likes company'; he is equipped for it, at least in a superficial way; he knows how to perform such convenient rites as making sympathetic allusions to a weather fortunately endowed with enough diversity to feed a whole conversation; asking the proper questions about holidays already taken or still looked forward to between March and October; Christmas trees contemplated or remembered from October to March; and holding a cup of tea with deft fingers, a performance which requires more social self-tuition than clutching a glass of wine with palm and thumb—though whether it is as gratifying remains questionable.

I have, in these past years visited many an English house or cottage. The old ones almost irrespective of their style merge, in colour and shape, into the landscape for which they were designed. The new ones, described as 'houses of distinction and character' by ironic advertisers, mostly 'belong' nowhere save on a ribbon-developed by-pass. Irrespective of aspect, wealth and class, they all have one characteristic in common which distinguishes them from Continental dwellings and stamps them, to my way of thinking as English. Once he has passed the threshold, the stranger has no feeling of intrusion into a realm either unprepared or over-prepared to receive him. To use an Americanism, he literally 'steps right in'. He does not penetrate a sanctuary as he may fear to do in a French provincial household. He is taken for granted and, once inside, once admitted into the circle, he also feels less circumscribed. He has plenty of elbow room. He will only become an intruder if he unintentionally forces the conversation in a direction he finds marked 'Private' and strains intercourse by giving it a personal turn. The 'no trespassing' seen on private grounds and fields, and little heeded there, will here be written in nascent scowls on every English face. The Englishman's mind is his castle much more than his house.

Indeed, self-defence against trespassers is not directed against the stranger only. Within the household itself, within that open household unguarded from without, there seems between its members to be a high degree of individual reserve and discretion, of individual self-defence against excessive intimacy. Where a French family will barricade its door against all comers but leave nothing untold within its walls, an English family will welcome the outside world, but each of its members will retain far more of his or her own privacy. There is something traditionally abhorrent to the English in an excessive sentimental or even mental intimacy. Against it, the individual must therefore find the last refuge in himself alone, not in the family. There is a far higher barrier between the individual and his family than between the family and society. Indeed, it has sometimes occurred to me in a suburban cottage that the house cat lying on the hearthrug was a sort of buffer state between man and wife, a barrier, as it were, against excessive promiscuity. In that respect, indeed, English individualism, if one means by it the antithesis of gregariousness, is undoubtedly the strongest in Europe.

There is far less prudery in England than is commonly assumed abroad. Little of it is now to be found in London itself, and in most parts, indeed, personal and even intimate questions are often discussed with surprising candour. Yet the 'personal recess', irrespective of language and habits or degree or morality, is still guarded and held with stubborn energy. Either intellectually, morally or sentimentally, wherever what Charles Morgan's Julie describes as one's 'integrity' may happen to lie, the type of reserve which the French call one's *quant-à-soi* (the region of oneself kept apart) is maintained against all encroachments. There remains in the individual Englishman a zone which he keeps 'out of bounds' to social or even kindred intruders, and for the safeguarding of which he will fight and may give up, if need be, the fondest association or the dearest relationship.

This characteristic stimulates another form of escapism which has an affinity with the English policy of non-entanglement in foreign affairs. It is an aversion from any human commitment from which no retreat is possible. 'Not to get involved' is a watchword which one hears time and time again, whether it applies to an invitation to lunch or to a sentimental attachment. Even when the commitment has been accepted as permanent, its binding character is seldom stressed. An English man and an English woman who share each other's lives interfere far less with each other's preoccupations (if not budget) than a Continental couple. Where the Continentals prefer a 'good quarrel' which may throw some light upon their actions or thoughts, doubts or suspicions, the English will choose to ignore a bone of contention, keep silence, or make 'an agreement to disagree' after the fashion of the Liberal Ministers in the National Government. Life will in most instances be quieter if less full; in other cases, there may be unexpected break-ups which a greater curiosity, a more exacting interest, might have averted.

It has long been a general assumption on the Continent that emotional life in England is somewhat 'underlived' and that the English live less intensely than their neighbours. It was the tradition that emotions were less discussed than in Mediterranean countries. But in these days emotional problems are discussed in very outspoken terms.

Stendhal once said that the French 'allowed their emotions to drop from day to day whilst the Italians let them accumulate until they overflowed'. It is tempting to apply the theory of accumulation and overflow to the English. There are few countries where emotional calm is more liable to be broken by a storm or prolonged silence to be followed by an outburst; or where feelings, positive and negative, are more likely to be suppressed till their accumulated force suddenly breaks through social convention and disrupts long-standing attachment or marriage bond. Yet the English disposition to control emotions until they become overpowering is perhaps less due to temperament than to the enduring effect of social education. After all, in civilized people, emotional processes are influenced by training and habits as much as by temperament, which itself is also, partly at least, a product of social evolution. Self-restraint and self-expression have not been taught in vain to generations of Englishmen. Nor were they taught solely in the name of moral or religious codes. Dandyism in the nineteenth century judged a show of emotion far more severely than the Church did a moral weakness. And Victorian fashion chastised demonstrativeness even in sentiments which it considered permissible on purely moral grounds.

What is still relatively constrained in English behaviour is often ascribed (by people who like the sound of the word) to the presence of 'inhibitions'. That irritating *cliché* means very little, for the simple reason that it can be applied to every creature under the sun. Inhibition, they say, is the product of repression; but we are all repressed from the day we receive our first scolding because our parents fail to share our delight in seeing the cat blunder away with a saucepan tied to its tail, to the day when our employer or a woman or the public fails to

appreciate fully our own shining personality. There is an inhibition in every dog whose springtime emotions must be restrained until his master has found a suitable match for him,
and in every one of the 615 members of Parliament when he
realizes that there can be only one Prime Minister at a time.
What do the 'inhibitionists' mean? That no human being ever
finds outlets for all his thoughts, sentiments, desires and appe-
tites; that many of these have to be repressed and that the
energy thus frustrated has to be diverted in some other direction? That is an obvious law of nature and it applies to the whole
of Creation.

It is probably true, taking the country as a whole, that relations between the sexes are not such an object of constant
attention, if not of unconscious preoccupation, in England as
they are in most Continental countries, and that less energy,
thought and time are expended upon them.[1] This is due to
several factors of which some are circumstantial and some
appertain to temperament: education or conditions of life on
the one hand, aptitude for moral isolation and natural reluctance to express oneself on the other. For those very thoughts
and emotions which the Englishman is inclined to keep to himself form the substance of all intimate human relationships
enjoyed by other nations.

Irrespective of the part played by physical attachments
('irresponsibly called physical', according to Colette), intimacy
here seems to set much store by things left unsaid, on a form of
understanding not unduly searching, on mutual regard and
respect of each other's 'secret garden', on tolerance rather than
overwhelming interest. The result is a lesser degree of moral
and sentimental interdependence of man and woman than in
other countries; and conversely far less subjection of the one to
the other. Indeed, that either feelings or sentiments should lead
to a state of subjection seems to be one of the most constant
fears of Englishmen and, even more so, of Englishwomen (who
would probably disagree with Plato's Pausanias that love, if
nothing else, does grant a temporary dispensation from self-
determination).

Most strangers to England are wont to make in the same
breath two contradictory remarks: the first is that 'it has a civili-

[1] War conditions excepted; and even so, the term 'attention', as against
pursuit, still holds good.

zation meant for men'; the other, that women have, in many respects, more privileges than anywhere else in Europe.

The fact is that both men and women attach a greater importance than is found in other countries to the safeguarding of their personal freedom. Attraction, love, companionship are all less binding, less exacting, and each side makes larger concessions to the other in order to retain a greater measure of independence. It is a civilization designed for men in so far as they have their games, their clubs, their life, in a sphere still kept out of reach of women, whose company is an intermittent and not an all-time feature of their existence. This applies to almost all classes, except that for financial reasons there is more 'mixing' in the humbler ranks. It is a civilization where women have acquired various political rights whilst also retaining most of the traditional privileges of femininity. It is a civilization where the interests, tastes, feelings, desires of both sexes are less interlocked and less fully shared in a human sense than they are, for instance, in France, even though the recent acquisition of rights and careers by women has increased the number of common pursuits. There is in England neither the French 'unitarian' conception of family life nor the sharp German distinction between manly pursuits and female servitude. It is, finally, a civilization where life within the family tends to segregation rather than promiscuity, with the result that English children depend on their parents for pastimes or guidance less closely than those of most other European nations.

It is in its emotional and private life that a people far from lacking in impetuosity and power, bold in enterprise and adventure, eager to take risks in action, shows occasional timidity and reluctance to face facts. The Englishman is most at ease either in society, or in nature, or when tackling a job or a physical obstacle, and generally in all situations where his *inner self* is not challenged. He is less at ease when at grips with a forceful human problem; there he does feel that 'a little of reality goes a long way' and seeks refuge either in adventure, sport, action, or in that singular moral isolation which is perhaps the source of shining achievements in lyrical poetry.

The term 'moral isolation' must, I think, be qualified lest it convey a suggestion of sulkiness or gloom which form no part of the picture as I see it. The reluctance or inability to express innermost thoughts or emotions, to let them spread out in words, to communicate with others, does not either blunt sensitiveness or response to human contacts, or turn 'isolation' into sorrowful solitude. The quality of friendship in England suffices to disprove such an inference. Friendship is neither searching nor expansive. It often confines its manifestations to minute occasions where it can find utterance in the most inconspicuous manner. For at its best it thrives on discreet watchfulness and timely care, in which more kindness is revealed than displayed, in which more is actually given than is outwardly tendered.

I have in memory a once familiar spectacle which, banal though it may be, I profoundly enjoyed before the war for its touching quality. In a quiet golf club in Surrey there were three old gentlemen, all well above seventy, who for the last twenty years had been going round the course twice a week as regularly as clockwork. They played very carefully and with great deliberation. They extended to each other every courtesy, far beyond the requirements of the most exacting codes of conduct. They talked little. When they did, as one was stone deaf and the others nearly so, you could hear them from a considerable distance. They had time-honoured little jokes, each appropriate to the successive hazards of the course, which made them chuckle in unison; if one of them failed to respond, the others would look at him with true concern. It meant that the sciatica had been particularly trying that morning or that the liver had reacted overnight to the daily glass of port. When one of them faltered in a bunker or sliced a tee shot—a rare occurrence, to do them justice—there was on the face of his companions an unmistakable expression of deep sympathy. It was before those minute accidents of fate and within the scope of their common pastime that these men expressed twenty odd years of friendship. Possibly they knew little of one another's private lives. Confronted with a family death they probably would have felt embarrassed and would have stammered unintelligible words of commiseration. Yet in the only language which came easily to them, that of the game which had brought them together, they had evolved the means of establishing a lasting human contact and of expressing a deep mutual care.

Their friendship, I feel sure, was real and ready to give. Yet none of them would have dreamt of imposing on the others the burden of his own preoccupations. Quite probably each of them, in adversity or simply in perplexity, would have preferred the company of his dog, who had over human beings the advantage of not inquiring into motives. For it is not only a principle but also an English disposition to share with others the little joys of life and confine the rest to oneself.

Before that 'self', that inner recess, the outside observer may well pause and stand as Balzac did before the closed shutters of many a provincial house, wondering what secret drama those quiet walls might enclose. There is no Gallup poll to record the trend of individual thoughts, hopes or dreams; they can only be guessed by the activities which they inform: from books read and tastes revealed or suggested. And yet in England more than anywhere, the 'unexpressed' is the most tempting field of exploration; for it is a wider field than in more self-explanatory nations.

There are two things, at least, which one may gather without casting one's net very far. The first is that, apart from the business of living and working and from obvious pastimes, pursuits or hobbies, day-dreaming occupies more leisure time in an English mind than in a Latin one; the second is that it generally has a more optimistic trend. Compared with the Latins or the Celts, the English, other circumstances being equal, are a nation of optimists. One of their truest national characters is Micawber and it is a very life-battered Englishman indeed, who does not show a touch of Micawberism, whatever may be the seriousness of his life and the efficiency of his work. There is hardly a Cockney in London who does not 'expect something unexpected to turn up' and this 'something' is pleasant; whilst a Frenchman's fancy might, as likely as not, drift towards prospective mishaps. Gambling itself is a sign of optimism and, in a way, an active manifestation of Micawberism. Nothing could reveal more optimism than the unparalleled success of the Irish sweepstake in this country in the years when it was permitted (and even later). For gambling does not begin at the moment of handing over the stakes or placing a bet; it begins in a kind of game of pretence played by oneself within oneself. To pretend that in a few years' time one will have the house, the car, the yacht of which one dreams, or that tomorrow the sweepstake will produce the dress, the coach and the lackeys of Cinderella; that is a true part of gambling as much as the lust for money. I often fancy that there is some such game of pretence, with or without gambling, in every one of these cottages which line the suburban roads of London, Manchester or Nottingham in endless rows. Are not those local pageants of the English themselves occasions for a game of pretence, in which the factory girl, even though she may not become queen of Ruritania or a film star in a few years' time, may at least be Mary Stuart for a whole day a fortnight hence?

Micawberism in England has survived all changes. Who can deplore it? It does not paralyse work nor does it burden the community. It may be fatal in politics but it proves absolutely harmless in daily life. Indeed, it is one of the greatest individual assertions of faith in life. Micawbers often are the victims of the perversity of things. Yet they bear no grudge to the world but, on the contrary, place an unshakable trust in Providence and they lend a sort of splendour to their shabbiest undertaking.

I once met in Cheshire an elderly mechanic whom I was most fortunate to find after a breakdown at nightfall. On board of what must have been the oldest roadster in England, he carried a set of indifferent tools and probably very little money. While at work on my car, he told me that he was looking for a good site on which to build the most modern garage in England. If he discovered the site, he would be able to borrow the necessary capital, and, given the capital, he knew where to find the equipment and the stock. His description of the scheme made my mouth water. Before we parted I warmly expressed the hope that he would find his Jerusalem and bade him not lose courage. 'Lose courage? What, me?' he replied, 'when I have been looking for it these past twelve years; I am more confident than ever.'

Near the South Downs, I spent a few days with a man who planned to set up near Steyning what he described as a 'crashing riding-school'. He had a one-eyed pony, so knock-kneed that the term 'breaking into a trot' applied to him literally, and a horse aged twenty-five whose coat looked like a winter sunset in Norway. The riding master, as he called himself, was absolutely convinced that he would draw to the shed which he used as stables, every tourist on the South Coast. The pink-grey horse had neither cantered nor trotted for months and was not likely to in the future. 'But', the proud owner assured me, 'he's got a rare good point which should attract those people who are not out for sheer speed and yet want to get on: he can walk up

Chanctonbury Ring and down again faster than anything on four legs, or, for that matter, on two.'

I met him by chance two years later. He had 'sold the stables' but was negotiating the purchase of five or six Dartmoor ponies which are used only in the pits and which cost at that time fifteen shillings a head. He swore he would 'train them to the saddle' and teach riding to every child within ten miles of Buckfast. He was beaming, and probably still is.

Who could wish to see those traders in merry failure slowly eliminated, as I fear they may be, by a world planned to the last dot? As for Micawberism in general, it can hardly die in England. When life falls short of the little man's expectations, it is his own compensation drawn from his own simple riches. And what politician will ever build up such an accomplished world that we could afford to live in it without 'expecting something unexpected to turn up' or ever playing a game of pretence? That in England the 'expected unexpected' should on the whole make pleasant thought, and the game of pretence be instantly renewed without bitterness, this is perhaps one of the traits which most accounts for the prevailing gentleness of life even under the deepening shadow of industrialization.

II. THE ENGLISH WAY

CHAPTER 6

FANCY AND ETHICS

Yet not your words onlie but mine owne fantasie. MARLOWE

THERE are, in all languages, words which, even isolated from any context, reveal much of the nation that speaks them, by their sheer power of evocation and graphic beauty. I once discussed with some French friends the suggestive value of French words in this respect. What was the most French word in our language, we asked; the word which was most distinctive? I proposed *lucide* as conveying at once light, clarity, and clear scrutiny. Had I to answer the same question in respect of the English mind, I should probably single out the word *fancy*, not as weakened by current usage but with its full and rich implications.

It conveys to my mind a combination of qualities which have been traditionally characteristic of the English: not only fantasy of which it is the contraction, but nimble freedom of will, dislike of rational obligations, whim and imaginative moodiness. The word has, so to speak, a propulsive suggestion; yet, like all others, it also has its brakes: reserve, a touch of shyness, some elusiveness, and an instinctive reluctance to follow any pursuit, cultivate any taste, or carry any belief to the point of mental strain. In two syllables *fancy* illustrates the contrast between the English and the German mind—fancy, not imagination which the Germans do, indeed, possess.

It also throws light on a controversial subject: the quality of the English imagination. 'We are not an imaginative people,' the English are wont to say. This statement calls for qualification. The gift of imagination in England has been proved beyond doubt in activities where it plays an outstanding part: scientific research, poetry, the novel, love of adventure and exploration. What is obvious to a stranger is that, in several directions, imagination in England is undertrained, underdisciplined, and therefore apt to become sluggish or erratic.

In the first place English education sets less store than Continental education by verbal expression and the discussion of general ideas, two effective stimuli of the imagination. In the second place insular England is not consistently brought into contact with certain realities on which the Continental imagination speculates from childhood, and consequently it appears less fertile in respect of them; in matters of European sociology, land warfare, architecture, theatrical production, an Englishman's imagination would traditionally find less scope than a Frenchman's, since England has, on the whole, seen less land warfare on a huge scale than France, made direct contact with fewer European peoples, been less of a theatrical clearing-house and of an experimental ground for generations of multifarious master-builders. A Lancashire weaver may be as capable as a Belgian farmer of realizing that a bullet through his body causes an unpleasant sensation. Yet a declaration of war will conjure up less alarming visions in the imagination of the former because he has not been trained for centuries to dwell on spectacles of invasion and havoc. Finally, irrespective of experience, each people applies its imagination to those pursuits for which it is naturally gifted, and not to all; each nation is unimaginative in some realm of thought, but imaginative in others.

Besides their shining record in poetry, there is a minor but charming art in which the English have excelled, an art which deserves attention because it throws into relief one distinctive aspect of their imagination: the art of telling children's tales. Here is a province of thought where fancy reigns absolutely, where it knows no other bounds than a certain relevance of the story to its own course and atmosphere, which is a very different thing from factual plausibility. It is *relevant* that we should learn why Mr. Toad in Kenneth Grahame's *The Wind in the Willows* yearns for a brand new red roadster (and we do: Mr. Toad is both a *nouveau riche* and a speed-worshipper); but it does not in the least matter to us whether in real life a toad would be likely to drive a car. It is, after all, on some such understanding that we expect the lines, words and rhymes of a poem to be relevant to the poet's own world, and not necessarily to strict, objective reality. In both instances, in the major art as well as in the minor, the English are supreme.

It is the peculiar quality of the English imagination which prevents English art from being at its mightiest when it courts realism. One of the characteristics of French art at any time is probably the constant relation of both imagination and emo-

tion to reality. I think English art is most original where both
rise above reality, shun it or, alternatively, take it with a grain
of salt. English humour is, above all, a mild revenge of individual escapism on daily reality.

To communicate the sense of life rather than to depict it in
all its particulars with ruthless accuracy, to express inclinations,
wants, yearnings, trends of human passions rather than objec-
tively to appraise their course and effect, to suggest what is
expected from life, derived from it or lacking in it, in moods,
hopes, warmth, illusion, frustration, such, I think, are the distinctive tendencies of English art. Even in the interpretation of
nature where English painters are more submissive than the
French to apparent forms and shapes, imagination plays its
characteristic part: not by stimulating scrutiny or broadening
its scope but rather by adding a wishful human touch to the
subject in hand. Before a French canvas you realize that the
painter has taken an armful of life and shown you as much as
he had seen in it. An English painter wants you to like not only
his painting as such, but also his landscape, his house, his portrait; and he describes them faithfully and fondly as though to
associate you in his feeling. The French and the Latin use their
imagination to increase their knowledge of reality; the English
to make it more gratifying. As a critic said of Rainer Maria
Rilke, they often 'use reality as a springboard'. It is no coinci-
dence that the French should aim at making the most of their
food while the English are more given to surround the eating
of it with a pleasant setting.

What is common to both is a deep appreciation of the value
of life and of the means whereby imagination can enhance it,
whereas a German imagination often expands itself in taking
arms against life. Between the English and the French the
difference is one of means of action and ways of approach. The
greatest means of investigation which the French possess is the
gift of sight. That of the English lies somewhere in the regions
of fancy. Almost every one of Dickens's characters discovers the
preciousness of life through dreams and want—of food, of
warmth, of affection, of what he has most lacked and therefore
most believed in. This is an approach to the world that Charlie
Chaplin in our own days has profoundly understood. Nor is
it solely due to the deep sense of frustration which weighed
upon the childhood of both men: it is a constant imaginative

short cut to the understanding of life which is natural to the English genius and which has been encouraged and stimulated in England by the presence of a strong Celtic streak in the nation's cultural development.

Some years ago during the revival of interest in the Brontës, three plays on the sisters' lives were produced at the same time on the London stage. Alfred Sangster's pleased me most, presenting a discreet cross-section of their development and the part of Charlotte being exquisitely played by Lydia Sherwood. In one scene Charlotte pays her first visit to her publishers in London: among several callers, Thackeray is there, unrecognized by her, for she is quite new to London. A literary critic takes advantage of her social 'greenness' to amuse himself at her expense and Thackeray's too: he asks her point blank what she thinks of *Henry Esmond* as a novel. Embarrassed at first, she gradually warms to the subject, makes a frontal attack on the book, and ends with a taunt at the author's analysis of feminine psychology: 'I am afraid Mr. Thackeray has a lot to learn about the heart of a woman. . . .' This little scene survived in my memory suggesting a tempting contrast. Here, on the one side, was Thackeray looking hard at reality with something like a French pince-nez and setting up from a wealth of experience two feminine characters which, for all the greatness of the novel, ring false to me too; on the other was the simple ambassadress of a fanciful world sprung not from experience but from imagination and rich passion, a realm magically reclaimed from the bleak waste-land of a Yorkshire parsonage. Did not she represent a combination of Celtic power of evocation and English fancy and art, in which the nation strikes one of its most characteristic notes? It has been a great English achievement to poise and balance various and apparently conflicting racial contributions. Even in characters created by writers of English stock there is to be detected something of the Celtic mood: from Dickens's Estella Faversham to Katherine Mansfield's Beryl Burnell.

Historically, English art and English thought have an idealistic orientation. Yet to say, as I have, that it strives to retouch or to sidetrack reality would be singularly to minimize its historic contribution to Western culture. It goes much further than that. It is greatest when it uses the passion and power latent in a sturdy nation to raise life above material reality; and for this particular bent English art is certainly indebted to Puritanism. In one form or another Puritanism runs right through English literature and art. By Puritanism I do not mean the arid and limiting formalism with which it is sometimes wrongly identi- fied, or into which it is apt to turn, but Puritanism in its ancient vein, which was above all passionate. Shelley's *Adonaïs* is full of such passion, an urgent striving to force life into a moral or ideal mould.

There is in this what might be termed an optimistic assertion of man, even in revolt. It demands much optimism to correct reality or even to tamper with it. And the English do believe in progress, progress in things, worlds, individuals, progress achieved by the action of man. Puritan thought tends to impose this by moral pressure; or, if it fails to do so, to record an empha- tic protest. This is perhaps the only sense in which the English are ethical revolutionaries, but it is capital. The English mind when it moralizes less manifests its optimism in other ways, in pleasant additions and amendments to reality: more warmth about the hearth, a deliberate overlooking of unpleasantness, hope that 'things will take a turn for the best'. In either way, whether passionate or quiet and smiling, English literature and art exhale a 'reformism' of life which may escape the attention of an observer who is only mindful of their apparent social con- formity and polish. Literary cynicism, the 'Cavalier' attitude in literature, flashes by, here and there; but it seldom goes without some moral preoccupation, as witness the lesson underlying the conclusion of Oscar Wilde's *Dorian Gray*, a Puritan end to a Cavalier novel.

What runs through English thought is the tradition of ethical romanticism which started with Milton's Satan and still pre- serves in our day part of its vigour; a tradition which Louis Gillet in an article posthumously published in August 1943 by the *Revue des Deux Mondes* holds to have inspired, directly or not, all forms of romantic revolt in Europe for three centuries; a tradition which has forcibly rejected the idea, born of the Roman Catholic philosophy, of man's resignation to his plight, together with the belief that the moral progress of the individual is an essentially spiritual problem not to be solved by the improve- ment of his temporal condition.

English civilization would not be intelligible without such an influence, which has left and still leaves its mark on English thought. Yet in order to understand contemporary England it is equally important to see how this tradition has also, in some respects, deviated from its original inspiration. The belief that circumstances as well as individual conscience play a determining part in the moral advancement of man easily led in practice to the conviction that a comfortable life is a factor in moral improvement and that, as the saying goes, 'a happy man is the best part of a good man'. In an age in which ethical preoccupations were changing to worldly and social issues, the old Miltonic inspiration thus indirectly fostered a general tendency to lay stress on physical comfort and to cultivate it as a prerequisite to moral progress. There is an 'odour' of comfort throughout the English novel of the nineteenth century which infers a growing connexion between moral behaviour and physical surroundings. Finally, since here as elsewhere and perhaps even in a higher degree, society was already regarded as a trustee for man's welfare, it also became saddled with the responsibility for his moral condition: an unexpected consummation for the Whig crusade on behalf of free will that it should thus have brought water to the mill of Marxist Determinism!

Should one infer from this aspect of her evolution that England has developed a materialistic civilization? And what has become in contemporary England of those traditional gifts and tendencies which, as I see them, were characteristic of the national genius?

It can hardly be denied that in all countries individual imagination suffers a setback as men become less and less self-reliant, as they depend more and more for their entertainment and even culture on collective spoon-feeding and 'canteens of the mind' such as the cinema, the radio, the press: all institutions justified in a political sense yet inevitably tending, at least for a time, to blunt the power of personal investigation and fancy. In England as elsewhere idealism is inclined to turn into wishful thinking, moralizing into a deliberate ignoring of unpleasant facts, and fancy into vague images informed by facile screen-memories or vague dreams of greater comfort. Nor can the inexorable process of specialization in all human activities fail to limit the scope of the imagination and to dull it. Such is, no doubt, the inevitable price of social progress, which may gradually be lightened if the world adapts itself to the change from individual to mass pursuits.

The very conditions of physical existence in England, with her crowded cities and dwindling rural life (a process which the war may well have decisively reversed), have made her especially vulnerable to the impact of such a transformation. Yet the old spirit of individual self-reliance in thought and craftsmanship, which the English share with other upholders of Western culture, is not, I think, likely to succumb to the threat of extinction. Indeed there are signs that England is outgrowing the first phase of gregarious materialism.

Look at the mournful geometry of building contractor's tenements: and at the thousands of houses almost identical in height and shape which are the horizon of the resident in Suburbia. And yet behind the façade, in the minute garden, English individualism manages to assert itself with spade, rake, mower, and clippers, and contrives to prevail over uniformity. No two gardens look alike; indeed they take pride in their diversity. Imagination may be dulled for a time; but it reacts in self-defence with such means as are at its disposal.

A modern Englishman may well believe that he will feel more kindly towards humanity if he has acquired a comfortable drawing-room suite, and, tempted by this short cut to virtue, may resort to the hire purchase system for the benefit of his immortal soul. But he will not believe for long that life's sole object is to provide the maximum number of well-fed citizens all provided with a car, a radio set, and a first-class season ticket from Twickenham to Waterloo. His own elusiveness, his own sense of mental elbow-room, will finally belie such summary conceptions of human destiny. Against them the Frenchman's safeguard is his individual respect for the solemnity of life. The Englishman may be more prone to intellectual nonchalance, but his fancy will keep him free from moral subjection to materialism; his fancy and also his humour, for there is as much individual protest against weakly materialism in the Grossmiths' *Diary of a Nobody* as in an ethical revolt.

There are, of course, other protections from the tyranny of materialism. One of them is mysticism, but this, clearly, is not a common feature of the English mind. Another is a sceptical disposition which the English possess. It is a quiet, congenial variety of scepticism, without a sharp edge; it is temperamental and not rational. Yet in the past it has proved a very effective weapon against intellectual and moral absolutism. It is the

Englishman's 'tongue in his cheek', equivalent to what in Germany would be a stodgy refutation. Without some measure of scepticism all minds would suffer from arthritis.

Scepticism accounts for the flexibility of the English mind and makes it immune from even dialectical despotism. Reason might occasionally overcome French individualism and make it bow, though only temporarily, before a dogma. Reason has less hold on the elusive English mind, which deftly evades the net cast upon it. Such agility also discloses a weakness; it often comes very near to intellectual frivolity, just as there is some frivolity in the fear of emotional entanglements, and again, in the political plane, in the fear of foreign commitments.

In second-rate fiction the English have made a liberal use of 'the novel with a happy ending'. Is it because the less-schooled section of the reading public considers a happy ending as truer to life? The shop assistant who buys a novelette for a train journey does not look to it for a life-like picture. What she does look for is the temporary pleasure of an agreeable conclusion. This is significant of a trait: rational scepticism would rebel against the enjoyment of something which reason belies. Not so English scepticism. While it will not tolerate an obstacle in the way of contentment, it traditionally draws the line at delusion in so far, of course, as it can detect it.

The distinction between conviction and enjoyment does not apply only in the case of inferior works and a comparatively unschooled public, but with almost equal force to the arts and the higher attainments of the English mind. In art, the French demand that it should teach them more of themselves and of their relationship to the outside world than mere experience can offer. The Germans go much further and take it with such seriousness and indiscretion that the whole nation periodically becomes the slave of a philosophy, a creed, a political dogma, so that any belief can be forced upon them by sheer didacticism. The English expect their art to be primarily gratifying, to open a field to individual tastes and curiosity; they wish it to make life richer. A *pièce à thèse* in England normally has little success and arouses distrust, save perhaps in war-time when it takes its context from inspiring events. It is only when English art has fulfilled its mission as a source of gratification that it may further claim an educational role; and, even so, whatever message it conveys will seldom be taken as all-embracing and final.

E

This disposition may not be without risks. It often encourages wishful thinking, which, in pre-war years, was certainly a notable intellectual weakness in England. There is a threat to the mind when the 'happy ending' ceases to be just a source of pleasure and becomes a form of self-deception which in England is at all times a greater danger than the forcible imposition of a dogma. The war, in the midst of which wishful thinking is a natural reaction to stress, is not calculated to restrain that tendency, for it allows hardly more in the way of creative activity than either a kind of imagery related to outward reality in the same way as photography, or else an intellectual diversion from the conflict.

A nation inclined to avoid realism when it interferes with its own way of appreciating life and of cultivating art, one which is alternately poetical and practical, escapist and earnest, has been able to maintain its high standards because its optimism never became complacent nor its idealism intellectually facile. And this success was largely due both to its powerful streak of moral 'reformism' on the one hand, and on the other, to the real richness and vivaciousness of its individual fancy, examples of which are still to be found everywhere in England even in these days of greater superficial uniformity.

These original qualities can only be seriously impaired, in this country as elsewhere, by cultural demagogy: by which I mean not only the tendency of the élite to serve political passions and popular controversies but also to placate the crowd instead of stimulating individual thought. Thus could the patient, robust, self-dependent and creative optimism of a people be turned into complacency and self-delusion. Art loses its integrity and does not serve the cause of the people when it lowers its standards or puts itself at the mercy of confusion, of political agitation and hand-to-mouth philosophies circulated from country to country, continent to continent. Nor does a nation serve the cause of humanity by losing its own character any more than an individual serves the people by adopting a supine anonymity.

English thought is neither conformist nor revolutionary. It is instinctively conservative in outlook and progressive in determination. To have shown that these two elements are compatible and that their combination can achieve much, is one of its original contributions to Western civilization. The English mind usually gains little by absorbing novelty at high speed or external influences in overdoses, and it achieves most when it follows its own disposition and its own pace, which is not to be forced. That pace follows nature, which goes no faster in its most startling transformations and which finds in contrasts the source of its richness.

. . . . .

At Newcastle-on-Tyne, in our own days, the Assize Judges are still presented with a gold coin of James I and Charles I: 'Dagger Money', for the purpose of providing a bodyguard to escort them along the perilous road to the next town on the Circuit. The survival of the ancient custom does not in the least impair the administration of justice; on the contrary it reminds Englishmen that they have a history of which they may thus occasionally take a glimpse elsewhere than in written records. That is the function of tradition. Far from hindering progress, it enables us to measure its strides and sometimes to make sure that we are not going back when we seem to move forward.

The English way of living has many faults, like that of all human communities. They are freely acknowledged as such. There is no attempt to attribute them to the perversity of fate or the malignity of the outside world; the English accept their responsibilities as individuals and as members of a society which recognizes the value of individual life and individual thought. They also understand that a little thing may sometimes be as important as a great conception, and to them a cup of tea may sometimes hold as much happiness as an architectural triumph. They have had a way of living which kept to the scale of man in its houses, its art, and its everyday pursuits, the way of living of a Western civilization drawing its strength from diversity, not mass, from balance rather than from extremism, not the breeding of *ersatz* supermen or the desolate discipline of the ant-hill. This civilization in England and elsewhere has been threatened not only by war but by many political impacts: yet the English in the political realm and in the institutions which they have evolved, as well as in their personal dispositions, have to hand effective weapons wherewith to defend it.

III. MEN AND INSTITUTIONS

CHAPTER 7

ENGLISHMEN AND POLITICS

I WAS barely twelve years of age when our old English teacher told his forty pupils the following story: Walking along the corridor of an English preparatory school a few years before, he had seen a child of our own age very carefully mending a damaged chair leg. The boy was alone; nobody was watching him; nobody had told him to repair it. 'But', explained our teacher looking at us severely over his glasses, 'that boy thought it his duty thus to contribute to the general welfare. Here,' that worthy man added with sadness, 'here I have often seen benches destroyed with a thoroughness equal to that which this English child displayed in a work of salvage. In this, my friends, in this, lies the strength of England!' he concluded defiantly, sure of finding no contradictor among us and drawing himself up with a vigour borrowed from such inspiring examples. For it is a habit common, I think, to all teachers of modern languages to overwhelm their pupils beneath the weight of virtues discovered abroad while infallibly overlooking the merits of their own people. Needless to say we soon made him sensible of so gross an oversight by putting his chair into such a hopeless state that even his model English boy would have had to give up any idea of exercising on it his sense of civic duty.

Once our wounded feelings had thus exacted a just retribution, the story was nevertheless duly recorded in our minds. I am not sure that my old teacher would find as many volunteers to-day as he might have in his own time for the repair of broken chairs. Yet, irrespective of the country's evolution in other ways, it is certain that the traditional English sense of responsibility to the community has endured and remains strong.

That society and not the state is the basis of English national life; that the power of society has hitherto supplied the surest political protection against the glorification of the state: these remarks have become truisms (although they may later call for some qualification). What is worth recalling is that the sense of individual obligations towards society, which is the condition of its power, is not only a tradition kept up by moral and dogmatic teaching; it is the natural consequence of the English way of living and, for this reason, it survives many changes and resists most ideological assaults.

An English child is trained to feel as much at home in the company of his school-fellows, at his sports club, on the playing-field, in the parks, as with his own family. His masters themselves do not treat him only as a child but also as a responsible social being. Whatever his parents' circumstances may be, he enjoys far more independence than any child on the Continent. He is less sheltered by his family in a human sense; on the other hand it constitutes no barrier between him and direct social experience. The spectacle of children making their own plans, arranging their own games, establishing their own codes, enjoying the freedom of a house, is common in England and rare on the Continent, just as the warm and inspiring atmosphere of a French family is seldom to be found in England.

The influence of the family on an English child does not altogether overrule that of his social environment; his allegiance to his family is less binding and his obligations to his own social *milieu* greater than is the case in other countries. The intellectual and sensitive development of the young Englishman is probably slower than that of the Latin; but he is fully equipped as a responsible citizen at an age when young men of other nations have everything yet to learn and do it suddenly through military conscription.

One might say that in France the family is practically the only intermediate stage between the individual and the nation as a whole, while in England it is society that plays this part. Social life in France is in the nature of an art. To the English it is the first test of citizenship and the basis of their political life. Both nations have in common an instinctive fear of the over-growth of the state; but French resistance is apt to remain that of the individual family, whereas English resistance is collective because society is a living body which incessantly supplies new forces.

Trained from childhood to social duties and functions by the habit of early association and responsibilities, the English are at ease in the field of politics, which they enter effortlessly as a new stage in social life, as a natural extension of social activity and social duty. Moreover, they enter politics with a sound sense of what is feasible and of what can reasonably be expected from men. 'Policy', said Bismarck, 'is the art of the Possible. . . .' That is an art which the English have cultivated by education and which accounts for their success in the government of men.

The chief characteristic of English home politics is, above all, their 'naturalness'. In most European countries political life is usually attended by a measure of stage-setting which marks its separation from individual or social pursuits. There is an air of solemnity about a Frenchman walking to the polling station, about his political meetings and assemblies. In Germany, even the nomination of a local councillor is not taken seriously unless it be surrounded with an atmosphere of drama. Not so in England.

In spite of the traditions which regulate political customs and of the pageants which adorn most great functions in English public life, there is little contrast between the attitude of English people in their political capacity and in their daily, ordinary behaviour. What struck me on my first visit to the House of Commons was not the wig of Mr. Speaker, the architecture of the assembly hall, or the singularity of a time-honoured procedure; it was the apparent casualness and homely atmosphere of the discussion. It might have been a club with the members comparing notes on the 'probables' for Ascot.

In the normal course of events a little town of the Home Counties is busier than a French provincial town of the same size and situation. Should municipal elections be held, the tempo of the French town will be quickened beyond recognition, while in England the change from daily routine will not be very noticeable.

Political talents and political habits are not superimposed on the English mind. They are not an additional, specialized form of training but one into which the people have grown through social experience; not only because of the trend of English education, but also because society produces in every conceivable field of action and business a number of associations, groups, clubs, guilds, unions, unparalleled anywhere else in Europe and rivalled nowhere else save in America. There is hardly a single occupation in this country which, provided it is shared by a score or so of people, does not supply a pretext for periodical gatherings, from the Singleton cricketers' annual dinner to the meeting of the 1922 Committee. In all of these somebody gets up to address, lecture, congratulate, thank or criticize others; and it is a poorly conducted affair indeed that does not also allow for one or two replies, proposals, counter-proposals, with seconding, backing, begging to differ, dissenting, minority report, vote, counter-vote and mutual congratulations to crown all, for this reputedly word-sparing nation becomes in its collective pursuits the most talkative in Europe. The result is that through such exhaustive practice in debating, from the 'specially appointed room for parties of twenty and upwards' at the Pig and Whistle to the Imperial Parliament at Westminster, the Englishman takes political life, so to speak, in his stride; he is completely at ease in a parliamentary atmosphere.

The English as a rule are not good orators, but they can make ready and pleasant speakers. In all classes there is to be found a high percentage of men and women who do not feel embarrassed before an audience and find its wavelength without difficulty. The speaker is expected to 'say' something, not to present a rhetorical work of art. Indeed, not only do the English forgive poor oratory and like conversational tones, but they distrust and fear eloquence as being out of keeping with plain and direct transaction of the business in hand.

Mr. Lloyd George, the greatest British orator I have heard, and probably the greatest European orator since Jaurès, has often suffered more than he gained from his supreme eloquence. I have particularly in mind the impressive luncheon which he gave to the world press in 1936 to herald his political come-back as the promoter of the 'Programme of Peace and Reconstruction'. Flowers, food and wine were provided lavishly and with rare taste. At the end he made a speech in which he used all the resources of his dialectical skill, all the inflexions and rich modulations of his Welsh voice. Yet the effect of it all upon the audience was aptly summed up by a journalist from Lancashire who had liberally partaken of everything, in one laconic sentence: 'Fare's too good; speech's too good; bodes no good.'

Had the great statesman fumbled for his words, stuttered here and there, served red wine with fish and made other such confessions of human frailty and unreadiness, he might have been more successful. As things were, they struck the audience as unnatural. There is in every Englishman an underlying belief that sound, practical politics express themselves plainly. Trimmings, stage-setting, even when they are the products of careful intellectual preparation, always seem to provoke the reflection: 'Methinks the lady doth protest too much.' Lord Baldwin's popularity as a speaker was largely due to his skilful avoidance of oratorical effects, to the impression which he conveyed of 'putting his case plainly' from man to man; his listeners always felt when he dealt with the most momentous problems that politics remained 'life-size'. His was the kind of approach which in normal times most closely corresponds to the English conception of correct outward behaviour in politics: a moral undertone, some reserve, absence of intellectual affectation, calm, simplicity of expression.

Such a conception of politics as a natural social function makes for moderation in methods of action and for realism in outlook. I remember the disappointment of a friend of mine who stood as Labour candidate for a Yorkshire constituency in 1935 at failing to stir up an attentive but impassive electorate: 'Mark Antony might come and make his speech here,' he said; 'they would listen to him, nod once or twice, and then go to the pub and have one!' I have occasionally seen instances of rough proceedings, but they certainly are not a feature of the nation's political life, which is more liable to be dull than passionate. Its moderation is totally different from the behaviour which is sometimes produced in Germany by herd discipline. It is a sense of order bred by social education and by a profound disbelief in the practical value of violence. Violence, in the Englishman's opinion, does not pay; and his aim in public affairs is to produce tangible results.

For, whatever their disposition may be in other pursuits, the English are realists in the realm of practical politics. They take stock of daily experience, human limitations, human resistances. The first reaction of the man-in-the-street to the general concept of 'Communism' is more probably to wonder whether and how the butcher, the grocer and the milkman would fit into a Communist state, than to speculate on the future implications of the dogma. To things political he instinctively applies the touchstone of his own social experience; this, more than his reason, guards him against the belief that any solution in local, national or world affairs can be absolutely good and justify unqualified adherence. In fact the expression of extreme views and the formulation of comprehensive systems in which everything seems to dovetail has a disconcerting effect on English people.

Should they be partly in agreement with some of the views and with points of the system, the presentation of a case which leaves nothing to chance usually induces them to reconsider their previous judgement and to back out.

Then the English seldom adopt an intellectual attitude towards political issues. They judge them on factual evidence and on practical grounds. In national affairs and national politics men and groups take their stand on specific questions. They seldom start from a theoretical, speculative basis. Continental parties are apt to grow as associations bound by a common doctrine or a comprehensive programme covering all problems set before the politician or the statesman. The plan of the building is laid down; then the human material is gathered to form the edifice. In England one is reminded of the Moroccan architect who, when asked by the local French Commissioner of Works to show him the plan of the house he was in the process of building, answered: 'The plan? What plan? How could I have made one? Why, the house is not even finished yet!' It is true that in recent years there has been a tendency among English parties to publish far-reaching programmes and to find doctrinal bases. On the whole, however, what the ordinary English citizen remarks in any given programme, including that of the Labour Party, the only one which might be called even partly dogmatic, is the answer of the party to some practical question, its proposals on a tangible issue immediately affecting his welfare. It is only in foreign affairs that emotional and quixotic reactions are to be found. Home problems are thought of and dealt with in terms of strict realism and of English local and national realities. That is why English politics are not exportable and English methods difficult to adopt elsewhere. They cannot be communicated as a rational system because they are a growth from nature and varying conditions. For the same reason, an Englishman finds it difficult to understand Continental conflicts of ideas and is apt to consider these as groundless and arbitrary. Being himself completely exempt from intellectual fanaticism in political matters, save, perhaps, and even then rarely, when they border on religious issues, he judges them accordingly on their immediate merits and ascribes either to intolerance or frivolity all contests in which the stakes are not concrete and positive.

The decision taken after the General Strike to render illegal all strikes which had a political and not a direct economic motive certainly corresponds to a profound trait of the English political character: it was considered normal that workmen should strike as a protest against insufficient wages, for that was a practical issue; but not that they should do so on grounds which might be purely ideological. As citizens, workmen should, it was held, express their political and ideological views through their official representatives and not attempt to make them prevail by resort to an economic weapon directed against the whole community.

Everything in its proper place and at its proper time: that is the traditional basis of English political life. In the past the English have always shown a great aversion to universalism in politics. They liked a man to talk of things which were within his own calling and experience; they did not like a tradesman to put the case for the miner or vice versa. They considered public opinion to be the cumulative product of views held by various categories of people on different subjects, in regard to which each category had a certain competence and justification to act within its own limits; public opinion is not the views of each man on all subjects. This is probably one of the reasons for the orderly conduct of English public affairs.

In this respect there was a marked change, perhaps only temporary, during the years which preceded the Second World War. A taste for universality was developed, under the influence of the press and the radio and often encouraged by politicians who led their constituents to believe that each of them was capable of passing judgement on any political issue. A daily paper went further and wrote in its leading article that every Englishman must be his own Foreign Secretary. It is a very dangerous extension of the principle of government by the people. What has perturbed French political life is not, as some people believe, the excessive influence of local politics but, on the contrary, the constant interference of citizens in the settlement of issues upon which they cannot be adequately equipped to form a valid judgement. It is for every citizen to decide whether his representatives at the local Council, in Parliament or elsewhere truly defend his interests and his convictions. It is not for him to riot if the national Government does not go to war in order to help Ruritania. Yet this is the type of excess to which claims of individual universality must eventually lead.

It is only fair to say that such tendencies in England have never yet reached the point of paralysing the action of the Executive. They have been checked on the whole by the traditional sense of responsibility; but they have gone far enough in such matters as the problem of the Indian Constitution, the Abyssinian crisis, the Spanish War, the reoccupation of the Rhineland, to be considered a new development in English public life. In these cases groups and individuals have intervened in state affairs not through the ordinary processes of parliamentary procedure but by such forms of direct action as the organization of an unofficial ballot or petition of protest. Irrespective of the merits of the problem on which a decision is sought by such means, the inevitable effect is to weaken the authority of Parliament and to create, as it were, a political black market outside normal institutions. Even during the war these tendencies have reappeared, usually stimulated by such generous impulses as the demand for the opening of a Second Front. As evidence of the trend of public opinion such manifestations may be useful. But should they assume the character of forcible demonstrations they might become a serious threat to popular government itself; for it is by direct appeals to public opinion and by sidetracking parliamentary institutions that Continental dictators have invariably succeeded. The totalitarian technique consists in overbidding popular assemblies in order to discredit them and to remove the obstacle which they place in the path of illegitimate power.

What considerably lessens the danger of dictatorship in this country is a combination of temperamental disposition and of political habits which characterize the English but not most of the nations where authoritarian régimes have prevailed. In the latter the personal factor plays a great part; whereas the English are not susceptible to the fascination of oratory. Such régimes demand a degree of fanaticism; and the English are at all times too intellectually nonchalant to reach such a pitch of intensity; fanaticism requires a dogmatic basis; and politically the English are too factual to be seriously tempted by dogmatism. These thrive on a measure of credulity; whereas the English, while very often wishful thinkers in foreign policy, are not gullible where their bread and butter is concerned. Finally, such régimes are especially successful where there is a certain disruption of society, which creates by contrast a yearning for gregarious action; but English habits of association produce a large number of spontaneous groups, sprung from society, which fortify the body politic against the full spirit of gregariousness.

In so far as we can judge at this stage of the war, Englishmen have resisted the temptation, and England the impact, of régimes founded on dogmatism, the conflicts between which have shattered Continental order and reasonable ways of living. That successful resistance is not due only to the disposition of the present generation of English men and women or, alternatively, to the sole fact of the Channel barrier, though this has, no doubt, played a great part in England's immunity; it is also the result of institutions which remained solid at the time when those of other countries collapsed. Their nature, their value to the people in our day, and the way in which they are affected by recent developments, certainly deserve reconsideration; and perhaps not solely from the English point of view.

CHAPTER 8

. . . Come, Demos, had you not best decide at once which is your truest friend and best disposed to the interests of the state, to your belly and you? Demos. *But how can I decide it cleverly?*

ARISTOPHANES: *The Knights*

IT was not only her own territory that England was left to protect, alone among the Powers of Europe, when in June 1940 Hitler secured virtual control of the whole Continent as far as the Russian frontier: it was also a certain Western order embodied in her institutions and traditional outlook. That order was described as democratic. Yet, although English democracy was deemed sufficiently real at the time to rally the hopes of a continent threatened not only by German military power but also by German political philosophy, its authenticity and value have been in the last three or four years repeatedly questioned both within and without Great Britain.

The reason for the controversy over the English system of government is that the very notion of democracy is now attended by the greatest confusion, and that the English order is judged according to conceptions of democracy which vary from man to man, party to party, nation to nation. No comment on British institutions is therefore possible without a definition of democracy, for only by means of it can the commentator's meaning be made clear and his reflections set in an ideological context both intelligible and honest.

There are those who are still satisfied that Lincoln's famous definition fills the bill and that the sense of democratic government has been made sufficiently plain when it has been called the 'government of the people, by the people, for the people'. Yet that definition, which had a profound significance eighty years ago when it was offered as an alternative to various forms of absolutism or arbitrary rule, provides in our own time hardly more than a starting point. Here are, for instance, a few questions of leading—even vital—importance to-day, which fall well outside the range of Lincoln's definition: Is it the object of

77

democracy to provide the maximum physical welfare for the greatest number regardless of the effects on individual independence of the means employed in the attainment of that aim, or is it to provide equality of opportunity for all by encouraging the spirit of individual responsibility and self-reliance? Should full social security be purchased if need be at the expense of individual freedom by general measures of coercion? Does equality take precedence over liberty? Does democracy endorse in 1944 the principle laid down by John Stuart Mill: 'There is a limit to the legitimate interference of collective opinion with individual independence. And to find that limit and maintain it against encroachments is as indispensable to a good condition of human affairs as protection against political despotism'?

These are but a few of the many questions which the contemporary man would have to answer in order to approach anything like a satisfactory definition of democracy. For the dominant problem facing the twentieth century is not so much, perhaps, the protection of the mass against individual or against aristocratic despotism, as the protection of the individual against manifold aspects of mass despotism. Autocracy in Germany and Italy has been installed and maintained through the spread of mass ideologies, by using the growing pressure of collective opinion. The only signs of resistance apparent in those countries have been given by individual consciences, by individuals resisting mass psychoses, and not by the enthralled community or by collective bodies opposed to the régime. We are told, to be sure, that in Italy and Germany the people were deceived; but in the possibility of mass deception on such a scale lies precisely the danger of any form of government which sacrifices the individual and his sense of responsibility to the cult of the mass. We have seen before our eyes the development of a technique of government which Raymond Aron aptly describes as 'Despotism by Plebiscite'[1] and which Napoleon III, in France, was the first ruler to exploit. It consists in creating a consensus of emotional opinion as a weapon for the establishment of personal or party power. It is unlikely that we have yet witnessed the last of such practices. They should suffice to indicate the vital need for the protection of individual independence against the ruthless interference of collective opinion.

The internal history of Western nations is largely associated

[1] *La France Libre*, August 1943.

with the struggle of the people against despotism. And one is inclined to identify the notion of despotism with that of tyranny. Yet personal or feudal tyrannies, whether dynastic, aristocratic or economic, are not the sole forms of despotism that men have to cope with. A whole nation can become despotic in its dealings with individual citizens; the individual in decadent Greece was as much victimized by the Demagogue who personified the mass, as by the most exacting of its former tyrants. There is a grave threat to the individual in the spread of bureaucracy, the anonymous power of which can be neither challenged nor miti-gated in its excesses, for it is not embodied in responsible persons and offers no visible target to rebellion or reform. In Western countries Trade Unionism, which is a necessary institution, often found itself defending the rights of the greatest number at the expense of the individual, by contributing to the elimination of independent artisans and small private enterprises. The fact that our contemporary world has therefore to face, is that the cultivation of mass opinion and the pursuit of mass welfare con-stitute in themselves, a danger to individual independence. To that danger all reformers should be alive. For the profound difference between Western and Mediterranean civilization on the one hand, and what we describe as Prussianism on the other, is not only our greater reluctance to bow before an autocrat: it is also our constant refusal to consider the mass as an end in itself, whether the mass be called race or nation or whether its power be embodied in the state or in a despot. It is our constant assertion that the human person has an existence and a moral and spiritual finality of his own; that a people is not a mass judged on its average standard of living, but a society of indi-viduals.

Yet, while few men would dispute that in principle, little attention has so far been given to its practical defence. States-men and politicians often speak at once of the collective and the individual aims of democracy, as though there were no incom-patibility between those two and no difficulty in balancing them, whereas in point of fact their adjustment and the balance to be found between the interests of the greatest number and the respect due to each human person, is the most puzzling question set to all political thinkers. Lenin himself was so well aware of it that in his political testament he presented state collectivism as only a phase of man's evolution, and individualism as its true end, thus justifying his own system of government by asserting its ultimate human objective. Democracy has in fact to reconcile a number of conflicting notions and natural aspirations or, if it fails to reconcile them, to choose where it prefers to lay the emphasis.

Politically, democracy is understood to offer two outstanding boons: liberty and equality (fraternity is a purely moral concept). The last century laid the stress on liberty, although it produced the first dogmatic exponents of economic equality, from Saint-Simon to Marx and Engels. In current practice, equality in the nineteenth century was understood as equality of opportunity. In the twentieth century the general trend of evolution and thought has been towards equality not so much of opportunity, but equality absolute. Even contemporary dictators have partly owed their success to apparent or real attempts to meet the demand for economic and social equality under the common Leader, who was alleged to play the same part in destroying economic feudalism as kings had played in overcoming medieval feudalism. To-day, most public men continue to associate the two notions of liberty and equality as though any progress towards one automatically entailed an advance towards the other. Yet experience proves this to be a fallacy.

Equality is not a state of nature. Desirable or not, it has to be established and enforced by some kind of coercion in order to achieve permanence. The instinctive individual tendency to assert practical, intellectual, spiritual superiority in the temporal realm has to be checked repeatedly, and this involves limitations on individual freedom, and even independence, whatever the methods of coercion, whatever the consensus of opinion whereby these are applied and maintained. It is of course for each nation to decide for itself whether liberty or equality is its primary aim; but it is also for its responsible leaders to point out (as Winston Churchill did in December 1942) that there is a degree of relative incompatibility between the two, and that statesmanship can only reduce the gap without necessarily bridging it.

Broadly speaking, the trend of thought in the Western world before the war was still towards the safeguarding of individual independence, whilst that of those countries which lie beyond the Rhine was towards equality, though in the case of the latter there were striking differences between nation and nation in the effective application of that equality. For the Russians it corresponded to a broad conception of human affairs; for the Germans it was no more than a social weapon wherewith to rally the nation and give German expansionism a pseudo-philosophical basis. Whichever tendency prevails in the end, one thing at least is clear: should we purchase economic equality by the sacrifice of the individual, all that is meant by Western civilization would be doomed. In purely collective attainments neither England, nor France, nor the Low Countries, nor the nations which are heirs to the Mediterranean culture, can ever hope to compete with Central or Eastern Europe, whose populations largely outnumber theirs and whose technical progress has caught up with theirs. Thus would end the superiority of Western Europe which formerly compensated for the discrepancy in numbers. In terms of mass, Western civilization would therefore not only lose the sense of its traditional mission: it would have no claim to assume any mission at all. It is by its championship of individual dignity, and by making converts for that cause throughout the world, that it can serve and therefore survive; thus and in no other way.

This raises a further point. Besides striking a balance between equality and liberty, there is another grave problem set to democracy in our century and one which previous definitions did not embrace: that of its own defence. There, again, events have shown what tremendous power can be mustered by nations that accept the sacrifice, temporary or not, of individual independence as we conceive it, to collective efficiency. Germany has proved it in her aggressions, and Russia in her defence.[1] It is true that their huge manpower partly accounts for their military might, but it cannot be doubted that their means of marshalling men and material were far greater and swifter than those of Western European nations. After more than four years of war the mobilization of British resources might be as 'total' as that of Germany, but this was the result of a slow process which went on behind the Channel barrier and the protective shield provided by the Air Force and

---

[1] Russia is already counteracting the effects of a mass conception of social economy by a wise process of cultural decentralization: she is well ahead of many countries in the encouragement of regional and minority arts, culture, and literature.

F

the Navy. It nevertheless remains true that the defence of
democracy sets a new problem to the political thinker: that of
the relative incompatibility between the respect for free institutions and the maintenance of power. The providential outcome
of the Battle of Britain, which saved an underarmed nation,
cannot blind us to the permanent gravity of that problem.
History allows such respites but threatened civilizations must
learn their lesson.

To reconcile progress towards social and economic equality
and the organization of defensive power with the traditional
protection of individual independence, such is the heavy
task of any democracy and more especially of Western Europe.
Our common civilization which spread from the shores of
the Mediterranean has always rated a well-fed and contented
slave below an underfed free man; and no state can truly be
called democratic, except in so far as an ant-hill is democratic,
if it permanently destroys individual liberty, or even if it does
not keep the nation constantly aware of the fact that equality,
liberty and power (in other words the welfare, the dignity, and
the defence of man) are three pursuits which are not naturally
compatible and which can be only partially reconciled. A
democracy is primarily a régime of conscious men, and the
realization of that inherent conflict of notions is part of the
ceaseless human effort to resolve it. All solutions adopted
hitherto have been no more than partial. Looking at them all,
I, for one, would value those communities where men remain
permanently alive to the magnitude of the task rather than
those where great improvements have been secured in one or
two directions whilst on the other hand the sense of individual
effort and responsibility has been blunted. For only in the former
can there be preserved the principle of freedom and the means of
defence against the recurrent threat of slavery which has grown
with the new weapons of assault provided by the ingenuity of
scientists. Defensive weapons are not supplied by the mere
economic contentment of the greatest number, but by the constant stimulus of individual thought and vigilance. After the
present war we shall no doubt witness many new attempts in
yet unpredictable forms to turn societies of individuals into gregarious communities whose sole preoccupation will be the index
of prices and wages. This cannot but be expected in a world
where the very notion of individual freedom has become com-

pletely meaningless for millions of young men bred and raised in dogmatic or materialistic hot-houses throughout the world.

In days like these, such a question as the value of British institutions is more pregnant than ever with meaning and consequence. To decide whether England or any other nation is a democracy is impossible. Democracy is an ideal state which we may conceive, but which no people has yet fully achieved with all its implications. Some nations have achieved progress towards it in one direction, others in a different way, according to their respective dispositions and dogmatic tendencies. What matters is to see whether a nation like England, which pursues a democratic ideal, has institutions capable of protecting and enhancing the advance towards that ideal condition.

In 1854 Montalembert, analyzing the reasons for many of the Continental attacks aimed at England wrote: [The reason is that] '. . . England has given such a striking rebuke to false logic, false science and to the ruthless passions of absolutism. . . . Her growing strength, her boundless freedom, her unrivalled prosperity have provided such formidable arguments both against a Socialist demagogy which would have everything mowed down under a savage equality and against an Absolutism which can only save people from discord and terror by throwing them back into silence and nothingness. . . .'[1]

Two years before, a young French historian and journalist, Jules Maurel, also made certain observations on English institutions which I must also quote, because of their striking relation to the present situation. They are extracted from his book *The Duke of Wellington*, published in Brussels, and refer to the Napoleonic wars: 'In her supreme struggle England's greatest strength lay in her institutions. The British Government conducted the war for twenty-two years—carrying on its back the implements of liberty, amidst the clamourings of the public platform and of the press, in the throes of commercial disasters, in spite of the meetings, the riots, the petitions for electoral reforms, and the breaking of windows—without surrendering any of its lawful rights, without ever feeling compelled to bow before the external or the internal foe. When the last free platform and the last free press had vanished from the Continent, all the passions, good or evil, were kept astir in the British Empire, and unwittingly, indeed unconsciously, all converged

[1] My own translation.—P.M.

towards the same goal. No one in England could deceive or be deceived for more than twenty-four hours. That animation, that din, which led Napoleon to believe that England was certain to blow up at any time like a powder magazine, was nothing but the life of a free people.'[1]

Jules Maurel was describing the England of the early years of the nineteenth century; Montalembert that of the Crimean War, fifty years later. In our own days, and more especially in the last ten years, the most striking phenomenon in English history is perhaps not that the country should have avoided invasion but that it should not have lost its political balance under the impact of conflicting ideologies. From 1932 virtually all English parties sympathized with, or espoused, causes which on the Continent constituted the elements of major civil conflicts; from the rise of Hitler until the war they were divided on every issue, and the foreign policy of the nation was perturbed by these divisions. Yet English institutions stood the test and in the end the nation that went to war had lost virtually nothing of its singleness of purpose. Even during the war such changes as took place were the result of specifically English experience and not, to any noticeable extent, the repercussion of external influences.

Now, once more, English institutions are the only ones in Europe, with the exception of those of Sweden and Switzerland, which have not been either broken by war, totally transformed by revolution, or thrown back into the melting-pot by enemy occupation. Once more, too, these institutions were attacked both before and during the war, for their archaism by dogmatic equalitarians, and for their excess of disorderly freedom by a new species of absolutists.

The attacks directed against them and also their surprising resilience can probably be explained by the same reasons: that at no time for three centuries has there been a complete break in the development of England; that English institutions are an historical growth, the cumulative effect of reforms, amendments, additions, corrections; that, being completely un-dogmatic, they never correspond to any given ideology prevailing at any time, and are therefore criticized on that ground as retrograde; that, finally, with all their faults and contradictions they are diverse enough to provide an antidote to political poison, to

[1] My own translation.

correct faults by amendment, and to create opposition to any form of absolutism.

'Nobody in England could deceive or be deceived for more than twenty-four hours. . . .' By keeping before its eyes the manifold elements and aspects of its development, the nation is protected against the illusion that changes necessarily mean improvement, or that, alternatively, no reform is possible without impairing the balance of the community. It has its own experiments recalled to it by its constitution, as its historical events are conjured up by its state pageants.

To-day, as often before, there is in many quarters a strong temptation to eliminate what appears to be obsolete, though the criterion whereby such matters are judged can hardly be absolute. The armour of our ancestors was considered obsolete when the fire-power of muskets was increased; yet the principle of armour has been applied to tanks after we had achieved an incomparably greater fire-power than that of the seventeenth century. The Upper Chamber was deemed obsolete in France in 1791, yet it was 'modern' a century later. So, while it may be absurd to accept literally Lord Balfour's suggestion: 'It is better to do a stupid thing which has been done before than an intelligent one which has never been tried,' it is equally absurd and even more dangerous to eliminate, on the plea of renovation, existing institutions which may not have exhausted their value.

During the last decade or so English institutions have carried the country through an economic crisis of the first magnitude, through a dynastic crisis, through the ideological storms of Europe, and finally through a war in which the country faced a powerful coalition. It is worth examining the main factors of their strength, both in themselves and in the attitude of the English people towards them.

CHAPTER 9

CONTROVERSIAL ASPECTS OF ENGLISH INSTITUTIONS

TO render the community the greatest possible service national institutions must possess the attributes of continuity, flexibility, adaptability and equity. Without continuity they cannot survive the impact of internal or external attack. If they are not flexible they provide no means of resisting excesses of other men or other bodies, for in order to guard against the misuse of one institution, another must be available to counterbalance it. If national institutions are not adaptable they cannot admit and assimilate changes within the body politic. If they lack equity, they are repeatedly challenged and the time must come when they can survive only by undue coercion and, finally, repression.

No existing system of government can claim to have fulfilled these conditions perfectly. The institutions of one nation may be equitable, yet too rigid; those of another may be at once equitable, flexible, and balanced, yet wanting in permanence. English institutions are at one and the same time flexible and endowed with the means of national continuity. Whether they are responsive to the need for change is a question often raised, and raised once again at the present juncture; but in the past, at any rate, it has been answered satisfactorily. As regards equity, they are more open to criticism since they have a markedly inequalitarian basis and serve an inequalitarian state of society.

It is certain that lack of continuity in the conduct of public affairs was a direct cause of the French disaster in 1940. Governmental instability may have been due to men as much as to institutions. Yet when these are so devised as to give men a sense of national permanence they can exercise a restraining influence on individuals and thus raise an obstacle to reckless change. English institutions are certainly well calculated to keep alive that sense of permanence and to encourage public deference, partly perhaps by reason of the decorum and traditional etiquette which attend their working. The Crown, the Church, Parliament, and the Law, as well as other lesser insti-

tutions, emphasize their permanence by the solemn ceremonies
associated with the discharge of their respective functions.
Englishmen may grumble about their government, their members of parliament, their lawyers, but they nevertheless submit
themselves to their institutions and take pride in them. Criticism
of individuals does not entail rebellion against institutions.

During the General Strike in 1926, a time when respect for
vested power was at its lowest ebb, Lord Simon (then Sir John
Simon) was called upon to demonstrate to the workers that their
action was illegal, and with his customary persuasiveness he
delivered a speech in Parliament to that effect. The tremendous
effect of that pronouncement upon the working class is well
illustrated by the reaction of one of the strikers on picket duty.
Having, in typically English fashion, made friends with his
opposite number in the special constabularly, he asked him
who 'this Simon' was. He was told that he was a leading King's
Counsel, a former Attorney-General, a lawyer who stood at the
very forefront of the Bar, and that he was one whose legal
opinions everyone accepted. 'Well,' said the striker, 'they've
had us! They told us this strike was legal. But if a man like that
says it isn't, we can't stay out.' Since this was England, that
speech demonstrating the illegality of the strike did more than
anything else to break it; but, as Simon's Irish wife afterwards
observed, in Ireland the notion that it was against the law would
have been not the breaking of the strike but the making of it.
Here, so long as it was merely a demonstration against the
employers and the Government, the men fought on. But they
had no wish to fight against the law of the land, one of the nation's
fundamental institutions, however doubtful its application to
that particular issue might appear to them.

The quality and power of continuity inherent in English
institutions and in their popular support were exemplified in far
more difficult and momentous circumstances when, at the close
of 1936, they underwent a perilous trial. I well remember that
afternoon of 10 December. A vast, silent crowd watched the
Houses of Parliament, fully aware that the world in its turn
was watching them. The world wondered whether an ancient
monarchy would stand the test. Not so the English public, who
never doubted that it would. The English public, with every
national fibre taut, formed on that day a wakeful family council
embracing every township, village, and hamlet in the land. It

looked to its constitution, whatever the final decision might be, to accomplish smoothly and delicately its natural function of national continuity, to leave the monarchy unshaken and the power of the people's institutions unimpaired, to settle a difference between men who must pass on, without impairing permanent values common to all.

On the same cold, sullen afternoon, in the House of Commons, Stanley Baldwin personified the nation as completely as any statesman could hope to do. The occasion lent him a rare dignity. His own nature gave his demeanour and tone the simplicity which alone could prevent his statement from reaching too high and unnatural a pitch; his discharge of a stern duty from stiffening into an assumption of austere self-righteousness. In such a grave national crisis few men can resist the impulse to borrow a temporary self-exaltation from the very drama in which they take a leading part, however undesired. It is to Baldwin's credit that, compelled by circumstances to play for a brief moment the hand of Fate, he did resist so powerful a temptation. As he rose from his bench, just before four o'clock, there fell on the Commons a silence so complete that one felt as though a magic wand had struck House and galleries into mute stillness. The reputation of time-honoured institutions was at stake. The Prime Minister walked to the Bar of the House with steps quicker than usual, turned round, bowed three times to the Speaker's Chair and said in a very firm and clear voice: 'A message from His Majesty the King, Sir, signed by His Majesty's own hand.' He went to the Speaker's Chair and handed him three sheets of paper bearing the Royal Arms. Captain Fitzroy began to read the message: 'After long and anxious consideration I have determined to renounce the throne. . . .'

When the Speaker had finished, the Prime Minister recorded the events of the preceding weeks: '. . . No more grave message has ever been received by Parliament and no more difficult, and I may almost say repugnant, task ever been imposed upon a Prime Minister. . . .' The tone of his voice hardly changed throughout his statement. An adjournment followed. When the House resumed only four members out of six hundred and eighteen expressed any doubt of the perennial value of those institutions which had appeared to be in peril. Those four were the members of the Independent Labour Party, who had made no secret in the past of their opposition to the monarchic principle. Neither in Parliament nor among the countless crowd which had tensely and patiently awaited the outcome of the constitutional debate had that value been seriously questioned. What had been feared was lest men should falter in the service of national institutions, thus exposing these and, with them, the people to a loss of prestige in world opinion.

Among those who have witnessed a few of the ceremonies, melancholy or joyous, which illustrate the continuity of the monarchy, its power to communicate a sense of national permanence cannot be disputed. The Royal Jubilee in 1935, the days of mourning which followed so closely upon it, the Coronation of King George VI, the contrasts of pageantry and of the attendant popular demonstrations, all have left on my mind a single impression: a feeling of 'out-of-timeness', by which I mean something very different from archaism. The sensation was not that the clock had been put back some hundreds of years because the rites performed, the scenes enacted and garments worn had not changed for centuries; it was that what I saw and heard did exist irrespective of time and present circumstances, and that both were transcended. Here was a national symbol of permanence beyond the reach of contingency.

These, of course, were only the signs of continuity visible to the onlooker, the heraldry of national identity. But between outward manifestations and living reality the borderline is not clearly defined. The handing of the seals of office by the king to his ministers, the right to summon party leaders in times of governmental changes and political crises, the opening of the Parliamentary session, the conferring of honours, and, by contrast, the traditional restrictions upon the rights of the Crown, all these are in part symbolical conventions, yet they are at the same time real and effective, for not only do they set against changing personnel an order which is not subject to variation, but they also persistently recall the principle of constitutional limitation of individual power and the need for balancing against each other the great institutions of a state. That the Crown by its assertion of national permanence has played a decisive part in rallying the peoples of the Commonwealth once again in the present war, is an incontestable fact which, by its unexpected swiftness, surprised not only the enemy but also many friendly nations.

Again, the Crown gives effect to the principle of continuity by reason of the fact that the essential English institutions are all in some way related to it. Every Liberal state practices the separation of powers: Executive, Legislative, and Judiciary, the spiritual power being sometimes State-established and sometimes not. In England the four powers, while distinct as among themselves, are all linked with the monarchy, partly through the House of Lords and the Privy Council where they are in a sense represented and active, but chiefly because the Ministers are the King's Ministers, Parliament is summoned by the King's writ, the judges are the King's judges, and the King is the head of the Church of England.

Yet however well vindicated this system may be in terms of national continuity, it is often challenged in contemporary England on democratic grounds. Its critics hold that it maintains in existence a social and economic order both unequal and arbitrary, or, alternatively, that it operates against any attempt to redress that inequality. No doubt many of its aspects, considered in themselves, are open to strictures; but, to be judged fairly, the system must be taken as a whole, just as a man's merits are assessed on the strength of his whole record, not of some isolated particular. My purpose in any case is not to judge but to compare; not to gauge the absolute value of the English order but to consider some of its most controversial aspects in their world context and in the light of experiments made by other nations.

English institutions are neither a dogmatic creation nor the work of theorists. They are an emanation from English society; they reflect its strength and weakness and change *pari passu* with its evolution. For that reason they, like society itself, lay emphasis on the notion of contract, between the individual and the community, between the community and its head; and for that reason, too, they embody the concept of hierarchy not as a deliberate principle but as a matter of social convenience at the present stage of human affairs. English institutions tend therefore to regulate by contract, convention, and tradition, an existing social condition, rather than to establish a definite and preconceived order (as did, for example, the French Constitution of 1791, the Italian Constitution of 1922, the Spanish Constitution of 1931).

Magna Carta was a contract settled by men of the thirteenth century according to their lights and on the basis of the social order prevailing at that time. Limited though its scope and application may have been, it established the principle that the subject was also a party to an agreement, that the monarch was both sovereign and yet bound by obligation. The sense of contract was further strengthened by the power with which the law was endowed and which raised it above the state itself. Through the law England thus established the power of society as against that of the central authority and against that of almost any vested power whether spiritual or temporal which overstepped its rights. To-day the general predominance of the Common Law still gives society a weapon against either absolute monarchy or any other form of despotism, including bureaucracy. On the spiritual plane, also, society asserts itself over the state; yet while through Church establishment the State authority has the means of achieving supremacy in ecclesiastical affairs, the religious history of England presents a remarkable phenomenon in the steady progress of Nonconformity during the last hundred years towards parity with the Church of England in influence and rights. Thus, even in spiritual matters, the state has had to recognize what society has built on its own initiative and by free association.

In every sphere the power of the state derives from society and can be checked by it; so that traditionally the English state is the exact reverse of the Moloch-state. This has its drawbacks. It has been observed that, time and time again, institutions created independently of the state have wielded excessive power in national affairs. In a world where economic feudalism has not abated this no doubt represents a danger. On the other hand, recent experiences have shown the catastrophic effect of total state supremacy over a defenceless society. And the capital lesson to remember is that it is far easier for any despot or despotic party to secure control of the central authority and therefore to use the state for personal ends, than to curb a living, diverse, and versatile society.

The war has caused an upsurge of opinion in England against this tradition. It is still difficult to appraise the force and depth of that movement. The effect of any conflict in which a whole nation is involved is naturally to impel it towards state control, which in war-time is a necessity. The arguments in favour of preserving and extending state interference after the war are based on the very obvious need for withdrawing from individuals or groups the means of controlling economic resources which must be available to the nation in emergency. A conspicuous example is that of war industries, where the demand for state interference seems not only founded in justice but justified by experience. Other arguments in favour of state control on a wider basis are advanced on grounds of economic and social equality: these are usually coupled with attacks on institutions which are said to perpetuate inequality.

That the English order, both social and economic is markedly inequalitarian is indisputable. Before the war Britain was socially the most completely hierarchized community in the West, while economically she presented the most striking contrasts of wealth and poverty. Yet social inequality resulting from the existence of prerogatives and the grant of privileges is one thing; economic inequality caused by capitalistic competition is another. Whether or not either is justified, the two conceptions are, at least in theory, on an entirely different plane. For it is possible to conceive a régime economically equalitarian and yet at the same time aristocratic in that it confers on some of its citizens and not on others permanent rights entailing a measure of political power. This distinction must be drawn in order to avoid a confusion of issues in the discussion of British institutions.

It may seem surprising that England should have been able to preserve her hierarchical order at a time when most European countries were irresistibly drawn towards social equality (although this tendency led in effect to the setting up of a new aristocracy, that of the Party). Perhaps one of the reasons of its survival is that the English order retained, in contrast to others, certain human values which considerably mitigated its illogicality: these values include respect for standards of fair relationship between individuals and the community, between the weak and the strong, a sense of moral responsibility, and, above all, thanks to the enduring independence of the Common Law, impartial arbitration in the Courts.

The very notion of arbitrariness so often invoked against English institutions must in any case be examined. In all states privileges are conferred on selected citizens. In England the granting of the privilege of a title lies in the hands of the Sovereign acting on the recommendation of the Prime Minister, who is the leader of the House of Commons, itself a projection of the people. The method of conferring the privilege is not therefore objectionable on democratic grounds; it is chiefly the idea of the perpetuation of privilege through hereditary titles which runs counter to contemporary thought. Yet the test of an institution is not simply its theoretical justice but its practical advantages to the community, whether positive in the services it renders, or negative in the dangers it averts. Hostility to any form of hierarchy is merely an imaginative aberration if it produces no more than a general notion of levelling without any practical improvement of human conditions, for, failing this, it can only breed envy, the most sterile of all political emotions.

The part played in the British system by privilege, from the royal to the aristocratic prerogatives, can best be understood if set beside the institutions of other nations. It is generally recognized that most European democracies have suffered from governmental instability; but what are the causes of that instability? First, the frequent overthrow of the executive power, whatever the reason; and second, the break in the continuity of the national ideal. Anarchy is rife when the central authority lacks initiative, when it is too frequently replaced, when the nation ceases to acknowledge the bond of common tenets or when institutions are not sufficiently well balanced to prevent one from growing to the prejudice of others. The flaw may be constitutional or functional: that is, it may originate in the constitution or in the men who work it. It may be prevented, alleviated, or compensated by the existence of national traditions and institutions, which themselves retain permanence while all other factors are subject to change. Alternatively, many countries have countered disorder, anarchy or instability by personal dictatorship; that is to say, by the oldest form of despotism, that of the adventurer who, from the start, establishes an arbitrary hierarchy, or founds it on a dogma. Apart from the external dangers always presented by this solution, based on the conquest of power, it is essentially in direct opposition to the principle of liberty. In the case of the modern dictatorships, continuity in national action has only been achieved at the expense of liberty. Even so, it has been shortlived.

The function of the English dynastic system and of the hierarchical order on which it rests is that of a homeopathic remedy, in the strongest acceptation of the term, against haphazard hierarchies or systems based on violence. It contains a principle of conciliation between the idea of national continuity and that of individual liberty, since the English hierarchy does not require the destruction of personal freedom in order to maintain itself.

The English hierarchy is obviously vulnerable to the arguments directed against social inequality. In England as elsewhere the cult of equality has recently tended to take precedence over concern for the independence of the individual, though it is a question whether this is a passing phrase or a fundamental feature of English development. It is not therefore surprising that social inequality in England should be the target for the criticisms of many reformers. It would be easy to show that neither Germany nor Italy had established true equality by methods described as 'totalitarian' (a word which, politically, means no more than most of the terms circulated by Germanic pedantry, and, in practice, only indicates total preparation for war). It can also be said that the Soviet system, although economically equitable, since the Soviet hierarchy is based on the capacity for work and production, is rendered socially unequal by the precedence given to the Party.

The English hierarchy is not based on economic efficiency, though it might in some ways claim to be so by reason of the elevation to the peerage of men who have distinguished themselves in the service of the state. Furthermore, when the privileges which it grants are hereditary, the principle of inequality is deliberately preserved. Having recognized this fact, one must judge it not absolutely but in its relative effects, that is to say on its practical advantages and disadvantages.

The great shortcoming of Western régimes called democratic is, to my mind, not the social inequality in itself but the particular nature and consequences of that inequality. They are oligarchies in which the real privilege is that of money, which entails no duty other than the payment of income-tax. The advantages enjoyed by the privileged class do not impose on it any contractual obligations, political, social or moral. Social inequality is governed and regulated by economic competition and by nothing else. The result, as Georges Bernanos observes in his *Lettre aux Anglais,* is often a complete divorce between the privileged classes and the national tradition with which nothing connects them. Striking instances of this have been seen in Europe during the present war, so that the Continent has seemed to hesitate between two types of hierarchy: one which was established by the rule of a party and imposed by it for the forcible attainment of political superiority, with or without progress towards economic equality; the other based solely on relative degrees of wealth, having no other link with the nation than economic interests which, according to circumstances, might or might not tally with those of the nation. The former produced in all cases a systematic suppression of individual and political freedom, the latter various forms of national disaffection and often economic and social disorder.

It is in this connexion that it is relevant to consider the traditional function of aristocracy in England, leaving aside for a moment its present trend of social development. Its privilege normally carried with it corresponding obligations towards the nation and duties towards the state entailing participation in national affairs. In this respect, it is only fair to point out that the House of Lords, whose powers were curtailed in 1911 in the name of democracy, to-day renders a service to democracy the value of which is perhaps underestimated. While the House of Commons embodies the principle of the popular majority and must defend the interests of the greater number, the House of Lords persistently pleads a cause which is too readily forgotten nowadays: that of individual independence and civil liberty. Thus the restrictions imposed on individual freedom by emergency legislation are watchfully surveyed by the Upper House. As an institution, the House of Lords can by its very nature be a useful complement to the Commons. Being less subject to the pressure of events and of political fluctuations it can devote more attention to a critical study of long-term problems and questions of national ethics.

Finally, a recognized function of aristocracy was to maintain a tradition of attachment to the land, which exercises a stabilizing influence in a manufacturing and banking nation where the moneyed classes naturally tend to abandon occupations which are less profitable than trade, industry or finance, and to consider the land only as a crowning luxury. (Incidentally, I have found a much truer and more human contact between the landed aristocracy and the peasantry in this country than between successful industrialists and their workmen.) In principle, therefore, the social order embodied in the two Houses served the purpose of national continuity. In the twentieth century, it has certainly stood against the establishment in England of ideological systems. Such an order could better be immunized than communities where national traditions were less deep rooted and where the urge to replace disorder by any kind of hierarchy could easily be exploited by adventurers. Thus the English order has fulfilled both a positive and a negative function since its very inequality has given it means of defence against political excesses.

At the present time, two contradictory charges are levelled against the English order. The first is that it perpetuates ancient privileges utterly indefensible in the twentieth century. A state chary of interfering with more than a minimum of the nation's activities naturally retains more of the burdens of the past than another; but, for that very reason, it also allows progress without compelling the individual to purchase every advance at the cost of new shackles. To be sure, tithes were abolished in England only a few years ago; while mining royalties and ground rents still survive as onerous burdens, though the elimination of those relics of arbitrary rule is not beyond the capacity of the reformer. The second accusation, which bears on a far more serious issue, is that British aristocracy is tending to become purely and simply a moneyed class. In that case, privilege would have the effect of perpetuating economic inequality and consecrating economic superiority, rendering it more formidable by giving it political backing. There is an obvious danger in thus strengthening commercial interests: the men who wield them would be in a position to set them against those of the nation not only in the field of open economic competition, but in the Upper House. At best, participation in all forms of economic speculation would tend to destroy that independence of judgement in national affairs which privilege encourages in those who enjoy it, placing them outside the range of petty daily controversies. This is undeniably one of the perils that confront the English aristocracy and, with it, the institutions to which it is related in the spiritual and temporal spheres. It is increased, moreover, by the gradual retreat of the aristocracy from the land.

It seems that, sooner or later, the English aristocracy, if it is to survive and play its true national part, will have to become dissociated, if not from wealth, at least from all competitive activities, and to assume or resume the character of an *élite*, which, while renewing itself to avoid anaemia, should attach itself more closely to the land and isolate itself from capitalistic competition. Under such conditions it would be able both to preserve its traditional role—which is to establish, under the Crown, a link of national continuity, to be a factor of national permanence without cutting itself off from the people—and to adapt itself to modern standards by a process of selection. The aristocracy would thus keep abreast of social reform, and avoid the risk of becoming a reactionary minority, of finding itself in conflict with the House of Commons, or of giving a class bias to English justice.

One of the sources of the strength of English institutions was certainly that this allegedly archaic system proved capable, in turn, of relying on permanent elements and of conforming to the laws of evolution. It is certainly not, hitherto, the survival of its ancient features which have retarded development. These do not make the economic régime unadaptable. If progress in general welfare has often been deemed insufficient, here as elsewhere the opposition comes more often from the new moneyed classes than from the old landed aristocracy; it has been economic far more than social, although the two ideas may be confused. Hostility to reform is never keener than in those quarters where economic competition is the only recognized law. Mr. Roosevelt's reforms in America met with far stronger opposition than rigorous taxation has encountered in England, even in the section of the aristocracy most affected. In England herself, the right wing of the House of Commons has sometimes been more obstinate in the face of reform than the House of Lords. Privileges of any description are justified in so far as they produce in return a sense of national responsibility. That sense is certainly fostered by tradition more than by competitive acquisition.

It is inevitable and necessary that the long struggle for economic and social progress should follow its course. In England as in other countries there are injustices and miseries to be redressed, reforms to be accomplished. The important question is whether in order to realize these reforms it is necessary to destroy the existing framework of institutions which, as compared with the rigid forms of a dogmatic hierarchy, have the shortcomings but also the resilience of society, or whether they are still flexible enough to admit of social progress to-day as

G

they did in the past. Recent developments have already affected unfavourably, albeit inconspicuously, not only the allegedly 'archaic' features of the English order but also the traditional balance of the English constitution.

CHAPTER 10

THE CONSTITUTION AND THE RISE OF ANONYMOUS POWER

Did not I warn you, señor Don Quixote, said he, to turn; and assure you that those you went to attack were no armies but flocks of sheep?
CERVANTES: Don Quixote

ONE of the most serious features of contemporary life in modern states, irrespective of their régimes, is the accumulation of power, both economic and political, in the hands of anonymous bodies and 'invisible' holders. Kings, feudal magnates, Church dignitaries, landowners of old, all these were recognizable persons, clearly designated to popular favour or censure. Parliament itself, although an assembly whose responsibility is collective, is a gathering of persons known by name and elected in their individual capacity.

The power of institutions vested in persons has been declining for centuries past. In the case of royal absolutism, or of feudal or ecclesiastical privileges, that decline is identified with the struggle against arbitrary rule. But the process of depersonalization has gone much beyond this. In our time the power vested in persons continues to decline even when it is legitimate; while that, whether legitimate or not, of anonymous institutions or groups grows steadily. More precisely, the persons who wield effective power become less and less recognizable and therefore less challengeable as such, while those who are supposed to exercise power by right tend, in effect, to lose it.

Economically, the substitution of company rule for individual ownership and responsibility makes it increasingly difficult to locate the sources of wealth, property, initiative and actual control of goods and services. Indeed, a friend of mine considers that the most sweeping, though inconspicuous, revolution in England was the passing of the Companies Act by Parliament in 1845. Politically, the formidable spread of bureaucracy renders part of the power vested by the responsible members of Parliament in the executive anonymous and often uncontrollable by the nation.

The risks attending such a development in all countries are

easy to assess. Assuming that the process goes on unchecked,
it is possible to conceive a state where, both economic and
political power being completely depersonalized, the ordinary
citizen would be left with no means of ascribing responsibilities
or redressing arbitrary rulings; or, alternatively, a state whose
executive would command unrestricted power by the mere
operation of an all-embracing administrative machine passively
accepted. In the former case the citizen would become helpless
and, in any attempt to trace and correct errors, would only lose
or defeat himself as surely as Don Quixote did in his charge
against those supposed armies of men who, when he found
himself in their midst, turned out to be flocks of sheep. In the
latter, bureaucracy would have created such a no-man's-land
between the citizen and the executive that his only resort, if he
wished to resume some measure of control over national
activity, would be insurrection.

In every nation the general tendency of those who wield
economic power—industrial, financial or commercial—is to hide
their effective strength and to make it inconspicuous by a process of dispersion, so as to evade the restrictions which the community would impose on them, to escape the full burden of
taxation, or even to overstep the limits set by the state to their
power for the prevention of its abuse. Dispersion through
anonymous bodies is a mode of concealment the advantages of
which are clear. It is far more difficult to prosecute the members
of a company than the owner-manager of a business. It is also
more difficult to control the wealth and power of an individual
when his interests are dispersed over several anonymous
enterprises, apparently unrelated. The most dangerous weapon
of economic feudalism to-day, therefore, is its elusiveness, its
ability to defeat opposition and restraint, and generally to
elude its obligations towards society.

It is inevitable that this method of dispersion should be more
easily applicable here than in some other countries, since wealth
and economic power in England are only partially vested in
tangible things such as machinery, plant and goods, and largely
consist in services and especially credit, the control of which is
most difficult of all. During the last few decades the banker has
gradually taken precedence over the industrialist just as the
industrialist had superseded the landowner within the national
economy. That transition from the power represented by

'things' towards abstract fiduciary power facilitates the growth of anonymous control of the national resources.

In order to stop evasion of fiscal and other responsibilities, the state in its turn spreads it tentacles further and further so as to reach economic power by tracking it to its retreats and blocking its ways of escape. This at present involves the building up of a bureaucratic machinery of investigation and control. The growth of anonymous power in the economic field is therefore a contributory cause to the spread of anonymous political power; and it may end in the remedy, at least the remedy applied so far, becoming worse than the evil, for this progress towards bureaucratic control involves dangers which are too often underestimated. It is not generally realized that the main difference between a democratic and a despotic state in modern times chiefly lies in the excessive importance given by the latter to anonymous machinery. Nor is it generally understood that, without frankly destroying free institutions, it is possible to render them inoperative by setting up beside them an all-embracing bureaucracy growing at their expense. Despotism does not always require the withdrawal of the means of popular control from the nation by compulsory action; it can also be enforced by superficially constitutional methods rendering that control impossible in practice.

The nature and dangers of such a method in England have been analysed in masterly fashion in a book which deserves more than passing mention, since it raises a problem of great moment for all contemporary nations. It is *The New Despotism*, published in 1929 by Lord Hewart, then Lord Chief Justice of England. The case made by Lord Hewart may be briefly re-stated.

The two leading features of the British constitution are the Sovereignty of Parliament and the Rule of Law. The predominance of the law excludes any other mode of determining or disposing of the rights of individuals. It is therefore the fundamental safeguard of freedom or freedoms against arbitrariness, since any act which is not an infringement of the accepted law is permissible and since no power but the law enforced by public courts *coram populo* can interfere with individual or collective freedom. 'But the supremacy of the law, as we know it, means something more than the exclusion of arbitrary power and something more also than the equality of all citizens before the ordinary law of the land administered by the ordinary Courts. It means that *in this country . . . the principles of the Constitution are inductions or generalizations based upon decisions pronounced by the Courts as to the rights of particular individuals*' whilst elsewhere '*the rights of the individuals may be said to be deductions from the principles of the Constitution*'. Thus while elsewhere the constitution can be operated in such a way as to restrict the rights of individuals, in England, so long as the predominance of the Law remains effective and not merely theoretical, society can resist encroachments upon its rights even by the state executive.

Parliament ensures the control of the people over its own government and its own legislation. The public Courts of Justice enable the people to survey the administration of the law and the foundations of the nation's constitution. Both are the instruments of democratic rule and the guarantees of civil liberties. How could their purpose be defeated and popular control be frustrated under these conditions? How could arbitrary rule be restored without a constitutional revolution? Lord Hewart's answer is: By the building up of bureaucracy and the abuse of its powers.

If by Acts of Parliament passed hastily under the pressure of circumstances or of the persuasiveness of the executive, excessive power is vested in the heads of ministerial departments, ministers may, by order, make decisions on points of law or fact which should normally come within the jurisdiction of Parliament or require examination and perhaps further legislative action by Parliament. 'There is', Lord Hewart contended, 'in this country a considerable number of statutes, most of them passed during the last twenty years, which have vested in public officials, to the exclusion of the Courts of Law, the power of deciding questions of a judicial nature.' Usually the power is given nominally to the Minister, but the matter is actually decided by some official, of more or less standing in the department, responsible to no one save a superior official. The result is in effect to place 'a large and increasing field of departmental authority and activity beyond the reach of ordinary law', and the consequence may ultimately be 'the accumulation of despotic power in the hands of anonymous officials'.

As the rights thus bestowed by Acts of Parliament on ministerial departments are extended, bureaucracy must spread correspondingly and itself create more machinery and more services tending towards virtual independence of both the Law and Parliament. Not only did Lord Hewart fear lest this process might 'reduce the Judges to a branch of the Civil Service' (a leading feature of totalitarian states) but he saw in it a threat of 'organized lawlessness' and of a resurgent arbitrariness through the anonymous weapon thus available at any time to the executive. He urged Parliament to take stock of the danger and to resist the easy temptation to lighten its burden by delegating part of its legislative power to state machinery: 'The old despotism, which was defeated, offered Parliament a challenge. The new despotism, which is not yet defeated, gives Parliament an anaesthetic. The strategy is different, but the goal is the same. It is to subordinate Parliament, to evade the Courts, and to render the will, or the caprice, of the Executive unfettered and supreme'.

Whether the late Lord Chief Justice was right in diagnosing wilful intent, where there may simply have been submission to a forceful process of bureaucratic centralization; whether the greatest danger of bureaucracy lies in the formidable weapon which it gives to the executive or in the paralysis of the national life; and, finally, whether his own concern with the strict maintenance of the prerogatives of the law did not lead him to overstress the peril: these are not easy questions to answer. What is certain is that he put in its true light and proper terms a problem of the first order for all nations and notably England, whose institutions may well be more vulnerable to the threat than those of countries traditionally adapted to constitutional centralization and less likely to be thrown off their balance by its excesses. Moreover his lucid definition of the contrast between arbitrary rule through abuse of state machinery and liberty through the predominance of the Law remains valid at any time.

From Lord Hewart's own analysis of 'the new despotism' it is clear that such a development can only reach alarming proportions if Parliament itself allows statutory laws to transfer rom the assembly to the state executive an undue part of its legislative power. Two questions therefore arise: Has Parliament in recent years shown a tendency to lose its grip on legislation? And how can the community exercise a proper and necessary control over the use and even the distribution of economic power without resorting to bureaucratic inflation?

As to the first question, while in pre-war England the potential dangers of bureaucratic despotism were not always clearly discerned or acknowledged as such, the anti-bureaucratic tradition survived, perhaps especially as a temperamental reaction. Parliament was watchful of all initiatives taken by the Civil Service in its own capacity and prompt to react with vigour to any alleged trespass on the prerogatives of either House by permanent officials. Stretching the point a little further one might say that there existed a latent rivalry between society as personified by the freely elected deputies of the people, and the state as represented by its appointed servants. This is not to say that members of Parliament underestimated the invaluable task performed by the Civil Service throughout the Empire (nor, incidentally, did Lord Hewart, whose book was by no means an attack on the Civil Service, the excellence of which he praised, but a warning against the threat of a misuse of its powers and a possible diversion from its initial purpose). But they denied it the right to assume the functions of the legislative assembly. Vigilance as between the representatives of different institutions is a healthy sign of their versatility. Yet while outwardly Parliament appeared to be alive to the need for watching state intervention, it did not in effect prevent a marked trend towards greater state interference and an increasing use of state machinery in the years which followed Lord Hewart's warning.

Let it be said at once that this warning ran counter to the main current of opinion which, in most countries, favours greater state control and considers the spread of state machinery the most convenient means of ensuring that control over the general economy. In the pre-war period the growth of public and social services, the implementing of social reforms, the rise of direct and indirect taxation, all resulted in the setting up of new systems of state machinery and led to the expansion of bureaucracy, a process accelerated in war-time when the greatest possible means of action must be left to the Executive.

Without regard to the issue of the controversy between advocates and opponents of state control pre-war Parliaments left considerable latitude to the executive. Although the successive governments of the last twelve years were not in principle committed to the extension of that control, the large freedom of action which they enjoyed encouraged them to rely more and more on state machinery and therefore to breed bureaucracy. An active and dynamic Parliament exercising detailed control over legislation leaves less to be performed by state officials, or at any rate, limits the scope of their initiative more than a nonchalant assembly is likely to do. For while it is normal for permanent officials to wish to enlarge their field of action, it is for the executive to delimit it and for the legislative strictly to define the powers vested in the executive and thus prevent any matter of national interest from escaping its supervision. Now, the activity of pre-war Parliaments suffered from three causes: first, the scarcity of men of outstanding ability, due largely to the last war; second, the tremendous pressure of external events which curtailed the time devoted to the passing and effective control of legislation; third, the huge numerical discrepancy between the Government benches and the Opposition, which inevitably engendered apathy and rendered the executive over-confident. The result was that Parliament did not keep the same grip on the executive as in the past. Consequently, a large amount of business which would normally remain within the province of the legislative was entrusted to departmental bureaucracy. The progress and expansion of bureaucracy was therefore far less attributable to a deliberate policy on the part of the executive than to the submissive and often passive attitude of Parliament in the control of institutions and laws. To resume the comparison used by Lord Hewart, 'the anaesthetic' was not so much given to Parliament as self-administered. That such pronouncements as Mr. Baldwin's 'sealed lips' speech on so momentous an issue as German rearmament, or as some of Mr. Chamberlain's optimistic declarations at the time of greatest danger, should have been almost unchallenged in the two Houses are sufficiently eloquent signs of parliamentary complacency in pre-war days. If such tolerance attended declarations of the executive's policy on matters of general knowledge, it is not surprising that a still greater tolerance should have been extended to its initiatives in far more intricate matters of legislation where the borderline between proper and excessive use of state powers is often hardly discernible.

In fact the House of Commons before the war was insensibly reverting to its old role of a House of grievances: that of a body making the granting of credits conditional upon guarantees and undertakings of redress given by the executive. Sometimes these guarantees were sought inopportunely, as in 1935 when credits for national defence were refused by the Opposition on the ground that the Government's foreign policy had not exhausted other means of ensuring the protection of the country. In any case its activity as a truly legislative body in constant touch with law-making, law-altering and law-safeguarding was notably weaker than it had been for many generations.

In those circumstances it is perhaps not surprising that such problems as economic control and social planning should have been approached only in their simplest form, in the shape of a controversy between advocates and opponents of state control by state bureaucracy, and that little attention should have been devoted in Parliament to the problem of securing that control without necessarily resorting to 'the new despotism' at the expense of liberty in the future. It must be recognized that foreign Parliaments did even less to solve the capital question of reconciling the need for curbing excessive economic freedom with the maintenance of individual and civic liberties.

Yet, whether legitimate interference by the nation in many classes of enterprise must inevitably result in centralized and all-embracing bureaucracy still remains to be decided. Perhaps it is too readily assumed that the interference is inescapable. Setting up machinery when new services are required is one thing; giving it excessive powers and allowing it to take an initiative which appertains to Parliament or the Law is very different. Whether in planning or control, the resources of both the judicial and the legislative power in this respect do not seem to have been either exhausted or even seriously tapped. Parliamentary planning and control by committees of inquiry and investigation have been applied with success to economic and constitutional undertakings throughout the Empire, and those often raised more complex issues than even the matters with which the post-war legislator is likely to be confronted. The idea of extending parliamentary methods to new fields and to different planes of activity has already been exploited in wartime and has resulted in the creation of such bodies as the Joint Production Committees in factories. These at present have purely technical functions, but it may well be that they contain the principle of a new development in economic control more in conformity with the English tradition and temperament than the growth of bureaucratic power and the setting up of an anonymous hierarchy. Finally, the resources offered by local government as against centralized machinery in many realms of action still remain available to the reformer. The Englishman likes to 'watch things working' and to have his say at the various stages of the national life. It is by being able to gratify that impulse and exercise that right frequently and successfully that he has so far avoided the two extremes of political apathy and political anarchy and both impulse and right would certainly be frustrated by bureaucratic rule on a national scale.

Besides the growth of state machinery at the expense of Parliament and the Law, other factors tend to affect the traditional function and balance of English institutions. Among them are the development of the press in recent years and the growing influence of the radio, an equally powerful medium of direct appeal to the nation. The function most natural to the press in a free and diverse country is to reflect all the tendencies of opinion and its contradictions, to be a kaleidoscopic image of its society, whose varying or even conflicting ideas and convictions are an assertion of vitality. Such was in the past the practice of the English press. Since the end of the first World War, however, it has undergone a process rather similar to that of industrial concentration. Newspapers have gravitated more and more into the hands of a few owners or groups or parties and therefore tend to represent sectional interests or opinions more than originality of thought. From a mosaic, the press has changed to a pattern of a few broad colours. The tolerance of editors towards the expression of views dissenting from their own has somewhat mitigated the dangers inherent in such a development. Yet diversity of opinion has nevertheless decreased in popular newspapers and sought refuge in the weeklies and periodicals, which retain a strong independence and exercise variety of judgement. Were it not that the political parties and religious groups with which newspapers associate themselves stand as barriers against excess of concentration or amalgamation, the process might lead to a veritable standardization of public opinion. Politically, the disappearance of an individually independent press, the grouping of newspapers and their increasing reliance on news agencies make for uniformity and encourage mass opinion as against individual judgement. That it has not led to a greater subjection of the public mind shows that the temptation has been resisted by those who wield such a power, and especially that Englishmen retain by temperament a lively scepticism even though their critical faculty may occasionally be overcome. But it is hardly disputable that were the press completely to lose its diversity through concentration, the effects of this on individual independence would not be very different from those produced by state control, and from an economic point of view might be worse.

The risk is rendered considerably greater by the present use made of the radio, which exercises a virtual monopoly in modern states—though to a far lesser degree in the United States where competition is permitted—and approximates more and more to a kind of bureaucracy in relation to the press. Indeed the radio sets a problem which no European country has yet settled; its function in a democracy would normally seem to be the presentation of the greatest diversity of views irrespective of their orthodoxy, official or numerical. Yet the state is in constant fear lest so powerful a weapon should be used against it. In most countries the radio has been put openly at the service of the government or party in office. In England it has been sought to establish a cautious balance between officialdom and moderate opposition. Although this is more equitable, the result is not very dissimilar in terms of standardization of thought. The mere fact that the means of radiophonic expression are concentrated in a single body, that millions of listeners are offered the same diet at the same time, that what is communicated to them is first reduced to a common denominator, and that all attempts at diversity in the output of the radio are nullified by the lack of alternative choice for individual listeners, prevents broadcasting from being anything but a mass instrument. Its educative value is indisputable; but so long as it does not contrive to meet the need for variety and contrast, to become a channel for all views whether official or not, accepted or not, backed or not at any given time by large bodies of opinion, it will remain elementary and may become a dangerous instrument of mental standardization. For one genius who may chance to speak five minutes at the microphone, there will be dealt out by the radio day in and day out, hour after hour, the product of an anonymous milling of news, views, general information and prevalent judgement. This is not to say that either in the newspaper press or in broadcasting England has come to a dead end.

Even in war-time she has maintained a freedom of expression surpassed only in America. But the effect of concentration of power in the diffusion of news and vulgarization of knowledge cannot be ignored in any assessment of English development; for it sets a problem which can yet be solved by those who still hold that democracy consists not in the maximum of uniformity but in the exercise of a responsible critical sense by the greatest number of citizens. This is threatened by a trend which tends towards the spreading of factual information but diminishes or dulls the means of using it.

In the long run the making and control of group opinion cannot but affect the working of national institutions. If the Law has hitherto remained unaffected by outside pressure, such was not the case with pre-war Parliaments. Debates in the House of Commons have sometimes been conducted in the shadow of press campaigns; and the marshalling of mass support by a group for the purpose of determining policy is a very different thing from discharging the duty of the press to explain and criticize. In one case the citizen is enlightened and stimulated, in the other he is doped, a form of arbitrariness not foreseen by constitutional theorists but practised in varying degrees in many countries. There again the marked passivity of Parliament in pre-war years played into the hands of those who had means of direct appeal to the public. It is a very remarkable testimony to the nation's political balance that the combined impact of organized mass movements and conflicting ideologies upon an institution temporarily weakened here and fiercely attacked in other countries should have left it almost unscathed. But the danger of press combines, the radio and even the cinema, if it achieved similar concentration, manufacturing public opinion and using it to outbid Parliament in the voicing of political grievances or demands has by no means passed; nor is it reduced, but only translated into a different form, when press and broadcasting choose or are compelled to submit to the policy of the executive.

Last but not least of the forces which influence the operation of traditional institutions in contemporary England, must be counted the female franchise. The extension of political franchise in England from property owners to all citizens had been up to the last war a comparatively slow process. Then at the end of the war, by a stroke of the pen, the electorate was, at least potentially, more than doubled. Twenty-three years have passed since conservative England took that revolutionary step with revolutionary suddenness. Yet it is still difficult, even for party agents, to assess the exact effect of the voting of women on the political mapping of the country. In constituencies which I have visited, my impression was that they voiced, and encouraged men also to voice, those grievances which have a positive and immediate bearing upon the welfare of the household. Their questions to the candidates in election time usually touched tangible issues such as food taxation, pensions, housing, retail prices, the means test. In the capacity of technical advisers on 'bread and butter policy', their influence although progressive was realistic. Women who share in the hard daily struggle for life, and these are the overwhelming majority, are not inclined to quixotry or dogmatism in matters of social or economic reform and usually consider a bird in the hand as better than two in the bush. On the other hand they are more given to extremes on issues not directly affecting short-term welfare, such as those of international policy. At the time of the ballot by the League of Nations Union, they showed uncommon activity and vehemence.

The extent to which women's votes are influenced by men is often overstressed. In England the influence is by no means a one-way process. Walking in a south London suburb on the eve of a by-election, I once overheard a brief exchange between two men standing on a doorstep: 'This time, it's a big issue, I told the wife. Whether you like it or not, I said, you'll jolly well have to hop along.'—'Lucky dog! *She* won't let me vote my way. Labour, and true red, that's my ticket; but they are all social pushies. Never mind, my vote's my own. She won't know!' The working class on the whole makes polling a household affair because the way the vote goes is of common and direct interest. This is a sound practice, since voting is performed as an act of consequence and not irresponsibly. I doubt if the predominance of either sex markedly effects on balance the outcome of an election. The only positive thing that can be said is that by increasing the electorate without noticeably adding to the diversity of opinion, the franchise of women adds momentum to the swing from party to party, and therefore makes for larger Parliamentary majorities; and that, for the same reason, it renders the nation more responsive to mass movements of opinion.

But then this last tendency is a trait, perhaps only a phase, of national evolution everywhere. In many countries political activity during the pre-war period was narrowed down almost to a conflict between large contending bodies of opinion, usually between two that prevailed in turn, or sometimes one which defeated and eventually absorbed the other. For several years English political life has lain exposed to the threat of an all-pervading uniformity, a threat which expressed itself in many ways and took many forms. It is that forceful tendency which English institutions had to meet by shock-absorption. Consciously or not, modern Europe has lately associated the notion of social progress and economic justice with systems of government or reforms all tending towards the destruction of diversity. Yet whether on a national or an international plane, diversity and liberty have a single and inseparable fate. This is too readily forgotten by many statesmen and politicians who pay lip-service to the tradition of liberty.

Any constitutional policy which did not include the protection of diversity as a fundamental element of progress would lead to despotism, 'the worst disorder of a state' as Socrates called it. For despotism is bred not only by the will of a man or a group but by the abdication of individual conscience. In our day the root of Totalitarianism has lain in the susceptibility of nations to mass psychosis, more than in the ambition of a few men, for any epoch produces a large crop of would-be dictators, and the immediate cause of despotism was invariably the prior emasculation of Parliament, the weakening of society, and the subjection of the Law. The threat in England was less conspicuous than elsewhere but by no means negligible. Essentially heterodox, English institutions had to resist the invasion of dogmatism; diverse, they had to stand amidst the stream of centralization; resting on society they had to prevent it from being mowed down by state machinery. They and the men who served them had in fact to resist a trend which makes for uniformity and gross simplification, as though by simplifying a political and social system one could at the same time simplify human problems which are, on the contrary, increasing in complexity and diversity.

Although British institutions bear the marks of the struggle, they still retain part of their resilience and versatility. In future their success or failure in preserving those qualities will largely depend on the vigour of Parliament in upholding both its own rights and the active independence of the law.

Apart from structural alterations and additions to British institutions, another factor came to bear on this country's national evolution during the pre-war era, namely, the growth of class-consciousness.

CHAPTER II

CLASS FEELING AND BOWLER HATS

Between England and Revolution there will always stand an army of bowler hats. . . .: SEAN O'FAOLAIN.

IN November 1935, during the General Election campaign, I was trying to make my way through a dense fog to the railway station of a little Yorkshire town, when I was accosted by a strange figure of a man: excessively tall and lean, he wore a black hat with a gigantic brim, a long cape of a colour recalling stale mustard and huge pointed moccasins of patent leather fastened with steel buckles. His face was so thin that the only features noticeable at first were thick ginger whiskers, a nose like the stem of an ice-breaker, and formidable horn-rimmed spectacles both covering and magnifying the whole upper part of his face. He was, apparently, also going to the station, for he carried a weather-beaten leather case, on which successive generations of owners seemed to have carved their initials, and a large cardboard portfolio stuffed with papers. 'Hello,' he said in a cavernous voice which, however, conveyed at least a genial intention—'don't you know me?' Having mentally stripped him of his outer garments and somehow turned him from a walking abstraction into a real person, I recognized one of the residents at the local inn where I had stayed for a few days and where the staff had enigmatically described him with a shade of respectful condescension as 'the Artist'. I acknowledged his greeting. He remarked in a sombre voice that the weather was as foggy as the issues involved in the General Election, informed me that he was travelling to Halifax, which was also my destination, and extending the compass of his long legs, walked alongside of me without further comment until we reached the station.

As soon as we had settled down in a carriage, he flung his hat onto the rack, removed or rather unwound his cape, stretched himself out across the compartment and without looking at me opened up with a flood of words, occasionally waving his angular arms as though he were underlining points

H

of his speech with semaphore signals: 'You wonder who I may be? Well, I am a teacher of colours. Not a painter, mind you; though I may claim to wield a pretty brush when I choose to, as a hobby. And I am also a staunch supporter of Social Credit. But first things first,' he went on very quickly, as though to wave off any query or interruption. 'A teacher of colours. Eh? Yes, a teacher of colours, a plain teacher of colours. I don't believe in painting. Painting is a despicable art. Why; now *why*? You are French. I like the French. Don't thank me! You would not guess why in a thousand years. Don't try. I like the French because they produced the only school of painting which is not contemptible: Impressionism. You know what that means? It means the elimination of the black line, the black contour. In other words' (raising a triumphant finger), 'in other words, the abolition of *barriers* between colours, and thence between realities, and one day between men. You are, I trust, beginning to see my point? Look at this.' He pointed at the scenery, as the train had by then moved out of town. 'Look at this cow in this meadow, although I admit you can't see much of it; but that's beside the point. A common sight, no doubt, yet gratifying. And I mean gratifying. Now why should such a plain, shall I say ignoble?—no—let it stand at plain, such a plain sight fill our hearts with exhilaration and secret joy? That cow is brown (so far as I can make out) and the meadow I take to be pale green. Two colours. But they merge. Why? No black contours, nothing to imprison colours. Therefore harmony, man, true harmony. Colours left to themselves are life. The black contour is death.'

'What if the cow were black?' I contrived to put in with humility.

He paused for a while, looking at me with sorrow. And then in stentorian tones, 'Ha, Ha. There you are. The trivial mind all over; what I have fought against all my life, for forty-three years. Sir, or rather Monsieur, whichever pleases most your appetite for distinctions between men, there is no such thing as absolute black in nature, for the reflection of the sun, the very light or, in this country, preferably the mist, supply the transition by disintegrating what in a painting' (he almost spat the word) 'would be a black contour! But let's be serious. I perceive from your expression that you wonder what connexion there may be between my advanced views on colours and social credit? The same principle, why, the very same identical principle: the abolition of the black contour. What are social distinctions? Black contours between men. What are economic classes? Groups separated by the black contours of an idiotic economic system. Parties, groups—black contours. Nations, religions, beliefs—black contours. Let's have a system regulated in such a way that no distinctions are possible in any permanent way; that the merger is possible at all times between different human beings as between different colours; that there is as much harmony between you and me (assuming that I am the humblest pedlar) in relation to each other as between this cow or any cow and that field—in the realm of colours,' he hastened to add. 'Eliminate black contours. Achieve harmony. Now I have never voted or taken part in any political activity—although there is little in that racket which escapes my notice. But I teach colours! And by teaching colours, I teach political impressionism, although the children don't know it and no authority could ever accuse me of subversive proselytism! My boys and girls learn Social Credit all the while without realizing it. And I enjoy it . . ."Je ris sous cape" as you say in French or indulge in *Schadenfreude*, if you prefer the German term. My children will step into Social Credit as easily as into their long trousers. . . . And that will be my triumph. Modest, inconspicuous, but decisive. In fact, Ibsenian; that is if you have read *An Enemy of the People*.'

He went on in the same vein until we reached Halifax where our ways parted. I wished to make a note of his name and address and asked for them. But he wrapped himself up in his mustard cape with the dignity of a dying Caesar and raised a forbidding arm; 'Names? Addresses? Black contours. Let Nature repeat the encounter. And when I say Nature, I mean my conception of it, not Ruskin's. Don't read the old whimperer!' He vanished into the fog, not without shouting a last warning: 'Class consciousness. That's what you must watch here from now on. The real black contour. Distinctions will get a lot sharper before they go. Never mind. Always darker before dawn! Good-bye.'

I had enjoyed his theory of life and generally the company of the fantastic creature, half dreamer, half buffoon. Apart from a collector's gratification, there was something to remember from his fantasies. It was true that class-consciousness in England was something to watch as a new development, though classes as such were no novelty. And his fanciful notion of black contours illustrated not, as he thought, the difference between a real and an ideal state of affairs but the difference between inequality as a fact and inequality as a pretext for clear-cut divisions between large sections of the population according to economic status. Political differences in England had traditionally cut across distinctions of an economic nature. Nor had English revolutions been prompted by purely economic and class conditions. Free Trade *versus* Protection had been an issue irrespective of individual status. Land taxation had found advocates and opponents in all classes. The nearest England had come to a class division was before the repeal of the Corn Laws in the nineteenth century, and even then a large section of the poorer rural population sided against what is known to-day as the industrial proletariat. Until the First World War, and even for a few years after, the 'class against class' slogan had little meaning and very few followers in this country.

The attitude of *a priori* challenge, of challenge as a matter of class principle, which is a familiar trait of Continental politics, was not a feature of English social feuds. Before the war there was comparatively little class hatred in England. This was remarkable enough in a country where the gap between extreme poverty and extreme wealth was greater than anywhere else in Europe; where unemployment was still rife; where, even though the general standard of living may have been reasonably high in theory, the contrast between slum life and opulence remained startling; where a few thousand university students would enjoy the unique privilege of spending their best years in the most lovely towns of Europe, whilst innumerable Welsh or Lancashire children were hurried away from a dreary school to a more dreary pit or mill. Yet whereas this state of things created a strong sense of grievance in many quarters, it did not breed systematic class warfare, partly because the majority of the working class did not share the worst evils, partly because grievances were not fanned by dogmatism, partly because Englishmen seldom keep up a feeling of abstract hatred, partly because the average English worker is more factual than imaginative in political matters and keeps subjects of dispute on a practical plane. My chance friend's 'black contours' as between two classes differentiated merely by their respective purchasing power and unequal degrees of economic control, were a dogmatic conception which had little currency in England.

Few English workers in the past were tempted to indulge in civil strife in order that a class doctrine might triumph, even though they were ready to act in order to secure an advantage or a specific reform. There have been occasions, notably just after the last war, when clear-cut systems have made a strong appeal to the workers; but these have been spasmodic and the effects of dogmatism have been impermanent. There has been more discontent and rebellious spirit against injustice, or alleged injustice, than fanatical adhesion to a creed. I once met in Glasgow a political agitator from Central Europe who had been watching the efforts of the Independent Labour Party and of the Communists in the only part of Great Britain where there is to be found something akin to a revolutionary tendency in the Continental sense. 'Even here,' he said, 'they are not really interested in political doctrine. It's not very different from England. They are not imaginative,' he added naïvely; 'once the workers have gained their point, they won't go on fighting!' Even among left-wing intellectuals such notions as Bakunin's permanent revolution have commanded very little attention. The English outlook on economic matters, at all stages of society, is traditionally factual. Socialism, to the average English workman, was not a systematic conception of the world so much as an instrument for tangible improvements in his condition. The English worker would, on the whole, be considered as 'reformist' by Continental revolutionaries; that is, progressive within an existing order rather than identifying his fate with that of an entirely new one. There is a strong streak of conservatism in every English workman. It is apparent in his tastes, in his craftmanship, in his private interests. That conservatism runs parallel to his natural aspiration towards a 'change for the better'. Revolutionary notions can only be superimposed on him; they are very rarely part of his mental make-up. And there is also a deep reluctance to destroy, which is both instinctive and encouraged by his distrust of ideas as a basis for novelty and reconstruction.

In Duhamel's *Club des Lyonnais*, a revolutionary intellectual having taken an active part in a discussion on the means of destroying the old order and expounded his views in detail, adds with some melancholy: 'Why in any case talk about myself? I shall not see our revolution.'—'Why?' asks another; 'Do you consider it unlikely?'—'No, but I shall be killed the very first day.'—'By whom? The bourgeois?'—'No, by my own comrades, whilst defending the Musée du Louvre.' An English workman might not be killed to save the National Gallery, were it attacked, but he might run a similar risk to protect the district bank manager 'who was not a bad bloke'. His conservatism is human and has a local scope. It is made up of daily habits, understandings, attachments, and practical rather than theoretical ambitions. It is also coloured with a marked partiality for a moderate degree of social climbing. To the workman the bowler hat of the foreman of old was more desirable than a brand new social order. It was indeed that bowler hat which stood between England and revolution. It served as a hinge between wage-earners and employers. It was in fact not a black contour but a connecting link. Perhaps the gradual disappearance of that variety of headgear from the workshop and the building contractor's plots is a sign of the times. . . .

For most of its dogmatic advocates, class warfare is not only a struggle for greater welfare or for the control of the means of production and distribution; it is also alleged to be a way of asserting the dignity of labour. But until recent years Englishmen, whatever their pursuit, however humble their task, had no inferiority complex about labour. Indeed each calling had its own dignity, and obligations, however lowly, towards superiors, were carried out merely as professional duties, never in a manner suggestive of servility. I remember in this connexion an anecdote told by M. Roger Cambon, French minister plenipotentiary in London. In his early days as a young attaché at the French Embassy he was once going out with his uncle, Paul Cambon, then French Ambassador, and his cousin, Paul Cambon's son. As they were stepping into the Ambassador's coupé, his cousin noticed a spot of white dust on the footman's livery and lightly wiped it as he passed. The footman said nothing at the time. Two hours later, however, as they came back from their drive and alighted at the door of the Embassy, he asked Paul Cambon's son if he could have a word with him. 'I must apologize, sir,' he said, 'for my carelessness in leaving a spot of dust on my livery. I assure you that it will not occur again. But if by any chance it should, I should be most grateful to you if you would draw my attention to it. I would then remove it myself.' It was the footman's job to attend to his employers. That was his contract. Yet even within his contract he asserted his right to equality of treatment as a man. And this is a very general trait of English behaviour in all classes. On the human plane therefore an ideology which encourages a sense of social grievance does not find very favourable ground in England, because English people in normal times do not consider technical subordination as humiliating. They couple respect for their job with self-respect within that job. This disposition sometimes borders on snobbery—another deterrent to class warfare. Many an English workman 'on a job' in a private house will prefer a cup of tea to a glass of beer, not from a queer aberration of taste, but because the very process and ceremony of tea-drinking establishes a sort of social contact and equality of status between him and his accidental hosts. These elements of the class problem are by no means to be ignored, for it is perhaps through the cumulative effect of correctness and benevolence on the part of the privileged class, and of temperate social ambition and tolerance on the part of the working class, that an uncommonly inequalitarian community has so far avoided extreme manifestations of class warfare. To resume the comparison used by my eccentric fellow traveller, in spite of the striking differences in 'colours' the 'black contours' dividing one from the other are made as inconspicuous as possible.

Sheer dogmatism having traditionally little hold on the English mind (a state of things maintained, for better or for worse, by education) and the sense of class grievance being normally little developed, most instances of social strife in pre-war England resulted from conflicts on practical and specific issues. Ideological influences may have been at work in the General Strike or the Invergordon mutiny, but, save in the period which immediately followed the First World War, they did not cut much ice: once a contractual basis of settlement was found, there was no dogmatic aftermath.

In the same year, 1935, I witnessed some manifestations of social unrest in the North of England. In Durham and Northumberland in particular there were political meetings which very nearly turned into riots. The issues involved were precise and practical: the means test and the 'betrayal' of the workers by the former Labour ministers. The very presence of Ramsay MacDonald and especially J. H. Thomas on a public platform incensed the miners, not so much because their government was considered a Conservative coalition to all practical intents and purposes, as because the Labour ministers had committed a breach of contract and 'let them down'. In the eyes of the workers their refusal to abolish the means test proved that when they had joined the National Government in 1931 they never intended to be a counterpoise to Conservative influences but had deliberately 'gone over to the enemy'. The cause of popular agitation was human not doctrinal. MacDonald and Thomas were not politicians with programmes to be discussed, but men standing before the tribunal of public opinion.

The sum total of social, economic, and political feuds, which are all a feature of national life in varying degrees, is not necessarily class warfare. In fact in England, although party divisions in the twentieth century have come nearer than ever before to representing social and economic divisions, they were not clearly drawn on a class basis, nor was class warfare generally preached from the platform. The Second International in Continental countries took 'the workers' revolution' as its first aim and as the first article of its constitution. This was not endorsed in practice by the Labour movement in England, whose policy was evolutionist and not revolutionist. The doctrinal basis for class warfare was not therefore established as a principle of British socialism. Neither in the attitude of the working 'class' nor in the tenets of the party to which on the whole it gave its allegiance were the elements of class warfare in England present as an innate tendency.

Yet class warfare, not only in its elementary and un-ideological form but as a deliberate instrument of change, has been such a portentous feature of Continental life in recent years that it was impossible for England entirely to avoid its impact and to follow a side path, applying local and pragmatic methods to issues which other nations treated dogmatically. And what was characteristic of pre-war years was that Continental influences exerted themselves on English life not directly through the absorption by England of extraneous social or economic dogmas, but indirectly and through the presentation before the English people of grave issues of foreign policy: the ascent of Hitler, sanctions against Italy, the Spanish civil war, the attitude of Soviet Russia to international questions. It was this series of problems, far more than the internal situation in England, or the spread in this country of alien dogmas, which chiefly made the English public conscious of notions of class and class-antagonism.

IV. IDEOLOGIES

CHAPTER 12

CLASS, PACIFISTS, AND 'BYRONS'

I shall not cease from mental fight
Nor shall my sword sleep in my hand
Till we have built Jerusalem
In England's green and pleasant land.

BLAKE

POLITICAL ideologies have played in our time the same part as religious creeds in the sixteenth century. They have divided Europe in similar ways, and have similarly been used by scheming rulers to further national designs. The upholders of Fascism (and kindred dogmas) and the advocates of Marxism not only fought for positions in Europe and sought footholds in states open to their influence, but also succeeded in convincing large bodies of opinion throughout the world that in future the choice would lie between these two extremes. Although the Western democracies officially refused to recognize the dilemma and persisted in attempting to steer a middle course, their own public opinion was partly permeated by foreign ideologies. In France Totalitarian and Marxist influences eventually produced a deep cleavage which fatally injured the political life of the nation. In England the impact of conflicting ideologies was felt less. Dogmatic Fascism achieved hardly more than the gathering of a few thousand followers whose meetings and parades ended in ridicule or shame. Marxism was considered as offering theoretical guidance to left-wing thinkers, and it influenced public opinion to some extent in two ways: first, by dividing it on important foreign issues involving ideological tenets; second, by raising within England class problems which English politics alone had never raised so acutely before.

This country was, indeed, in recent years made conscious of the idea of class warfare chiefly by its own reactions to external events. The struggle between Marxism and Totalitarianism in Europe had all the appearance of class warfare on the international plane; and as such it divided opinion within democratic nations and aroused dormant class feelings everywhere. To some extent ideological and class feuds on the Continent revived in England, in a new form, an old ethical conflict: that between Order and Justice, the former understood as social order, the latter as social justice. It was as proclaimed guarantors of social order that authoritarian régimes found supporters here among the privileged class and the middle class; it was in defence of social justice that these régimes were primarily challenged by the working class. Thus, the Continental spectacle led parties and groups in England to regard one another with somewhat the same sentiments as those of contending factions abroad. As a consequence, the English system was itself questioned. The Left, like a modern Electra, was ready to upset the existing order rather than accept the perpetuation of social 'injustice'; the Right, like a modern Ægisthus, opposed demands for social 'justice' on the ground that they threatened the existing and necessary social order. But the antagonism in England never reached the same pitch as in other countries. Nevertheless, the English—who had not in the past shared Continental conceptions of clear-cut divisions between classes, whose society was a hierarchy rather than a community roughly divided between 'haves' and 'have-nots'—acquired for the first time a notion of social and political relations founded on class contrasts. This may be a temporary feature in English political development. Nor is it certain that class warfare and forms of government which take account of the class factor are more than accidental elsewhere. But, however that may be, class consciousness did manifest itself in England before and during the war. In the years 1935, 1936 and 1937, class feeling certainly played a part, if not in the national life of the country, at least in its international conduct.

Ideological reactions to external events, to be sure, had already been apparent in the early 'twenties when sympathy with the U.S.S.R. was aroused among the English working class by Allied intervention in Soviet Russia. Yet the danger of a class conflict, which had not been negligible, eventually subsided. The rise of Fascism in Italy also caused a surge of popular feeling inspired by class hostility to that régime, but the effect of this on English policy was not decisive either. Finally, the growth of National Socialism in Germany shocked England but did not affect the class issue at once, as the German question was regarded as involving a menace to peace rather than as one to be considered in ideological terms. The first great occasion on which England truly and broadly reacted ideologically to a foreign issue and on which class sentiments played a decisive part was the Italian menace and subsequent aggression against Abyssinia in 1935.

It was not unprecedented for England to display in her general policy the effect of popular reactions to external problems on ethical grounds, nor even to show a degree of quixotry in dealing with these problems: the German aggression against Denmark in 1863 aroused crusading instincts in sections of the British people. The Midlothian election fought by Gladstone in 1880 was, as Mr. Francis Birrell remarks in his *Gladstone*, a striking example of 'leading a party to victory by an appeal to nothing but moral standards'. An outburst of feeling on the Abyssinian question would not, of itself, have been a new phenomenon in English political life. What was a departure from precedent in that instance was that the moral and sentimental surge of opinion corresponded to a confused but powerful awakening of class consciousness. And the phenomenon was all the more remarkable since it then contrasted with the relative calm prevailing on the English home front at a time when everywhere else social strife had already developed into open or chronic class warfare. The cumulative effect of the Abyssinian affair and of the Spanish civil war was not only to render the English public aware of class problems but to transform its attitude to the issue of war and peace. Abyssinia destroyed the remnants of pacifism and substituted for them in the English Left a strong urge to intervene abroad. Spain kept that tendency alive and broadened the class cleavage between Right and Left by rendering the Right class conscious also.

The importance of these developments can best be appraised in relation to the English attitude to the international events of 1933 and 1934. In those days, despite the rise of Hitler and the periodical sabre-rattling of Mussolini, the mood of the average Englishman remained markedly non-interventionist. His tendency was to avoid foreign entanglements. It is true that British statesmen and officials devoted considerable time to external affairs, but their policies were truly popular at home when it was thought that they would lead to the elimination of irritating difficulties affecting the English tranquillity. Englishmen took an interest in foreign policy only in so far as they still believed that diplomacy could keep them immune from serious complications, and their natural inclination to avoid problems rather than to participate directly in their solution caused them to indulge liberally in wishful thinking. Thus the English public had approved the wiping out of reparations at the Lausanne Conference in 1932 in the belief that it would usher in an era of economic peace in Europe; thus, despite the Hitlerian threat, they went on hoping after 1933 that British policy could contribute to peace by securing concessions from Germany's neighbours to the new German state and by rendering the German nation more reluctant to follow Hitler if he went too far.

Despite the activity displayed by their Government in the foreign field, the English, until the Abyssinian crisis developed, only showed an intermittent interest in external events; or, more precisely, that interest was awakened but it was vague, inconstant, and occasional, expressing itself, at times, by outbursts of feeling on some international subject such as the Disarmament Conference or the debt to America. But on the whole the traditional indifference of the English to foreign thought, events and people, quickly reasserted itself and prompted them to return to their own business after such demonstrations. The latent xenophobia of the English worker in town or country, vividly analysed by George Orwell in *The Lion and the Unicorn*, encouraged that indifference. Xenophobia in England is passive and never aggressive; it is a snug and deliberate unawareness of the outside world, a way of expressing the attachment of the English to their own peace of mind. Its result is, and conspicuously was during the early 'thirties, to render the English very sceptical as to the ability of foreigners to disturb their tranquillity. Consequently xenophobia in England leads the nation to underestimate external menaces instead of overrating them, as the Germans do. Another effect is to encourage a mild form of pacifism. Paradoxically this latter disposition often coexists with a readiness to feel and act pugnaciously if after all, contrary to all expectations, the English peace of mind is disturbed. So that a people truly cool, collected and deliberate in its own pursuits, is apt to become temperamental and emotionally erratic in its reaction to international events by the mere contrast between its normal state of detachment and its occasional outbursts when detachment is no longer possible.

Just before the Abyssinian question began to assume the seriousness of a first-class international crisis, the English mood was non-interventionist with a touch of sulkiness about it. Many things had happened on the Continent which irritated the man-in-the-street without rousing him. A genuine, unsophisticated example of that mood was presented to me in the late autumn of 1934 when Hitler was already beginning to show his hand. I was spending a few days in the Lake district and stayed near Ullswater with an old Cumberland gardener who for a few shillings had let me a very tiny hut adjoining his house. In the days of horse-drawn traffic he had spent twenty-seven years driving a four-in-hand on Lakeland tours. At about seventy-five he was still as strong as an old birch tree. He had seen many foreign visitors in his time and had reached definite conclusions about them, which he would insist on communicating to me in the course of long walks. 'We're tougher 'n 'em,' he would say; 'we're tougher 'n all of ye put tagether. It's ur climate. Makes us stick anythin'. Feinest climate ye can have to breed guhd men. No, sir, my lad, ther's no fear of war. And we mawn' go to war for anybody; nor for yer leik, least-aways. Once was enough and more'n enough. If the Hoons want us le'em coum raight here. Y'll watch. Us're slow in gittin' garn' but we'll give 'em an owgly roghin'. . . . Reight here in these hills of urs we'd trounce 'em guhd and hard. . . . No sir, my lad, us woon't git on the move for ye agin, nor for anythin'. No war for us. . . . But, nuh, see ye, I'll get the old goon when I see 'em Hoons coum op fram Appleby way, but nat before, not a minute before. Tchek! But they woon't! They kna better! They kna we're tougher. . . . It's ur fein climate that is. . . .'

The old man was expressing in his own odd way the contradictions thus existing within English minds between tendencies which the pressure of threatening events had not yet sufficed to reconcile; for men only attempt to think clearly on things which seriously matter to them and, on others, they merely react according to their circumstances and natural dispositions. Furthermore, pacifism, either in a theoretical form or as a political attitude, was still in 1934 a factor to be reckoned with in the English nation. For many years, both during and after the First World War, the pacifist outlook and even pacifist ideology had played their part in the national life. By the pacifist outlook

I mean conscientious opposition to war on grounds of moral or religious conviction; by pacifist ideology, a refusal to wage war for the defence of a particular national order. The former is ethical and unconditional, the latter is a form of class warfare and it is conditional since its exponents accept the arbitrament of war on behalf of their own beliefs and only reject it as a purely national undertaking. Both were still to be found, chiefly among left-wing thinkers and among the working class, in 1934. To all intents and purposes, both were defeated and destroyed in 1935 and replaced by a strong tendency to class intervention, by a kind of collective Byronism in which class solidarity played the part of cultural affinity: the Left was thus tempted to crusade not, like Byron, to defend a kindred civilization but to serve common class ideals, a common conception of social and economic justice, and to protect these ideals from the ideological enemy. The change from indifference or even pacifism to interventionism was not illogical; it was for ideological and proletarian reasons that pacifism occasionally spread among the Left as a protest against the alleged buttressing of upper-class interests involved in a 'national war'. It was in support of ideological principles that working-class leaders supported régimes that seemed to embody their ideals, or took up the challenge of régimes that threatened social justice and class progress.

The change resulted from or rather was precipitated by, the international dispute on Abyssinia in 1935 and its most spectacular demonstration was at the Labour Party Conference at Brighton on 1 and 2 October when the delegates voted by an overwhelming majority in favour of sanctions against Fascist Italy. In spite of assertions to the contrary, class feeling was then the greatest stimulus in the British surge towards interventionism. What class sympathy for the Soviet Union had not done in the early 'twenties, class hostility to Fascism achieved in the middle 'thirties: it was at the Labour Party Conference that pacifism received a fatal blow at the hands of Trade Union and Labour.

When the Brighton Conference met on 1 October, the result of the struggle between interventionists and abstentionists was almost a foregone conclusion. The three Executives, Trade Union, Labour Party, and Parliamentary Labour Party, had already passed at the Trade Union Congress at Margate a resolution strongly recommending the resort to sanctions against

Italy. Yet the issue was finally joined and fought out at Brighton. The Labour delegates met at the huge Dome Palace. It was as though a skilful producer had set the stage for a truly historic debate and created a suitably dramatic atmosphere. The countenances of the members of the Executive, ranged behind a table set on the platform and covered with red cloth, added to the ominous implications of the gathering: they looked somewhat like a tribunal of the great Inquisition passing sentence on the Mussolinian heresy with the Margate resolution for their articles of faith. And Mr. Hugh Dalton, whose natural geniality easily hides behind a grave and austere mask, could well have been cast for the part of Chief Inquisitor. Jimmy Walker on the other hand looked like a powerful county auctioneer bent on outbidding the local squire at the sale in retaliation for his Conservative politics. Among the assembly, responsive to the point of frenzy throughout the debates, there were three schools of thought. The most important by far was in favour of sanctions at any cost, though in point of fact the cost was expected to be light and Italy an easy nut to crack. Another group felt that the Labour Movement should not support sanctions which were to be carried out by a capitalist government, for it would thereby entrust the Conservatives with weapons the use of which could neither be limited nor controlled. This was Sir Stafford Cripps's thesis. Finally, George Lansbury contested the very legitimacy of a policy of coercion at any time as contrary to socialist thought. Both conscientious objectors and class objectors of the Cripps persuasion eventually joined forces but suffered a decisive defeat.

George Lansbury's personality justifies a pause at this stage because he was the last spectacular illustration of a pacifism which, though it has now practically died out, had deep roots in the ethical history of England. The sincerity of his pacifist faith has since been questioned. It has been said that whilst Lansbury was admittedly an opponent of force as a means of action, he would not have gone so far in his advocacy of total abstention at the Brighton Conference had he not realized that his days as a party leader were numbered, and had he not wished his defeat to assume the tragic splendour of self-immolation to his creed. I think this judgement very unfair. Often before and after the Conference I had long conversations with him in his little house in Bow Road, in the East End of

London, where his welcome was warm and his kindness unfailing. He was in many respects a shrewd man and this was put forward by his detractors as evidence against the genuineness of an idealism bordering on naïvety. Yet shrewdness in him was no whit exclusive of a profound humanity. In an iron age when human causes receive lip-service from abstract theorists rather than true sympathy, when the people's welfare is far more often a pretext for commending conflicting doctrines than an object of real concern, Lansbury believed in men, not as symbols of a particular ideology, not as creatures a thousand miles away, but men on his own doorstep and within reach. He was, above all, a Christian and instinctively conservative, inasmuch as his revolutionary tendencies were never allowed to overrule Christian beliefs which forbade him to advocate retaliation or to comply with any policy, however justified its temporal aims, which were capable in practice of endangering spiritual values. A great believer in human progress to the point of credulousness, he was, however, sceptical as to the ability of any group of men at any time to hold a measure of truth warranting violent proselytism and fanatical action. He was naïve enough to tell me, when embarking on his journey to catechize Hitler in 1938: 'After all, every man is born of a mother'; which made me remind him of the paradox of Macduff's nativity. Yet in 1935 he had been clearsighted enough to understand that sanctions could only be effective if the Western powers were ready to face Germany as well as Italy, and that the issue went far beyond a rehearsal of the League's powers—as many of his colleagues were inclined to believe. A man of humble extraction whose simplicity of habit bordered on asceticism (he lived on vegetables and water and did not smoke), he had, like many of his proletarian constituents, a middle-class respect for home comforts and he understood that the poor in England, rightly or wrongly, are more tempted by a good coal fire and walls with pipes which do not burst than by doctrinal abstractions. His sentimental horizon was worldwide, his long-term dreams almost Utopian; yet in his constituency, where he was loved, he appreciated daily practical wants and the need for achieving what improvements could be secured within a lifetime, for he did not set dogma above facts. Elected leader of the Parliamentary Labour Party at a time of great dearth of men, when many had gone over to the National Government, he did not over-value himself and, while he was proud, I never found him envious of others' fame. With his broad face framed by grey-white whiskers, his generous blue eyes seldom without a good humoured twinkle behind steel-rimmed spectacles, with his heavy shoulders and his swaying gait recalling an 'Old Salt' and stiffened in later years by an accident to his leg, with his grave, husky Cockney voice, Lansbury was above all a lovable human figure; not an outstanding parliamentarian perhaps but, even in his contradictions, a man whose very mistakes were an assertion of man's dignity.

Such indeed was the respect that he commanded by virtue of his disposition, that the very day when he made the profession of faith which led to his downfall as a party leader was also the day of his greatest personal triumph. Few of the delegates at the Conference expected Lansbury to survive the debate, but all wondered what he would say and who would finally break him. When he rose, he was cheered as I have heard few men cheered by an assembly; and the whole congregation as one man struck up 'For he's a jolly good fellow'. This tremendous welcome moved him; but he was too much of an old-timer on political waters to have any illusions. Perhaps for that very reason he burned his boats and spoke without any concessions to his opponents, setting forth without reservation an extraordinarily bold and unmitigated profession of pacifist faith.

He recognized at once that it would be difficult for the party to retain at its head a man who did not share the official view and he certainly did not enhance his chances by taunting Trade Union leaders, suggesting that their own 'and other influences' had been brought to bear on the Labour Party, whose members had not always been in the past whole-hearted supporters of sanctions. As for himself, he had never believed force to be a remedy. On that point he had never changed. In his own country, in mining districts and elsewhere, he had often talked to people who were nearly starving. He had never told them to revolt or to riot; he had asked them to wait, however strained their patience might be—to wait for the eventual triumph of socialism. Force would only breed force and change without progress. What he had said when his own countrymen were starving, he would for a stronger reason apply to international affairs. History was but a long succession of changes brought

I

about by forcible means, of injustices brought forth by the violent removal of injustice: 'All they that take the sword'—he quoted—'shall perish by the sword.' Sentence after sentence, in a voice which gathered strength in its very hoarseness, he built up his case against force as an instrument of redress and justice. Socialism, in his view, could only succeed if it prevailed by virtue of conscience and reason; otherwise it would only degenerate into a dogma akin to those which it attempted to combat. If, however, truly socialist methods should fail, if all should prove useless . . . then—Lansbury concluded with passionate exaltation—'God is my witness that I should be ready to say with the early Christians: "Such is my Faith; I have no other; I remain true to it, and here, if need be, I will die".'

Such words had never before been heard at a political meeting in the twentieth century. It was easy enough to challenge the speech on rational grounds and even to deride it. Yet the orator received an immense ovation, which went to the man if not to the party leader. But the assembly had been stirred, not persuaded, by his swan song. That song marked the death of pacifism, for by the very act of raising it to a mystical level Lansbury destroyed it as a practical policy.

Among the sanctionists, it was Ernest Bevin who really carried the day. It was he who stood out as a rising tribune of the people at a time when the English Left hesitated to assert its dynamism in foreign policy and contributed to turn the Labour movement into an international force of its own which, misguided or hesitant though it might occasionally be, would henceforth have to be reckoned with. It was Ernest Bevin who personified what could well be termed an Imperialism of the Left, if the word Imperialism could be divorced from physical conquest. Hardly had he begun to speak when all felt the impact of his formidable oratory, which did not seek to charm but to arouse, which despised fine shades but made points with the might and also the accuracy of a sledge hammer, which ignored all emotions save when they prompted action.

One after another, the old tenets of a moral socialism were knocked down like skittles: the sharing of the world's riches, the throwing open of colonial territories to hungry states. In such an international atmosphere, it would merely start a new goldrush and precipitate a world war. Pacifism as a means of action? China was the most pacific country in the world. Her territory has been overrun and defiled by the warlike Japanese. Every civilization which threw away its shield in the past had eventually been destroyed and the clock of progress had been put back. For years the British Labour movement had worked to build up the League of Nations as an instrument of law. Its strength was justice and true morality. Would Labour disown its own professed convictions at the time when at last there was a chance of asserting the might of law over the rule of force? Would Labour desert the very path which it had pointed out to others? 'Lansbury has quoted the Bible: "He that takes the sword shall perish by the sword." Mussolini has taken the sword. And we are here, faithful to the Covenant of the League, so that, having taken the sword, he shall perish by the sword!'

To wield the sword, the sword of Justice; such was precisely then the ambition of British socialism. It is true that at Brighton most of the orators disclaimed any class bias in their crusade against aggression, and that Herbert Morrison, who wound up the debate, made a special point of asserting that the action of the Conference was not directed against Fascism but against international lawlessness. No doubt most of these assurances were given in all sincerity. Yet on what other issue than the chastisement of Fascism would such a consensus of opinion have been formed among the representatives of the working class?

To be sure there were more motives and inspirations than one at the Brighton Conference to account for the overwhelming majority which eventually voted for sanctions. There was in fact a little of everything in the minds of the delegates: a sense of outraged justice; a degree of xenophobia expended the more willingly on a nation which the English working class is inclined to scorn; a pugnacious reaction to the disturbance of peace by a second-rate power; a quixotic desire to become the champion of the weak, together with the hope that Abyssinia might by her resistance make a laughing stock of Italian arms; and also a strong anti-papist feeling stimulated by the passivity of the Vatican before the prospect of an act of Italian aggression. Yet, had it not been for class hostility to the Fascist order and its social record, the large section of the population still concerned for its own peace of mind, still reluctant to take unnecessary risks or to seek international adventures even on behalf of justice, could not have been so easily stirred to challenge the transgres-

sor of the Covenant. The case on its own merits no doubt
justified active reprobation. But the *macte animo* rang a class
note. What Trade Union and Labour leaders, the latter perhaps more hesitatingly, clearly realized was that the working
class had then its chance of wielding the sword of Justice: they
could point the way to a Jerusalem that could only be reached
if the English working man defied the heathen. And in 1935, the
heathen in class terms, was the Fascist order which threatened
the world with its evil proselytism.

Outside the Labour and Trade Union movements, the Abyssinian crisis had aroused diverse sentiments and preoccupations
which all converged for a time towards the same goal, contradictory though they seemed: the sense of a menace to permanent
imperial interests, the hostility of the Liberals to Fascism independently of class considerations, the crusading instincts of the
English Protestants. Indeed the Abyssinian question typified
a phenomenon frequent enough in England and invariably
misunderstood abroad: a genuine surge of public feeling coinciding for a while with national interests. This is interpreted in
foreign countries as revealing among the English people as a
whole a keen appreciation of the country's particular interests
and a remarkable readiness to defend them, whereas in fact
the cool calculation of statesmen may for a time turn to good
account a consensus of emotional opinion and attempt to reverse
the stream when circumstances have changed and require
caution instead of enthusiasm. It was thought in France
throughout the Abyssinian crisis that Britain used the League
machinery against Italy for the defence of her imperial interests, and the genuineness of popular feeling here was grossly
underestimated. In this connexion it is amusing to recall that
Gaston Bergery then advocated help to Great Britain on that
very assumption, holding that France should take sides with
England despite the nature of England's motives. The misunderstanding between the two countries on the Abyssinian issue
caused a breach which was never repaired. French traditional
policy had always considered Germany as the only serious
threat to European peace and held that civilization was to be
defended on the old Rhine-Danube barrier to German expansion. To count Italy as an enemy when no preparations were
made to meet the German danger was, despite Italy's guilt, a
difficult decision for the French to make. Moreover, in June

1935, French opinion had been incensed by the conclusion of the Naval Treaty between England and Germany at a time when France was protesting against German rearmament under Hitler. So that the same French Government which had upheld the League as an instrument of collective security refused to support the League to the full in the face of an Italian act of aggression, unless guarantees were given that England would assist France if Germany took advantage of the situation to attack her. This was logically sound but a grave mistake in practice, since, in so doing, France estranged European nations which counted on her when the Covenant was to be enforced. England on the other hand rightly thought that an example should be made of Italy in order to assert the executive force of the Covenant, but ignored the further implications of a resort to sanctions and the seriousness of the German menace. Indeed I heard members of the House of Commons at the time suggesting that perhaps Germany might join in the enforcement of sanctions! British policy was sound in principle but inconsistent. Focused on the fact of Italian aggression, it either took for granted that Germany could be intimidated by a mere deployment of strength against Italy, or forgot the German danger altogether. French policy was realistic in its assessment of the consequences of sanctions and in its demands on Great Britain, but grossly underestimated the moral issue and the effect on the world of its refusal to uphold the Covenant unconditionally. In London and elsewhere German diplomats were in the best of moods, delighted that the English bull should rush at the Italian red cape whilst their own country was quietly rearming, and that France should wreck her own system of alliances on the Continent through forgetting the diplomatic repercussions of her complacency towards Italy. The result was that the two Western Powers had the worst of both worlds. Italy was neither curbed by the weak sanctions eventually imposed on her, nor impressed by Laval's attempt to mitigate the application of the Covenant. Germany was encouraged in her plans of aggression both by the weakness of the League and by the prospect of bringing Italy into her own camp. The stage was set for a new episode of the European drama: the alignment of the Totalitarian states on ideological pretexts, but with aggressive national aims, with the Spanish civil war to test and cement their alliance.

Throughout the year 1935 and during the early months of 1936, the Abyssinian crisis weighed heavily on the relations between Great Britain and France. Fascist aggression had aroused the French Left as it had the English, but the French Left was then in opposition and its influence on the policy of the government was not sufficient to carry the day. Furthermore, France, Left as well as Right, had been shocked by the naval agreement between England and Germany and by England's apparent reluctance to treat Germany as a potential danger. Paradoxically, the French working class, far more class-minded than the English in regard to the home front, was less deeply class conscious on the international plane. Indeed many Labourites in England privately, though not officially, criticized the moderation of their opposite numbers in France on that issue—criticism which, doubtless, was seldom heard.

In both countries the outbreak of the Spanish rising against the Republic on 18 July 1936 gave class consciousness a tremendous impetus. But while the Abyssinian question had stirred English class feeling to action in an external field, the effect of the Spanish war was deeper because it divided the country from the start. With the Spanish war, in fact, the sense of class interest passed from the ideological and international plane to the national and internal one, and class mindedness was equally conspicuous on the Conservative side which, through part of the Abyssinian affair, had had little opportunity to assert itself on social grounds. Indeed, one of the important consequences of the division of sympathies was that non-interventionism and even pacifism shifted from one class to another, from Left to Right, at least for a time, and that the 'No war' slogan changed sides. The effects of the change were later to be revealed at Munich. From 1936 onwards the dread of any disturbance to public order largely influenced the attitude of the right-wing parties; so, perhaps, did the conviction that, contrary to an old left-wing prejudice, war destroys and does not enhance class privileges and vested interests, a thesis expounded by Montesquieu two hundred years ago.

In 1935, in the case of the Abyssinian dispute, popular feeling against Fascist Italy had been encouraged and stimulated 'from the top' of the Labour movement and especially by trade union leaders. In the case of Spain, in 1936 and thereafter, leaders and politicians were far more cautious: the crusading impulse sprang from sections of the people. The early speeches delivered by Labour politicians at the beginning of the Spanish war were cold, uninspiring, certainly not calculated to stir public feeling: they sounded as though the Labourites were performing, dutifully and reluctantly, an inevitable ritual, rather like the sending of condolences to a provincial aunt or congratulations on the marriage of a cousin three times removed. Later on, parliamentarians and trade union leaders warmed up and even complained that Non-Intervention in Spain should have been initiated by a French left-wing government (the Popular Front was then in power in France), but in 1936 that policy suited their book admirably. This moderation on the part of the English Labour movement, or this indifferent solidarity with the Spanish Republicans, can easily be explained. In the first place the Labour party was in the condition of a wrestler out of wind who must recover his breath. Its vain efforts during the Abyssinian quarrel left it tired, perplexed and dispirited. In the second place the movement knew or believed that Communist influences were at work in England on behalf of the Spanish Republicans. Labour leaders, fearing they might become involved, were eager to show that their own policy steered clear of the Communist reef. My remarks on the hesitation which marked the attitude of British socialism in the first stages of the civil war do not therefore imply criticism of the attitude of British Labour at the time; still less do they betray any regret that there should have been no intervention in Spain on a *class* basis. They merely record the fact that from the beginning political Labour and trade unionism were not deeply stirred by events in Spain and that, without openly recognizing it (which they could not do) they dreaded rather than desired intervention on ideological grounds. The reaction to events in Spain was stronger among the workers themselves. Working-class opinion, which had been awakened and then frustrated at the time of the sanctionist campaign, had kept alive both a sense of class solidarity and a combative disposition towards socially antagonistic régimes. The political temperature of the English Left was thus, so to speak, raised from below. The conspicuousness of Italian and German help to Franco, the story of German savagery at Guernica, the bombardment of Almeria, and other incidents, gradually prompted Labour leaders to show more fire in their defence of the Republicans. What perhaps rendered them even more pugnacious was the undeniable fact that English conservatism also reacted by a 'class against class' attitude to events in Spain. This time the class challenge did not come only from the Left, from the section of the population which is traditionally more inclined by its very condition to adopt a class attitude, but also from the Right. The Spanish war inflamed class feeling on both sides and created a fairly clear-cut division between the two. It was indeed the first occasion on which a cleavage occurred on a nation-wide scale and truly entered the consciousness of the English people. Films, photographs, radio and newspaper stories, all brought the Spanish war within the purview of the man in the street. The very vocabulary used by newspaper commentators and cast into their headlines emphasized a class intention. Thus the *Daily Mail* at first described the two Spanish parties as 'Government' and 'Insurgents', then as Republicans and rebels, then as Government and Anti-Government, then as 'Reds' and 'Anti-Reds'. Others went further and referred to battles between Reds and Patriots. Part, though not all, of the English middle class, like the French drawing-rooms at the time of the great Revolution, saw no more in the Spanish war than a struggle between well-thinking and well-groomed officers and a rabble. It was on the side of 'order' and again forgot Germany and Italy rehearsing their parts for 'Der Tag'. The working class refused to admit that excesses had also been committed by the Spanish Left and that, apart from the Fascist clique of mercenaries, there were against the Republic men who were genuinely dedicated to the defence of a tradition, retrograde perhaps, but worthy of respect. Despite the remarkable capacity for detachment from political preoccupation of most Englishmen, it then dawned on them that there might be in the 'class' opposite the same potentialities of hatred or repression as were turned into bloody realities by the Spanish drama. And that realization had a dual effect, indeed two contradictory effects. One was to inoculate the people against similar excesses: the sight of the unfortunate Spaniards on the screen had the premonitory force of a warning. The other was to reinforce class consciousness which, in the political sense, was still merely tentative when the Spanish war broke out. The old English conviction that 'It can't happen here', almost an equivalent to the *Civis Romanus sum* as a naïve assertion of unbounded national self-confidence, never allowed the horrors of the Spanish war to become completely *real* for the English public. Or rather, its reality was that of a nightmare which troubles one's imagination and causes physical reactions not altogether different from actual happenings, but from which one can retreat by passing from one state to another. English fists might be clenched at each other but in intention only. Save for a few thousand men who demonstrated their political convictions in arms on Spanish soil, the tragedy of Spain remained far away. Yet it created sentiments which lingered on, suggesting a chronic antagonism between classes which, mild or not, would henceforth become part of the political set-up. Like Adam and Eve after they had eaten the apple, the two classes knew that they were different. The Spanish war left behind it in England if not a class feud at least a class sense of embarrassment.

The end of the Spanish struggle in 1939 coincided with other European events so serious that they eclipsed for the English people all other considerations. And the Second World War brutally interrupted the process of English development, leaving a question mark at the end of its latest chapter. Yet class consciousness did reappear during the war and, this time, not under any extraneous influence, but under the impact of the conflict itself. The fact, inevitable in itself, that bombing from the air, however indiscriminately it struck England, caused incomparably greater sufferings among the poor than among the rich or well-to-do, was bound to create a sense of class resentment. Envy, social or other, is not at all an English characteristic. In Latin countries the visible, daily apparent inequality in suffering which aerial bombardment causes to a far greater extent than any other form of warfare, would probably have fanned class warfare. Such was not the case in England. Indeed I find class feeling less conspicuous now than it was in 1940 and 1941; but, milder though it be, it has become a problem not to be ignored by post-war rulers, a heavy legacy to post-war legislators. There again, England has shock-absorbed contemporary tendencies which on the Continent were given full expression in open feuds or rankling enmities. But she did not avoid their effects, nor solve the problem they set. Nor did Parliament or the parties and men who served it prove equal to the magnitude of their task in this or in other fields of national activity.

V. THE DECLINE OF PARTIES

CHAPTER 13

THE DROOPING TOP HATS AND THE BUSINESSMAN'S ERA

May one be pardoned and retain th'offence?: Hamlet

ONE memorable September morning in 1938, a platoon of Hitler's bodyguard, drawn up fanwise flanking the doorway of the Peterhof, presented arms as a tall, lean figure emerged from a huge car and stood up with affable shyness in the autumn sunshine of the Rhine Valley. The Peterhof was a large hotel, the grey bulk of which crowned the top of Petersberg, one of the Seven Mountains, facing the little town of Godesberg on the opposite bank of the river. It was there that the British delegation at the Godesberg Conference had been accommodated. The man to whom the Black Guard presented arms was the Right Hon. Neville Chamberlain, Prime Minister of Great Britain. The blue serge suit and light felt hat which he wore told of seven hundred years of Parliamentary tradition. The soldiers in black uniform, their heavy helmets riveted to the flat napes of their thick necks, were the heirs of those Teutons who, nine centuries earlier, had sacked Rome and brought Gregory VII to a miserable end, avenging the German Emperor Henry IV. At Canossa, German temporal might had had to bow before the spiritual power of Rome. In Rome, German might had taken its revenge and redressed the balance. At Versailles in 1919 German pride had again been curbed. At Godesberg it was silently asserting its rebirth and determination before that representative of the Western Powers, and his attire must have strengthened in those warriors standing at attention there a belief in the advanced state of decay of nations which still insisted in 1938 on dressing *their* Führer in civilian clothes.

Like all visitors to the Siebengebirge, Mr. Chamberlain had no doubt been told the story of the Christian virgin of the Drachenfels who, offered as a tribute to the Dragon, had finally destroyed the monster by brandishing a crucifix before its flaming eyes, through that miracle converting to the Faith the heathen tribes of the Seven Mountains. German tourist literature omitted to say, however, that the conversion had never struck so deep as altogether to discourage the indulgence of those tribes in warlike and predatory pursuits. The fact being lost sight of, well might the British Prime Minister on his peace-seeking errand present to the Press photographers a reflective smile, as he watched the formidable display of German military power with the steady eyes of a missionary making his first contact with the natives whom he has come to catechize.

Mr. Chamberlain paused for a while. He looked at once shy and self-possessed, embarrassed and benevolent, thrilled and flattered, as though he felt that the Dragon had been somewhat maligned and might after all be talked out of the bad habit of eating people up; and also as though he nevertheless wondered how to create the proper social atmosphere so soon after the jarring note of Berchtesgaden.

The scene, which lasted but a few seconds, remains vivid in my memory. Was Mr. Chamberlain conscious of the impression of uncanny power conveyed to the onlookers by the very simplicity and frailty of his appearance set against such a background of paraded force? For who but a man conscious of tremendous albeit secret resources, which he might release at will, would thus display drawing-room amiability in this Temple of War where nothing but physical might could inform and load the words which he was to utter within the next few hours on the other side of the Rhine? Who but such a man armed with hidden weapons could so much as make sense in war-clad, war-bent, war-yearning Germany whose inexorable intent was featured in the stubborn brows and pale obsessed gaze of the Führer's bodyguard?

Perhaps the Prime Minister's big eyes—those eyes almost without whites, which, like those of giant birds, changed their focus by sudden, transitionless motions—were musing at that moment on the question which of the two Powers would prevail, the ostentatiously displayed or the latent, should his mission end in a fiasco. But it was not in his nature to consider failure. He seemed to enjoy the contrast between armour and blue serge. He may have been toying with the idea that, at that precise instant, crowd and soldiers were acknowledging the leading part which the Prime Minister and party leader played in a drama that must have a happy ending. Perhaps they were acknowledging the greatness that was England, in thus endowing his own businesslike appearance at a Rhineland hotel with the solemnity of such a stage setting. . . . It was with the same odd capacity for producing fatefulness and for conjuring up grandeur out of unreality, that he was later to return from Munich with the scrap of paper that meant 'Peace in our time'. Having paused for a brief moment in the pool of light which the sun shed on the threshold across the dark, high, ominous trees, the Prime Minister slowly walked into the Peterhof, on his way to his suite, to the Godesberg Conference, and eventually to Munich.

That Neville Chamberlain carried with him the sense of his country's greatness, there is no doubt. That his use of that greatness as a weapon, as an asset, was perverted in practice is equally certain. Some of his shortcomings were truly his own, some he largely shared with other men. His conversations with French leaders in 1938 evinced a sound knowledge of military and strategic problems, a power of practical discussion, and an ability to grasp the material points in issue—qualities which he did not so clearly display during public debates in the Commons. The Anglo-French discussions also showed him to possess a reasonable acquaintance with foreign affairs and a considerable ability in dealing with the economic aspects of international questions. Mr. Lloyd George's sarcastic remark that 'he would at best make a good mayor of Birmingham in the lean years' was more witty than just, although the man who had risen to such colossal stature in the last war was entitled to set all statesmen high standards. Neville Chamberlain was far from greatness; yet he was well above the average parliamentarian. He suffered from a deep-rooted contempt for small nations dwelling outside the field of daily British interests, from self-confidence to the point of vanity, from a total lack of psychological sense, and from a profound stubbornness. Intellectually he had a clear mind on matters with which he was conversant (and they were many), but a marked inability to imagine and to understand what previous experience had not already taught him. As with other English politicians at the time, his chief defect was incurable wishful thinking in most international matters, this contrasting oddly with his realism in the economic field. A business man at heart, he readily believed that realism in foreign policy consists in getting the other man to state his views, giving him his fair share, shaking hands and then turning to serious work. Finally, in common with most of the world's inhabitants during these fateful years, he suffered from the fatal belief that discussion can change the nature of things and the course of events. In this respect the chief difference between him and Ramsay MacDonald was that the latter pinned his faith to the motto 'the more the merrier', and appeared to think that the more intricate the issue the more people there must be around the proverbial table, while the former preferred a *tête-à-tête* on the ground that two is company and three a crowd.

Well cast as a Conservative Chancellor of the Exchequer, Neville Chamberlain was miscast as a national leader. But then the casting was not his own. Prime Ministers in this country are not self-appointed nor are they chosen by accident. Why was he selected for that exalted part? Why, if not because his views and even his prejudices largely reflected those of his party at the time; because he represented, to say the least, a large body of sympathetic opinion? Indeed, anyone who in 1935 had chanced to attend the Conservative Conference at Bournemouth could bear witness to the tremendous popularity which he already enjoyed and which somewhat baffled dispassionate onlookers. A creation of his party, Neville Chamberlain was then the heir-apparent to Stanley Baldwin whom he was beginning to over-shadow in Conservative councils. Throughout his tenure of office he enjoyed the firm support of his party. Whatever mental reservations there may have been were never given proper utterance save by a courageous and unheeded minority headed by Winston Churchill. For many years Neville Chamberlain truly expressed a trend of thought. It was only towards the beginning of 1940 that many of his followers recanted his gospel and that he became their scapegoat (the inevitable and just fate of the man who rises to power). Yet the question remains: what and whose sins was he redeeming?

During these anxious days of 1938 when the Prime Minister was travelling across Germany in search of a 'settlement', I was curiously reminded of a remark that I had heard several years before. It was in the early days of 1935 when Mr. Eden was sent to Moscow and held conversations with the members of the Soviet Government. As it happened I was paying my first visit to the lobbies of the House of Commons, though not to the House itself, when his forthcoming journey to the U.S.S.R. was announced. I was anxious to know what some of the Conserva-

tive members thought of the new departure in British foreign
policy, and, upon being introduced to Sir Herbert Williams,
who was regarded as a staunch Tory, it was to him that I first
turned for enlightenment. I rather timidly asked him what he
felt about Mr. Eden's trip. My 'greenness' in parliamentary
customs led me to expect a philippic against the Soviet Union
and I braced myself for an outburst of right-wing russophobia.
Sir Herbert, who was in the act of negotiating a large ham sand-
wich that he might face his constituents with a stouter heart
later in the day, considered my question for two seconds, man-
fully swallowed a formidable mouthful and answered in a stifled
yet powerful voice: 'I'll tell you what I think. I think the place
of a British minister is in London, right here [he extended a
hard forefinger towards the ground] and not in Moscow or in
any other capital. And I think that if the jolly Russians want
to have a look at Eden, they jolly well should send Molotov or
Stalin or anybody else to London and let us know what they
have to say for themselves.' Upon which comprehensive statement he went off to catch his train for East Croydon.

His reply, disappointing though I found it at the time, rang
the Palmerstonian note. Indeed it was the last echo of it that
I was to hear in the House of Commons (for one could hardly
describe as Palmerstonian the weekly question, put on the order
paper by a certain die-hard, 'Whether, before undertaking any
negotiation with the Soviet, H.M. Government would secure
the restitution of the silver plate stolen from the British Embassy
after the October Revolution of 1917?' It was a long way from
the Tory overconfidence which prompted Herbert Williams's
remark in 1935 to Mr. Chamberlain's perambulations in 1938.
But even in 1935 such remarks amounted to little more than
sallies. The Conservative party was already undergoing the
change that made its acceptance of Munich possible and almost
enthusiastic. The tall, gaunt, erect figure of Austen Chamberlain—in his frock coat and top hat, with his silhouette which
retained at seventy the elegant ease of youth, with his impassive
ivory face so smooth, despite the stamp of age, that it looked
like a monocled mask, with his grave affability of manners and
address—still passed from the lobby to the House evoking the
great days of the Conservative party. The elder of the two
Chamberlains had had his Locarno in 1925. The younger had
his own in 1938. The former had tried to build a dam against

the German flood. The latter thought he could open the sluices and control the flood. But then from 1936, when Neville Chamberlain took office, to 1938 the Locarno policy, or any policy aimed at restraining Germany, was just as much out of fashion with the majority of the Conservative party as Austen's fast-disappearing type of headgear was with the House of Commons.

Munich marked the nadir of British prestige and power, of that prestige and power which it was the traditional purpose of the Conservatives to uphold. Yet the Party had virtually ruled England for seven years under the National Government. From 1931 to 1938 it had enjoyed a huge majority, reduced but no whit impaired by the General Election of 1935. And from 1935 to 1938 its two successive leaders were Prime Ministers of England. It is therefore in that period of years and against the background of the party's evolution during that time, that the policy which led to Munich (in so far as Great Britain's responsibility was concerned) must in fairness be considered, and not on the sole shortcomings of Neville Chamberlain's conduct of affairs.

It seems to have been a feature of political life among the Western nations during recent years that the various parties exercised an ever increasing influence on one another's programmes and policies and that this influence usually exerted itself for the worse. This may have been of less consequence in England than in some other countries, but the fact was nevertheless noticeable. Under the National Administration from 1931 to 1938 the interpenetration of parties was all the more influential because sections of the Liberal and Labour parties had migrated into the ranks of the majority and brought with them some of their convictions and most of their habits of thought. There was consequently a daily reshuffling of ideas and tendencies. This encouraged the already growing practice of right-wing parties in democratic states of borrowing from the Left any suggestion or scheme capable of enhancing its sponsor's popularity at small cost. Indeed, stealing a march on the opponent has recently become a method of political warfare freely indulged in by public men. Its consequences can hardly be good. Each party has its own programme, which is the sum total of its convictions, beliefs, and competence. Adherence to that programme may narrow the field of vision but it makes

for intellectual honesty and efficiency. On the other hand, a
policy which gradually turns into a patchwork of projects and
notions, grabbed here and there for their publicity value and
hastily assembled, is likely neither to be successful nor to be
punctually carried out.

British foreign policy from 1931 onwards reflected the perplexities and contradictions of the Conservative mind which
questioned its own principles, doubtfully and half-heartedly
tried others, fumbled after new notions, was the prisoner (albeit
ashamed) of old ones, and stood by none. In that respect but
alas! in no other were British and French policies conspicuously
akin. Never in English history had a parliamentary majority
been so secure; secure even to the point of immunity from any
attack. Yet never had its members been more divided in their
minds, not by reason of deep contrasts in their beliefs, but owing
to their susceptibility to fluctuating influences through lack of
considered convictions, unreadiness to adopt a line of action and
keep to it, and consequent inconstancy from week to week and
month to month. With very few individual exceptions a record
of public speeches made by members of the majority over the
fateful period from 1931 to Munich would show remarkable
inconsistencies and changes not only on specific points or problems but even in fundamentals. In matters of Home policy the
majority occasionally showed determination (although it had
few opportunities to display it after England had emerged from
the financial crisis of 1931, when the true sense of national
responsibility had superbly asserted itself). On international
issues no clear inspiration ever came from the Government's
followers. The parliamentary debates were occasions for the
expression of multifarious individual tendencies unrelated to
any definite policy and from which it was almost impossible to
guess the speakers' political allegiances or convictions. This
lasted until the Government put an end to it and silenced everybody with a promise of better things to come.

Influenced but never stimulated, sometimes stung but never
aroused, by an Opposition weak in numbers and spirit, the
Conservative majority slowly solidified from year to year into
a complacent body whose heterogeneous opinions seemed to be
voiced in a purely tentative manner, as though they could have
no bearing on the Government's decisions, let alone on international events. Conversely, the Government itself developed

an uncommon self-confidence, used as it was to seeing its most vehement critics meekly shepherded, at the end of a debate, into the division lobby where they voted loyally as one man!

Thus it was that Ramsay MacDonald could during his last year of Premiership make pronouncements on international affairs which defied all understanding and were so abstruse that the official translators in foreign chancelleries had to re-write them from beginning to end for fear of being sacked as saboteurs of their country's relations with England. Thus it was that Stanley Baldwin, a statesman of fine intellect and noble vision but not a strong executive, could be let off scot free after a speech in which he asserted, without troubling to produce evidence, that British air power was still well ahead of Germany's. Thus it was that in June 1935 the Conservative majority endorsed without batting an eyelid the Anglo-German naval treaty which legitimized the right of Hitlerite Germany to re-arm; that no one took notice of its catastrophic repercussions in France, where it made Laval's pro-Italian policy tolerable and, in the very midst of the Abyssinian crisis, dealt a disastrous blow to the pro-British majority—no one save the few members of a clearsighted minority, including Sir Austen Chamberlain, Winston Churchill, Anthony Eden and, later, Harold Nicolson. Thus it was that the majority readily embarked on a policy of sanctions against Italy and gave it up with equal readiness when the Government changed its mind. Thus it was that the reoccupation of the Rhineland was philosophically accepted and even justified on moral grounds by most of the Conservatives. Thus it was, finally, that Mr. Chamberlain's expression of confidence in a lasting peace, on his return from Munich, when Germany was bristling with bayonets and tanks, elicited hardly more than a few counsels of prudence from the 'solid' benches.

What had happened during those years to render the members of the Conservative party so docile, so uncertain in mind, that they were cowed into submission by a mere crack of the whip? Or that, whilst in a state of constant though placid disagreement, they only differed, contrary to a famous precedent, the more easily to agree when the Government lulled them with half-measures? In the past the party had shown at least an acute sense of any threat to British interests and security, a traditional, often over-sensitive awareness of dangers to the realm, and a

K

pride which had its drawbacks but also its dignity. Yet for a period of years, indeed until the terrible awakening of Dunkirk, it had lost the scent, underrated obvious perils, grudged all effort and repeatedly swallowed its traditional pride.

This temporary blurring of the party's external vision, strangely coinciding with a long lease of unchallenged power, seemed to become a Conservative malady from the time of the advent of the National Government at the end of 1931; and one cannot escape the conclusion that the two happenings were closely related.

Ramsay MacDonald, who headed the National Government for nearly four years, was a great believer in the League of Nations and in its methods of action not only because, as an idealist, he warmed at the thought of world-embracing schemes, but because as a politician he was partial to large audiences and to the new, exotic pleasure of having delegates from sixty-three nations as potential constituents. The World Economic Conference of 1933, Mr. MacDonald's glorious, albeit abortive, offspring, bore witness to both inclinations. His tenure of office immeasurably enhanced the popularity of League phraseology, even if it did not altogether raise the stock of the League itself, throughout the country. Under Mr. MacDonald's leadership League-consciousness certainly reached its high-water mark.

The League of Nations was undoubtedly a great idea and could have become a great institution (though the weakness in its very conception was that it failed to take account of the basic fact of profound discrepancies in degree of political maturity between its member-states). Yet so long as nations were not ready to act unreservedly on the principle of 'one for all and all for one', so long as the League could not muster full executive powers, its very existence had two unfortunate effects. The first and obvious one was that in each case brought before it none save the interested party was prepared to work its machinery to the full, and that consequently it added nothing to the means of self-defence possessed by each state in its own capacity. The second and less obvious fault was that, although ineffectual in practice, the League nevertheless encouraged large sections of opinion in most countries to believe that their own urgent problems could be left for settlement at Geneva; so that League-omania undermined the sense of national self-reliance without creating in its stead a sense of collective solidarity or collective responsibility. The idea of a League of Nations is admirable but such a league can only be either omnipotent or impotent; in the latter case it creates dangerous illusions of which the well-meaning are the dupes and the scoundrels the profiteers.

Until 1936, when the Abyssinian crisis confirmed the League's failure to check aggression, the foreign policy of the Government's parliamentary majority was a prolonged game of see-saw between traditional conceptions based on national self-dependence by means of armaments and selected alliances on the one side, and partial resort to collective solutions on the other. Ramsay MacDonald's and, later, Stanley Baldwin's premiership did not succeed in making the Conservatives out-and-out crusaders for the League but succeeded well enough in clouding international issues for them. Both prime ministers rendered the Conservatives conscience-stricken enough to doubt the propriety of a purely British policy, but their proselytism achieved little more than that. For a long time those Conservatives who paid more than mere lip-service to the League saw in it, above all, a precious device for disposing of unpleasant problems; what would have worried or unduly burdened London might as well be dumped into Geneva. Thus in 1932, whilst Conservative eyes turned eagerly towards the real business of the Imperial Conference at Ottawa, they left MacDonald and Simon a free hand to eliminate such international embarrassments as the Franco-German quarrel which stood in the way of sound Conservative Empire-promotion—whereas at that time a genuine Conservative policy, even though governed by the narrow demands of exclusively British interests applied to European problems, would have been far better than no policy at all. The Conservatives did not trust the views of MacDonald and Simon far enough to let them play with the Empire, but they trusted them far enough to let them try their hand on Europe. Moreover there seemed to be a tacit understanding between the former Labour and Liberal ministers on the one hand, and the Conservatives on the other, that so long as Labour and Liberalism did not interfere with Conservatism in things British they could 'get rid of their political inhibitions' on foreign policy. And the comparatively League-minded Conservatives probably fancied in their heart of hearts that, after all, the League of Nations, if it did happen to solve international problems, might thereby provide an honourable short cut to isolation: an odd destiny for the Temple of World solidarity!

By helping to make the parliamentary majority League conscious and League-tongued if not League-persuaded, and therefore helping to spread the gospel throughout the country (as witness the famous Peace Ballot of 1935), the Labour-Liberal enclave in that majority certainly contributed to the perplexities and divisions of the Conservatives in parliament as well as outside. Between tradition and novelty the Conservative mind was left as hesitant as Buridan's ass between his measure of corn and his bucket of water.

In October 1935, at the very time when the League was standing its greatest and final test, like hesitations were again apparent at the Conservative Conference which immediately followed the Labour Conference at Brighton. Among the Conservatives, of course, the question of sanctions against Italy was raised in an entirely different spirit. For Labour the question had been: Must our international and class solidarity lead us to take the sword? For the Conservatives it was: Can the League, on the Italian test case, prove its ability to help in the defence of England?

Indeed it fell to the lot of Neville Chamberlain, then Chancellor of the Exchequer, to sum up the issue in some such terms as these: 'We are not supporting the League because it is the League,' he said; 'we are supporting it because we expect it to prevent war by collective action. If it cannot fulfil that hope we must give up that hope and turn somewhere else.' Mr. Chamberlain reminded me of the peasant who was ready to believe in God if God helped him to sell his eggs. Was an association with the League a practical proposition or not? That was his point. In those early days of October 1935 he was the only leading Conservative to put the problem in such crude terms. Many of his fellow delegates at the conference probably shared his views but lingered a few steps behind in expressing them. The emphasis, throughout the proceedings, was definitely on the need for British rearmament and British security, but the wording of it took into account the desirability of collective action, of which so much had been heard and said that few members of the party dared as yet to omit it from their speeches. Characteristically, the resolution adopted by the assembly asked for an increase in armaments, but justified that increase not only by the need for ensuring the nation's defence but also by the general desire to honour the country's international undertakings. To this was added a pious reference to the delegates' faith in an ultimate reduction in armaments. A dual purpose was thus achieved: the qualms of conscience of genuine supporters of the League, like Lord Salisbury, were appeased; and the Conference gave a lesson to the Labourites, for the Conservatives not only preached collective security (with whatever mental reservations) but provided the weapons for its enforcement. Yet when the Conference ended and everybody had carefully added to the Conservative programme a leaf borrowed from the Labour book, the ambiguities of that programme persisted. The man in the street still heard the Conservatives using the phraseology of collective security, which could not fail to impress him, but he was not clearly told that the League had in fact been given a final chance which, if missed, would close the era of Conservative toying with Left ideologies and lead them back to the path of party tradition.

Nor after all was the Conservative mind itself clear on this vital point, for, a month later, the failure of the Western nations to enforce oil sanctions against Italy marked the end of all hope of coercive action against the aggressor; and yet from the end of 1935 to Munich no clear Conservative policy emerged from that important decision. Rearmament, the only item on which all Conservatives were agreed, proceeded slowly and the Government's majority did little to hasten it. The German menace grew to staggering proportions and the majority persistently hedged on the methods whereby it might be tackled, even when they did not court the puerile hope of diverting it from English shores.

At the very time when Germany was building up her power with predatory intent, the Conservatives were put off the scent by their own class fears. The class feelings aroused among them whenever the Soviet Union appeared to play a part in international controversies, as in the case of sanctions against Italy, were deeply stirred during the Spanish Civil war, from July 1936 onwards. If class bias did not eventually take precedence over national duty, it certainly diverted Conservative attention from the real peril during the two vital years when Germany's rearmament ceased to be a controllable process and became a *fait accompli* which only war could thenceforward alter. It was the greatest triumph of German political strategy that by waving the red cape at the bull, it everywhere distracted the energies of those who had, traditionally, shown acute awareness of all threats to the national interest. Conscious of the fact that Germany and Italy were supporting Franco in Spain, yet biased in their judgement of the implications of that fact by the accounts of Bolshevization of Republican territory, the Conservatives spent two years wondering whether it was not possible after all that Germany's sole objective was the destruction of Communism. Meanwhile, Germany was producing and testing in Spain those weapons wherewith she intended to undeceive her dupes when she felt strong enough to throw down the gauntlet.

One of the paradoxes of the Conservative attitude at the time was that although it had ceased to take account of the League and all the League stood for, it unconsciously retained certain illusions born of League ideology and even in a perverted fashion applied some of its methods of approach in their worst form. One of the characteristics of the MacDonald touch had been a certain 'mateyness' with foreign peoples, an adaptation to the conference table of the 'heart to heart, mate to mate' touch as well as a high belief in the virtue of discussion. A tendency developed among Conservatives also to make contacts with the 'other side' in the same matey spirit, and to discuss things with an assumed air of outspokenness; only their mateyness was directed chiefly to the Germans, partly out of a desire to peep into the enemy camp, partly in keeping with the chivalrous tradition of drinking a cup before meeting in the field, partly because there were common sympathies on class matters and the cultivation of such affinities might possibly become a factor in preserving peace after all. It must not be forgotten that class rivalries encouraged in many Conservatives a distorted pacifism opposed to the left-wing interventionism, similarly stimulated by class consciousness. Just as there was in the Conservative party a recent tradition of friendship with the Magyar landlords of Hungary who knew how to run a pack of hounds and had put down Communism in the early 'twenties, so there grew among them at least an interest in those Germans who claimed that once Communism were defeated they would turn out to be the friendliest of neighbours. The Anglo-German Fellowship in London was a popular association, until the meeting at Godesberg dealt it a mortal blow. Mammoth parties at the German

Embassy had an atmosphere reminiscent of the Geneva mateyness; but it had a subtle class flavour, even though the English
guests found a few upstarts among their hosts. While the Hitlerite gang was thus pulling the strings behind the scene, every
manor and hall in Germany had been combed to find present-
able persons for the English market, figureheads with better
table manners than Hermann Goering, and introductions at
the German Embassy kept British visitors gaping with 'Howdye-
do' on their lips whilst they listened to the cascading enumera-
tion of 'Vons' and 'Zus' indicative of the fresh arrival's numerous
country seats, places of origin and ancient associations. Hosts
of dusty Junkers, barons of the Holy Empire, descendants of
free citizens of Hanseatic towns, were dumped on the London
social stage to do the crowd work, while good Nazis with
shorter names but longer arms were working at the back
door and cultivating such real pursuits as the installation of
radio apparatus and telephone wires. In their stage-management
the Nazis went so far as to choose for their ambassador in
London the ineffectual but well-mannered Von Dirksen after
they had realized that the Ribbentrop type was too revealing
and that even the head of their Embassy must be a puppet.
Well might the ambassador's interlocutors be impressed with
a man who, in the quiet language suited to a British audience,
suggested that if it were not for the Soviet and for the Franco-
Soviet Pact, the kindred souls of Germany and Great Britain
could be bound in harmony till death did them part. Similar
conversations, with a slight change in the names of the countries,
were probably going on in Paris at the same time. In both
capitals they made some impression on a good many Conservatives, for whom the class bogey temporarily eclipsed the
national peril.

It was in the same spirit that in 1938 Neville Chamberlain
embarked on a policy which can only be expressed in the formula which he himself made famous: 'Try, try again.' 'Try,
try again' was definitely Genevese in its underlying implication
that endless conversations can produce endless peace. But it embodied a more businesslike conception of things in that it reduced the principle of the world-parley to the level of a talk
between two commercial travellers who need not tell the public
about the tricks of the trade and the weak points of the mer-
chandise. It was Genevan in that it postulated that, peace being

a normal state of affairs for normal citizens, those men or
nations who threaten peace must have a good reason for doing
so; and that, consequently, all the well-meaning had to do was
to find that reason and remove the wrong. (The notion that
'what was wrong' might be either too complex to be doctored
or too deliberate to be exorcized by words struck very few
people, whether advocates of collective security or of the
business method.) Yet Chamberlain's policy was non-Genevan
and truly Conservative in that it rested on a conception of
bargains between the strong, whether or not such bargains
were acceptable to the weak. It was as a strong man that he
fancied himself, 'as one who would impress Hitler'; it was as
a strong man that his party had fancied him ever since the
Conference of October 1935 when he had shown apparent
realism in stating that if the League could not deliver the goods
England would find other means of protecting her interests. But
his party, like himself, did not seem to remember that realism
consists primarily in the knowledge of the realities one has to face
and not simply in a disposition to face a situation with a degree
of cynicism. His party, like himself, put the wrong construction
on both realism and idealism, understanding the former to be
a certain selfish sense of one's own immediate interests, and the
latter as wishful thinking and a capacity for believing that the
business transacted at Munich would yield everlasting dividends. From twenty years of League terminology and seven
years of association with extraneous parties the Conservatives
only seemed to have assimilated enough to dim their vision and
to weaken what was soundest in their national tradition. And
when the League had failed and the businessman's era had led
to Munich, they had not yet regained enough of their once
genuine realism to realize that peace was lost. It took six months
of winter hagglings over what remained of Czechoslovakia to
awaken them, yet still not so fully that the German threat to
Poland did not arouse in their hearts hopes of another business
settlement of the Munich type. They were still in power, still
the strongest majority ever known in a British Parliament; they
and their leader had been pardoned. Yet they retained that odd
mixture of realism and ignorance of realities which could only
be described as cynical self-delusion.

Most of these Conservative mistakes were to be retrieved
later, when they and the whole country found a leader whom

they had ignored for nearly twenty years, as they had ignored their own real self. But the question is: why had he been ignored? Why had the Conservative party been led for so long by men who represented only a passing tendency, or a concession to a prevailing ideology, or a temporary expedient? The answer to the question is wider than the question itself. It is that the so-called Right parties in England and in other Western states suffered from an inferiority complex during the years between the two world wars. They hesitated to abandon their attachment to certain vested interests, and attempted to purchase peace at home by concessions to the mere letter of democracy, chiefly in external affairs. They gave way to the Left when the Left was most vocal (which does not mean that it was necessarily right), but in general resisted reforms even when these were justified. Traditional defenders of national interests, they confused these with class interests, and faltered though the threat was aimed at the country and not at a certain conception of social order. Those honest and courageous men who rose above such considerations either were not heeded, or, alternatively, suffered from a sense of shame at the idea of being what they were, namely Conservatives, at a time when unscrupulous reactionaries sought popularity by resorting to left-wing slogans. The Conservatives confusedly thought that they had to pay danegeld to the Left, and did so reluctantly and inappropriately, instead of adapting themselves to twentieth-century conditions as they actually were and not as they were interpreted by partisan salesmanship.

The Conservative party, in any case, is only one example of a phenomenon which was not confined to its ranks, but was part of the general confusion of political thought remarkable in all democratic states and probably inherent in all periods of swift change, economic and social. That phenomenon was the depersonalization of parties, each losing its true identity and real purpose and fumbling for new ones—too often, alas! for no better reason than attractive window dressing. In France, it led to such shuffling and reshuffling of parties and groups as led to a complete imbroglio. In England depersonalization produced quieter and less conspicuous manifestations. Yet it was there, and it affected men, parties and Parliament. That a man of such high moral integrity as Lord Halifax should have espoused Neville Chamberlain's foreign policy and needed

several years to realize its implications, is significant enough of
an utter loss of political bearings among the very best elements
of English political life. That, contrary to time-honoured principles, a parliamentary majority should have allowed a civil
servant like Sir Horace Wilson, to discharge a vital diplomatic
mission to Germany[1] in complete secrecy and with catastrophic
results (as was to be expected considering his utter ignorance
of international issues); that, previous to this, the same majority
should have shut its eyes to Mr. Chamberlain's systematic resort
to semi-fascist bureaucratic methods for the purpose of sidetracking the Foreign Office, thereby endorsing what British
traditions reject as an abuse of power: this shows how parties
and Parliament has been thrown out of balance. It is true that,
contrary to what happened elsewhere, parties and Parliament
preserved a superficial dignity and order. But within the outer
shell, despite the labels, the process of depersonalization went
on.

[1] When Neville Chamberlain, who had used him to build up a little
Foreign Office of his own at 10 Downing Street, sent him to see Hitler
and deliver what should have been, but never was, a stern warning that
England would go to war if France honoured her undertakings to Czechoslovakia (September 1938).

CHAPTER 14

DEPERSONALIZATION OF PARTIES

ONE of the most significant and, to my mind, regrettable developments in English politics during the pre-war period was the decline of the Liberal Party. Indeed there is more in this than concerns England alone. For the shrinking of the party to a mere token of its past glory coincided with the decay throughout Europe of such values as political tolerance and intellectual freedom. The Liberal tradition runs counter to absolutism not only in the obvious form of personal despotism but also in its disguised manifestations to which democratic countries are still in danger of yielding, however unwittingly. In recent years, when the Liberals, had they mustered sufficient strength, might have been the guardians of individual independence and political consciousness, when they might have led the struggle against facile slogans, mental laziness, ready-to-wear ideologies and mass irresponsibility, a mere handful of them was left in the English arena to keep watch. Nor was that small group in any position to carry weight, however light the weight might be. Assailed from every quarter, subdivided by disaffection within its ranks, threatened with political extinction, the Liberal Party had to apply the precept *Primum vivere, deinde philosophari*. They had to attend first to their own survival and leave ethical crusading to happier days.

Not the least of the causes for regret in this Liberal eclipse is that it fostered a general tendency of the public to oversimplify political issues. Just as a General Election in England practically reduced itself to a straight contest between Labour and Conservatism, so did public opinion come to consider most world problems as capable of only two kinds of solution, one vaguely described as 'progressive', the other hazily fancied as conservative (or 'retrograde'). Their usual distrust of clear-cut conceptions failed the English then. There is little doubt that the disposition, current in pre-war England, to regard the world outside as roughly divided between Left and Right, corresponded to the trend of evolution at home towards a similar grouping of forces. During such a process the Liberal Party could not but suffer and, with it, England as a whole. For when political alertness and flexibility in action were most wanting in Europe, the English reserves were depleted in quantity and improverished in quality by the loss of a genuinely English contribution.

In the crisis of 1931 which marked the beginning of their decline, the Liberals themselves, acting in what they held to be the nation's interest, had brought about the fall of the Labour-Liberal administration and had thus been instrumental in the consequent setting up of the National Government. Yet it was the very fact of the national composition of that government which later caused the splitting of the Liberal Party into two groups: one which maintained its support of the Government, while the other went into opposition and was further divided by the schism of the Lloyd George family. This partitioning clearly accelerated the decay of the party if it did not cause it. The members of the old party who remained within the Government's ranks no doubt felt that they were thereby serving the best interests of Liberalism; but there was courage, rare in our days to be sure, in those men who chose to cross the floor. They had given up office under the second MacDonald administration because they placed the general interest above sectional interests in a time of national emergency; and, again, they gave up office, party unity and all hope of an early comeback when they broke with the third (the National) MacDonald government, to take their stand on Liberal ethics. The national emergency had passed and circumstances ceased to justify the 'agreement to differ'. This may well come to be regarded as the last known instance of a great parliamentary party jealous enough of its moral integrity and political identity to sacrifice political power to ethical principle. Conversely, it was a sign of the times that such courage not only went unrewarded but was cruelly penalized by the electorate. It is true that the Liberal Party, like others, lacked men just when, even more than others, it needed a powerful crew to row against the tide; yet the chief reason for its failure at the polls was not so much its shortage of outstanding men as the very force of that adverse tide.

Liberalism, in every sense of the word, had ceased to be a public preoccupation in pre-war years. The vast majority of people came to consider politics as a contest between a so-called Conservatism (which had lost its essential characteristics) and a so-called Socialism (which in England had no doctrinaire programme). In England as elsewhere an implicit conviction grew among the general public that the struggle of the century was between individual privilege on the one hand and collective welfare on the other, qualified though this rudimentary issue may have been by the flexible quality of English political consciousness. Few men wondered, as true Liberals naturally would, whether there might not also be an underlying feud between the notion of mass interests and the defence of the individual: not the privileged individual but the ordinary man whom both sides appeared to ignore. The adherents of the Right were inclined to identify the cause of the individual with the preservation of personal privilege; those of the Left to attack personal privilege on the exclusive behalf of mass privilege.[1] Caught between the opposing forces of such prejudices, Liberalism was smashed; nor perhaps did its exponents, bold though they proved themselves to be in the field, show sufficient initiative in setting clarity above confusion.

The fact is that Liberalism was taken for granted as an achievement of the past, a milestone on the hypothetical road of progress, and one which had already been left behind. Few politicians felt that true Liberal tenets, far from being accepted once for all, were in incomparably greater danger from the enemies of democracy than were the social achievements or expectations of Socialism. Lip-service was paid to the Liberal tradition by both Labour and Conservatives, who seemed tacitly to agree that occasional professions of faith in the rights and freedom of Man were all that need be left of Liberalism. Both also borrowed from the Liberals what suited their respective books, invoking the Liberal tradition against each other when it provided a convenient argument, and generally disregarding the confusion of contradictions which such haphazard borrowings brought into their respective programmes. Thus Labour fought Protection which imposed tariffs on the poor man's food and crusaded on Liberal principles in defence of the English breakfast table, while all the time pressing its claims for state control of the national economy, which can only be

[1] The tendency of contemporary Labour to cater for mass interests as against individual or minority interests, even when those were the workers' own, was underlined in the war waged by the T.U.C. against independent trade unions. Here is a clear instance of mass politics directed not against the privileged classes but against wage-earning minorities.

enforced in practice with the help of protective tariffs. Thus, too, the Conservatives took their stand on Liberal principles to reject most forms of economic control[1] within Britain itself, while nevertheless demanding state control at her borders in order to shield British enterprise from outside competition. Both antagonists thus appropriated from Liberalism what might be palatable to their own followers. Finally the Liberals themselves, squeezed as they were between two contending bodies growing at their expense, tried to regain elbow room and living space by broadening their own programme and making predatory incursions into Labour territory.

Not only had the sense of Liberalism been obscured by those outside the Liberal tradition who had made frequent misuse of the term, but it was also confused by the Liberals themselves who secretly wondered whether they had not become reactionaries in 'a new world'. One is, of course, always reactionary from something. Having in the past been a forward party, the Liberals had for twenty years seen Labour grow to colossal stature in the country, even when (as from 1931 to 1935) it was inadequately represented in Parliament. The Liberals therefore suffered from the classic inferiority complex of once-advanced parties overtaken by more advanced ones. They too, like the Conservatives, though from very different motives, were ashamed of being their true selves. They had accepted political penury for the sake of upholding their convictions, and then begun to wonder whether Liberalism should not extend its scope, enlarge its horizon. The majority Liberals (Liberal-Nationals) were deliberately instrumental in encouraging such fears and deepening such complexes among the orthodox Liberals. A clear case of this was a speech by Sir John Simon at the National Liberal Club in February 1935. As leader of the Government's Liberal contingent, Sir John had been invited by the Opposition Liberals, his former friends and now antagonists, to explain his attitude and the alleged inconsistency of his position. The invitation, or challenge, had been made with true sportsmanship and was accepted in the same spirit. The occasion was a luncheon at the Club. An oratorical joust was to follow the luncheon and neither hosts nor the guests were disappointed with it: Sir John Simon's speech was a dialectical

---

[1] Most, but not all; since in agricultural matters the Conservatives did accept or advocate controls: e.g. the Agricultural Marketing Boards.

delight, though few pronouncements did more damage to the Liberal Party and Liberalism in general.

The gist of his argument was this: Why was the Liberal Party weak in numbers? Because its days of conquest were past. Political parties represent a tendency towards something, a progress towards a certain achievement. After years of struggle traditional Liberalism had achieved its ends; it had pervaded the political consciousness of the whole nation. The nation had absorbed it. Englishmen's every political thought, notion, conception, gesture, prejudice exuded liberalism. Liberalism was an English *fait accompli*; it was no longer at stake. The opposition Liberals were preaching to the converted, besieging an open fortress. It was true that under the pressure of circumstances alien to England's will, economic Liberalism had been transgressed by the enforcement of Protection. But tariffs were only temporary; the very reluctance of the country to erect such barriers to trade had shown its Liberal-mindedness and guaranteed a return to normal economy as soon as international conditions warranted it. Indeed, the presence of Liberal ministers in the Government and Liberal members in the majority would hasten that consummation. In every other respect (for Liberalism after all vastly exceeded the scope of economics) the nation was Liberal at heart. To turn Liberalism into an opposition party when its principles had triumphed was a contradiction in terms. In opposition to what? To a state of things which was the outcome of the party's historic exertions? Or were the Liberals so short of ideas that the mere act of opposing temporary tariffs was the sum total of their programme, that fighting on behalf of Free Trade constituted the beginning and the end of a once-great party's contribution to the national life? Let them stand for new achievements and, as a party of government, of responsibility, bring their minds to bear on the performance of the nation's great tasks.

This was but the core of a long argument in the course of which the position of the majority Liberals was reviewed and explained in detail, Sir John contending that any further collusion with the Labour Opposition would infallibly lead to the whittling away of the Liberal party. But his thesis that Liberalism was no longer a controversial issue in this country, save for those points of the old doctrine not practicable under prevailing conditions, gained considerable currency and strengthened the

belief that the public indifference was largely justified. He and
his followers were thus bringing grist to the mill of all those who
thought that Liberalism must either merge with the parties of
conservation, whose wild oats had long ago been sown, or find
a new lease of turbulent life through the infusion of revolutionary blood: in other words, Liberalism would be all right if it
were something else! That it was perhaps the chief point of
attack in Totalitarian states, that the enemies of freedom
troubled less about Socialism, which they had discovered how
to pervert, and Conservatism, which they found an easy
opponent, than about what was left of the truly Liberal spirit
in Europe: this consideration commanded little credence or
attention among the general public and hardly more among the
political pundits of pre-war days. The clear path of Liberalism
in the twentieth century was and still is that of a party setting
political freewill against two forms of economic and social
despotism—that vested in individuals or groups, whose economic power frustrates or threatens the community, and that
vested in a tentactular state growing at the expense of individual
freedoms. That the Liberals sensed the problem, was shown in
many of their pronouncements; that they were not in a position
either to find solutions or to make them popular is equally
obvious. In any case, compelled as they were to wage a ceaseless
tactical war, they could hardly keep their minds on long-term
strategy.

The general election of 1935 was marked by the signal defeat
of their leader, Sir Herbert Samuel, at Darwen and by the
dwindling of their parliamentary party to about a dozen members. Henceforth Liberal politics would be shaped by a hard
struggle for life, moulded by opportunity and existing possibilities rather than by clear-sighted determination. Neither the
quality of the small phalanx nor the independence of mind of
its new leader, Sir Archibald Sinclair, could prevail over circumstances which loaded the dice against the Liberals. They
came to be regarded as a more mildly pink replica of the Labour
Opposition, in which situation they found themselves repeatedly
outbidden and overtrumped by Labour. On the supreme issue
of war and peace, they shared with Labour several inconsistencies, such as advocating coercion of Fascist Italy whilst still
denying Defence credits to enforce that policy, and denouncing
Hitlerism while failing to take responsibility for any bold

counter-measures when Hitlerite Germany transgressed the law.[1] Yet the Liberals were among the first to come to their senses. They retained enough of their great tradition to stand for the rights of the small nations and to resist, in September 1938, the peace psychosis which drowned for a time the conscience and even the sense of realities of most politicians. When on the 27th September Mr. Chamberlain brought the House to its feet by announcing the forthcoming conference at Munich and relieving the terrific pressure of impending war, the Liberal leader was one of the few men who issued there and then a grave and unheeded warning that peace could be too dearly bought.

In the meantime, since 1937, the success of Independent candidates at by-elections may conceivably have expressed a tendency of the English public to seek an alternative to the two big parties which had crowded the political stage for nearly twenty years; and that development could, perhaps, be construed as heralding a slow revival of Liberalism in the future. The pre-war and war emergency has, however, interrupted most domestic political processes and the chances of any 'middle-party' remain a matter for conjecture. The dominant fact of pre-war years was that Liberalism came very near to political extinction and that, under duress, it failed to evolve and to lay down a programme inspired by its traditional ethic, yet adjusted to the needs of the times, and sharply distinct from both Labour and Conservatism.

Whilst the Conservative Party, when war broke out, had been steadily losing its political identity through lassitude, excessive security, and overgrowth to the point of unwieldiness, the Liberal Party had been losing its identity through paucity of numbers. The Labour Party on the other hand was not exposed to either danger. Being in opposition to the Government it had to fight all along and, depending on a fairly reliable body of supporters, ran no risk of debility. Yet Labour also was confronted with a problem of its own. Traditionally undogmatic, it was clearly wondering in pre-war days, and apparently still is, whether its political empiricism was not out of date in the contemporary world; whether, in other words, English Labour in

---

[1] The long-lasting influence of Lloyd George, whose distrust of French foreign policy led him to consider Germany with lenient eyes and to find in French 'intransigeance' excuses for her behaviour, still weighed with the Opposition.

L

its turn should not find a doctrinal basis for its political activity. In the past, Labour's task had been to defend the rights and welfare of working men on practical issues. Was the Party to go far beyond this, and oppose a comprehensive system of its own to the existing social and economic order? Was it to turn from a merely reformist into a revolutionary movement? Such was the dilemma which exercised Labour minds when a doctrinal battle was raging throughout Europe, and ever-increasing contacts with Continental men and problems added, day by day, to their perplexities. That dilemma persists. Labour has not taken a definite stand. From dogmatic socialism it has borrowed such principles as the responsibility of the state for the physical and mental welfare of all men 'from the cradle to the grave', the need for economic control, a marked tendency towards state enterprise. In practice, however, the Labour Party is not of one mind on the extent to which the enforcement of such principles must or can be carried. All that can be said is that more recent speeches, notably those of Herbert Morrison, indicate a disposition to apply comprehensive socialist solutions to English and world problems; it may perhaps be added that such speeches are flavoured with that dogmatic imperialism which could already be detected in Labour pronouncements at the time of the Abyssinian crisis. Yet one doubts whether this disposition is general throughout the Labour movement. At present Labour's supporters seem to be at variance not only on issues arising from their participation in the Government—such as the precedence of the war effort over social planning—but also on points of long-term policy, such as the powers to be vested in the state for the direction of the national economy. Labour has ceased to be the pragmatic party that it once was, without, however, decidedly crossing the Rubicon and turning into a dogmatic movement. Its personality is not yet firmly established.

That no English party should have stabilized itself or established a firm political identity during the pre-war era, was largely due to the constant pressure of external events, economic as well as political. The world economic crisis, the ideological feuds in Europe and, finally, the threat of war, all would in any case have prevented English political groups from finding their proper balance. No question set to any party or even, for that matter, to the nation, was capable of a purely English solution. There was a loose end to every internal issue. How could one fix wages schedules when the fluctuations of prices could not be controlled? How could one plan an employment policy well ahead without any guarantee that British industries would retain their markets? What priority should have been given to social services and Defence credits respectively? Those were only the most elementary questions which party or government had to answer and would have had to answer under any régime. By the very nature of her economy and geography England could not, even if she had wished it, resort to autarky and shut herself off from the world to cope with her own difficulties in her own way. Economically, socially, politically, nothing that occurred outside her shores could fail to have a bearing on her domestic affairs. To a degree, the perplexities of English parties, their intellectual restlessness, the impossibility of finding their respective focuses, were therefore due to causes independent of the English will and beyond the nation's control. There were also, however, purely English causes, for this unsettled state of affairs.

'For so many years now', R. B. McCallum wrote in his *Asquith*, 'we have been accustomed to see the highest place in the King's service filled by persons who, for all their qualities, cannot be regarded as pre-eminent in intellectual power, that we incline to forget how high a standard had been achieved by the late Victorian Prime Ministers. . . '. That high standard was certainly not upheld by the Prime Ministers who held office during the fifteen years preceding the Second World War; nor did they make up for lack of intellectual pre-eminence by exceptional strength of character. This in itself would account, to some extent, for the hesitancy of English pre-war policy. Even more relevant is the fact that from 1931 onwards none of the three national leaders followed a policy truly characteristic of the party which he represented. Ramsay MacDonald, a Labour man, headed a government supported by an unprecedented Conservative majority, and his social views were seldom so vocal as to cause serious controversy between him and his new associates. Stanley Baldwin turned out to be one of those Conservatives whose nerve can be shaken by bringing against them a charge of 'Toryism', and he was constantly looking to the Left for letters patent of good moral character and progressive broadmindedness. As for Neville Chamberlain, he was a Conservative chiefly in the narrow sense that he disliked change, proved adamant to most plans for reform, and displayed more prudence than imagination during his stay at the Exchequer. He was Conservative in a negative way. Confronted with the worst threat ever aimed at his nation's existence, he was found wanting in his party's traditional reactions to danger—resilience and pugnaciousness. That the three successive heads of the National Government were not strong party leaders and did not act as such was a very important factor in pre-war England; for, in consequence, none of them brought to bear upon the matters in hand the driving force, experience and matured conviction which great party leaders should derive from their years of experience and from the resolute backing of their followers, with whatever shortcomings these advantages may be qualified.

It was, needless to recall, the very object of government by a 'national' team that party politics should be set aside, since the National Government was the result of a compromise or arrangement between three parties and, though the national character of the Government was regarded as purely formal by most foreign countries, it was taken more seriously by the English themselves. That the executive should adopt a co-operative rather than a partisan programme of action was certainly a popular project in the 1931 emergency. Was that aim ever attained? Was the new combination a success? Was the Government national and was the sacrifice of party vitality, inherent in an administration founded on compromise, compensated by advantages accruing from genuine teamwork? Events rather seem to warrant the conclusion that, once the financial crisis had been overcome, the 'National' system gave the country the worst of both worlds because, although parties were devitalized, the evil aspects of partisanship persisted.

Let us consider the political situation after the general election of 1931. The polls had returned a Conservative majority of over two-thirds in the House of Commons, while the extraneous groups associated with it, in order to justify the National label, amounted to some four dozen members who were no more than the rump of the Opposition parties. The Conservatives were the unquestioned conquerors. Only angelic virtues could have persuaded them to draw on the spoils for no more than a one-third share, and they showed no sign of growing wings! The result was that the social, economic, fiscal and imperial policy of the National Government bore the Conservative stamp and little else. In all these fields of action a Conservative Government backed by a smaller Conservative majority and persistently challenged by a powerful, active, threatening, Opposition would no doubt have made more concessions and proved more progressive than an omnipotent group which could afford to ignore all critics and even appease its own qualms of conscience by the mere process of calling its legislation 'National'. Not that the presence of non-Conservatives among the majority was not felt; it was, but seldom in a constructive way. That influence was profound in undermining the Conservatives' purpose in all matters which were not of immediate and conspicuous interest; and those happened to be mostly connected with defence and foreign policy. If neither National-Labour nor Liberal-Nationals succeeded in opening Conservative minds to necessary reforms, they did succeed in clouding the Conservatives' perception of danger to the country. If the Conservatives did not succeed in opening their colleagues' eyes to the potentialities of the international situation, they did contrive to turn their thoughts away from those social and economic problems in which Liberal or Labour interference might have caused embarrassment.

The compromise failed to draw out the best that each party could offer, and maintained prejudices while weakening convictions. Each party seemed to sacrifice on the National altar what was traditionally sound in its own tenets. The left-wing of the coalition retained its ideologies but not its social and economic alertness; the right-wing protected the vested interests of a certain section of its followers, while forgetting its sense of national tradition. Meanwhile, behind the National screen, party machinery was omnipotent. Seldom had the average member been more sensible of party etiquette. Captain Margesson, the Chief Whip, wielded for years the power of an overlord. His three-line whip overruled opinions, convictions, purposes. Tentative dissidence there might be; divergences there were; conflicting, varying, anti-Government opinions might well be voiced in open debate. But the unruly section, having had its say in the House, went Captain Margesson's way into the lobby. Or as somebody put it:

> *In open country as bold as a ram*
> *But in the lobby as meek as a lamb.*

The notion of compromise had been perverted by the National administration. It ceased to mean a process of give and take; it merely meant a tacit agreement not to disturb.

Now, the best means of avoiding, or postponing, disturbance between people who may happen to disagree is to remain vague about points of policy likely to become a source of contention. Any two men may disagree as to whether a specific reform is desirable, as to whether it is advantageous to conclude an alliance with a given country; but if you ask a man whether he is generally in favour of reforms conducive to human happiness or whether he approves of a world understanding that will prevent war, he is unlikely to answer 'no'. By raising the problem far above the limited and contentious issues at stake, a point will be reached somewhere in the clouds or stratosphere where disagreement is rendered impossible. This method of avoiding controversy was carried to a fine art by Ramsay MacDonald. There was no insincerity and probably little calculation in his case. He liked to broaden questions until everybody agreed, although by that time there was little left that was worth agreeing about, save such notions as the need for peace, world happiness, or world plenitude. Thus at the World Economic Conference which was to be a resounding failure he made an opening speech which was unanimously applauded because there was nothing in it substantial enough to be a target for criticism. The question of whether the Liberal principles which inspired his address had not been slightly infringed by the recent enforcement of Protection and the more recent system of Imperial Preference instituted at Ottawa, in no whit restrained his prophetic fervour. He had placed world issues so far beyond the range of frail human practice that at that dizzy altitude contradictions vanished into thin air and earthly storms became caressing zephyrs. Thus, too, his association with a Government that opposed the abolition of the means test did not prevent Mr. MacDonald from making his veto on this matter an occasion for a world-wide appeal to improve human conditions, though his own constituents displayed a prosaic tendency to consider the point in itself rather than its moving context.

It is idle to suggest that 'MacDonaldism' had no influence on the House of Commons. As the head of a Government resting on a Conservative majority, Ramsay MacDonald had given up Labour as a practical proposition. But in his dreams Labour came back with a vengeance. The narrower his field of daily action as a former Labour leader, the broader became the imaginary field of his humanitarian visions. And the Conservative majority in its turn gradually learnt from him how to embellish Conservatism with pleasing effusions on human welfare, and how to invoke nebulous ideals in justification of a loan to a shipping company. Few members at that time dared to make a speech on the promotion of beetroot cultivation without asserting their faith in the regeneration of the world, or to suggest that the fate of a plague-stricken handful of Patagonians was less dear to them than the forthcoming dividends of their brewery in the Midlands. From a Government headed by Ramsay MacDonald and his colleagues they learnt the trade of make-believe, of focusing their attention on immediate interests whilst letting their gaze wander hopefully about an arming world whose problems 'bold initiatives', 'world conferences', 'heart-to-heart talks', 'a little goodwill', 'general understanding', 'give and take' and 'meeting half-way' would perhaps exorcize like evil apparitions. As for home policy, the migrants from the Opposition pointed the way: increases in salaries, pensions, economic freedom, all would be granted 'when the world had broken its economic shackles', when other countries had realized the folly of tariff competition, when the distribution of riches became more equitable, and when British industries ceased to be the victims of dark hostile forces. For the Left, the world provided a field of vision, a screen on which to project its frustrated emotions; for the Conservatives it was a heaven sent scapegoat on which to cast the sins of government in social policy.

I last saw Ramsay MacDonald in November 1935. He was staying at a friend's house at Easington, in County Durham. His fine, pale, sad, dreamy face; shaded by dark spectacles, was worn by days of rough, even rowdy, political campaigning against his own unpopularity as well as against a bitter opponent. He was convinced and remained convinced to the last minute that all he had seen, heard, and endured amounted to no more than a conspiracy against him organized by extremists. He said so and I believe he was sincere, for he urged me not to consider the scenes of disorder which I had witnessed as typical examples of electioneering methods in England, and added that all this would boil down to nothing when the attempt at intimidation had failed. For four years he had lived in his own thoughts, his vast plans; against a hostile audience he still showed superb courage and something of the flame of the Tribune. Then he would, one guessed, dismiss the unpleasant memory from his mind and, afterwards, before a quieter audience, ready to eat out of his hand, return to his hazy addresses, his conjuring up of harmonious future possibilities by vague, non-committal words and promises: the kind of address which his enemies described as 'a powerful edifice of fog solidly founded on a bedrock of mist'. Yet for four years his presence at the helm had been characteristic of the type of compromise then achieved between English parties which had once stood firm, each on its own chosen grounds; and it had been contributory, in so far as any single influence could be, to the evasiveness and ambiguity of British policy.

Nor was Stanley Baldwin, his successor, a cutter of Gordian knots; rather did his mind—fond of fine shades and delicate poise, full of scruples, averse to clear-cut solutions, dreading all accusations of Conservative bias—work for the safeguarding of the precious national gift of equivocation. His leadership was a sleeping draught rather than a stimulus for an already dozing Parliament, which the general election of 1935 did not shake into awareness and in which the parties came to tolerate each other's little weaknesses all the more readily in that these were less and less related to firm-set convictions. The rise of Neville Chamberlain in 1937 was hailed by many of his followers as the promise of a return to an open party policy; but events showed what construction the new Prime Minister put on Conservatism and to what extent the weakening of party character had mollified Parliamentary life. Neville Chamberlain was followed to Munich.

On the 27th September, five days after Godesberg had shown him and the world what Germany meant, the overwhelming majority of the House hailed the dramatic announcement that a Four-Power conference was to take place in Munich the next day. At the end of a speech which began like the preamble of a declaration of war, the Prime Minister sprang upon the House the last-minute news of the meeting, prolonging by this theatrical effect an era of mental confusion and self-delusion.

On the afternoon of the next day, in beflagged Munich, Neville Chamberlain and Edouard Daladier joined Hitler and

Mussolini in the last full-dress conference of the pre-war period. When they went back to their hotel in the evening the only delegate who refused to smile was the Czech envoy: it is true that he had been neither invited nor received. The conference table had shrunk since the days of Ramsay MacDonald. The field of wishful thinking had been narrowed. The size of the table did not matter much to the groups of Germans we met singing in the streets of Munich: both round-table and business *tête-à-têtes* had helped to make them what they were. The single party in Germany had not met its match in either France or England: not in France, because there were too many parties; not in England, largely because for seven years there had been none—none, that is, prepared in the traditional way to choose a pilot and back him doggedly in any emergency.

VI. NATION AND EMPIRE

CHAPTER 15

THE NATIONAL OUTLOOK

PREDOMINANT in British and even European history is the fact that for three hundred and forty-one years[1] this island has been the only country of the old Continent with no frontier disputes. Many threats have been aimed at the power of Britain in the course of centuries, but her land itself has never been a bone of contention. Attempts have been made to subjugate her, but not for the purpose of wresting a province from her territory, of tearing a limb from her body.

Because of this paramount fact, the English have evolved a national sense and outlook radically different from that of other nations. No Englishman can remember in his bones that his ancestors ever fought for acres of grass or corn, that his field was ever 'fattened', to use Virgil's robust term,[2] with the blood of the invader. The unity of population and abode, that essential factor of national life which is repeatedly challenged elsewhere, is taken for granted here. There is no Alsace, no Silesia, no Macedonia, no Transylvania to cast a shadow over the national consciousness. Fear, primitive fear for one's own flesh, one's own kin, plays therefore no part in English nationalism, which is innate and so deeprooted as to defeat self-recognition in peace-time. Only Englishmen could say, 'Why do we always belittle our own achievements? After all we've nothing to be ashamed of and a lot to be proud of,' without realizing that both question and answer reveal a serene national self-content so high above the storms of vociferous self-assertion that it can afford to smile down upon them. English nationalism is quiet, Olympian, sometimes (though rarely, but then almost unbearably) arrogant, but it cannot, by the very nature of things, be touchy, vocal, nervous, argumentative. The English people's reaction to external menace is slow and deliberate because their purse and larder are usually threatened before their heart, and

---

[1] For 237 years if one considers the Act of Union with Scotland in 1707 and not the *de facto* Union under James I.

[2] bis sanguine nostro

Emathiam et latos Haemi pinguescere campos—*Georgica*, i, 491-2.

there is a time-lag between the first scratch and the deep thrust.

The absence of quarrels with other nations over the boundaries of Great Britain proper has, or had at the beginning of the present century, removed from the English outlook the most common kind of national prejudice: that against the hereditary foe, he who periodically grabs part of one's land or challenges one's right of ownership to it.[1] One state or another might in turn be The Enemy; English sympathies or antipathies might go one way or another according to ethical or other particular inspirations and emotions; English views might be biased from a thousand subjective motives, and they often were: but English policy was not predetermined in its course by recurrent external threats assuming the inevitability of a law of nature and introducing into the country's life a sense of fatality. To that extent and in that respect English policy enjoyed a large measure of freewill and the people's vision of the outside world was less predetermined by history than that of any Continental nation.

Needless to say, factors other than the people's land come into play in the shaping of the national attitude. In the case of England her large dependence on supplies from abroad has created a sea-consciousness unknown elsewhere. English policy, like others, has biases and 'imperatives' of its own: the freedom of the seas, the guardianship of ocean routes, the two-power standard in naval building, the clearance of all approaches to straits or narrow seas. Yet these are ideas for leaders, technicians, or, at least, the instructed; they do not penetrate the ordinary man's daily consciousness with the same force as would the presence of millions of potential invaders on the opposite bank of a river or upon the other half of a plain. Looking from his cliffs after the last war towards the mainland of Europe, an Englishman would no doubt remember that from time to time a despot had risen from amidst her crowd of nations to defy England; the despot came in turn from Spain, from France, from Germany. In each instance, though it involved a bitter struggle, it was yet no more than an episode in history. Perhaps once more the strong wine of power would go to someone's head on the Continent. Who would it be? From

---

[1] The Irish question, which might be quoted against this view, is in fact a confirmation of it. English national self-confidence is such that its natural impulse when a border problem arises outside Great Britain itself is to treat it as 'colonial'.

which land, this time? The Englishman did not know, he did not locate the threat beforehand; his history text-books were liberal and diverse in their interpretation of the past; judgements varied according to moods, contingencies, philosophies. He loved peace; disliked foreigners in general and those who were nearest, noisiest, or most dark-haired rather more than the rest; hated nobody, not even the Irish whom he had often wronged; and was inclined to the view that wars were caused by adventurers, potentates, dictators, economic conditions perhaps, rather than determined by nation-wide dispositions.

The First World War certainly did little to alter the unprejudiced outlook of the English people. The notion that there remained a specific zone of danger in the central plain of Europe, approximately between the Rhine, the Vistula, the Baltic sea and the Danube, was not only alien but barbarously so to the average Englishman. Indeed, if the war had any effect, it tended rather to the opposite conclusion. Sympathy was felt for the defeated enemy, all the more so since that vanquished foe happened to be German. The Victorian tradition of amity and supposed kinship with the Germans had not been broken by the Edwardian era; the Entente Cordiale with France itself, an Edwardian creation—one might say an Edwardian fashion —had not cut very deep. Comradeship-in-arms with the French (who drank wine, were Roman Catholics, were light or grave out of season) engendered little popular friendship between the two peoples, whereas the contrasts with the Germans, although far more material, were less perceptible to the English, since the Germans were in the other camp. Alleged incompatibility was put down to war propaganda and mentally dismissed as such from English minds as soon as the war was over. So long as the Weimar Republic survived, the English as a whole felt that the French were prolonging a dispute which was finished and trying to involve Great Britain in it. In the eyes of most Englishmen there was no prospective enemy on the Continent; only political or economic provocation could lead Germany or any other state to acts of desperation and deeds of violence. Even when the Republic was overthrown or, rather, frightened away, there persisted in England a strong tendency to consider its downfall and the subsequent rise of Hitlerism as the result of intransigeance and mismanagement of German affairs on the part of other nations, namely France, Poland, the states of the Little

Entente, who correspondingly suffered in the esteem of the
English public. That the German Republic had never taken
root; that it had vanished with an ease and by a process incon-
ceivable in any country where democracy was more than a
name; that Hitlerism had been heralded by over a century of
German philosophers whereas Weimar was right outside the
German historic context: all this counted for little in the judgement of most Englishmen who regarded as a mere prejudice
any belief that a nation's behaviour might in many respects be
predetermined. They frowned, therefore, on those states which
raised the alarm; and the lack of *a priori* prejudices in the
English people led to temporary animosity against nations or
men who played the unrewarding part of Cassandra. France
and her allies were unpopular in England until at least 1938
(that is, until France had ceased to have any allies) for the
same reasons that Mr. Churchill was unpopular in the House
of Commons: because they tried to provide a focal point
for English attention, because they exercised mental coercion
on English political thought which strove to retain its elusiveness
and its freedom to wander, at a time when concentration of
energy was becoming essential. Indeed the English fought as
stubbornly against the tyranny of factual evidence during pre-
war days as they were to fight later against a reality that
threatened them with extinction.

The waverings and indecision of British foreign policy in the
'thirties are sometimes attributed to a decaying sense of national
loyalty, a weakening of the national consciousness. The upholders of the motto 'My country right or wrong' often expressed
that view and blamed left-wing ideologies flavoured with 'inter-
nationalism' for an alleged decline of the national conscience.
Both the judgement and the assessment of responsibility are ill-
founded. In their conduct of affairs or appreciation of dangers
both Right and Left did err; but it is not true to say that the
Left was lacking in national sense. On the contrary, its inclination in the middle and late 'thirties was to display a quixotic
spirit in which a 'Jacobin' nationalistic mood was clearly
recognizable, whereas during the same years the sin of pacifism
was, tentatively at least, committed by a right-wing school of
thought. Furthermore, the belief that the vague emotional inter-
nationalism which has become fashionable in recent years
amounts to much more than a pious sentiment or that it has

destroyed the fundamental 'Britishness' of the people, rests on a false diagnosis of the English character. The English national sense, or nationalism (if one may use that word in its proper sense, which is not derogatory) is not at the mercy of theorists or ideologies, the influence of which may be spectacular for a while but does not cut very deep. The striking fact which emerges from class or party controversies in England is certainly not a deprecation by any side of national virtues or abilities (such as could be witnessed in France during the early 'thirties) but rather a naïve exaltation of them. Whether one hears Mr. Bevin praising the achievements of British workers or one of his antagonists recalling the moral value of Public School education in this country, whether the superficial emphasis be placed, for the sake of political argument, on one or another section of the population, the real stress is on the epithet 'British' irrespective of other points at issue. Nor is this a special feature of war-time politics. Long before, it was among trade unionists and in Labour circles that I found the most implicit faith in the national virtues, a faith revealed in such paradoxical pronouncements as 'Our British workers have too much common sense to let themselves be hoodwinked like yours by jingo politicians.' For all the weaknesses of British foreign policy and for all the contradictions between quixotry and lingering pacifism displayed by public opinion in pre-war years, it was no process of denationalization that accounted for the timid spirit in which, until September 1939, England faced the most serious challenge to her national existence. If explanations of that timidity are sought elsewhere than in party confusion, class ambiguities, and lax leadership, they are more likely to be found in national over-confidence than in national disaffection. The English national sense was by no means in jeopardy during pre-war years, though it was unprepared by its nature and tradition to perceive and meet the new threat with which England was confronted. Nor did that sense rightly assess the country's relative strength and possibilities in a new world. Both these statements must be elaborated.

All foreign wars fought by England since the Battle of Hastings have been fought on foreign territory; nearly all have been waged in answer to some threat, but not, since the Armada, under the direct impact of an enemy onslaught. Almost invariably England had the option, at least temporarily, of giving battle or of standing aside. The memory of past wars is therefore associated in English minds with the idea of deliberation. The country's decisions were not dictated by events but by herself according to her judgement and calculation of dangers or advantages. Finally, although, contrary to a common belief, England occasionally lost a war, her homeland never suffered much, save from the financial burdens imposed by war. This long immunity, coupled with the fact that England had always surveyed the field before joining issue, had several effects on the national outlook of the English people: they regarded war as an enterprise their participation in which could be limited in extent or regulated in time by their own will,[1] instead of being solely determined by the bulk and pressure of enemy forces on the frontiers; they retained to some extent the power to withdraw (although they seldom availed themselves of it) since they could usually do so without loss of life or limb; they could go to war with less military preparedness than Continental nations, provided their fleet was adequate to the guarding of the seas; they had more freedom to choose their allies in peace-time and were no more obliged to have hereditary allies than hereditary foes. Further, they relied in war on technical quality rather than on vast manpower, since their security did not depend on a mass rush to the frontier. In many wars, this technical quality did in fact amount to pre-eminence, though it was less in evidence during the Napoleonic wars, disappeared during the Crimean campaigns, and was recovered only in certain directions during the first world conflict.

Up to the crucial stage of the Second World War the very concept of total warfare was not only alien to the English people but practically unintelligible to them, and this for two reasons. The first is that the condition precedent to total war is the total preparation of the nation in peace-time, a thing traditionally abhorrent to Englishmen as intolerable in England; the second is that the English were completely unaware of the importance of the demographic factor in war because their country's contribution to past conflicts, however notable, had always consisted of expeditionary corps and not of her entire manpower

---

[1] A remarkable book showing how the fact of insularity has led England to evolve a strategy of her own certainly deserves to be read or re-read at the present juncture: I am referring to Sir Julian Corbett's *Some Principles of Maritime States*.

thrown into battle to protect every inch of coast. England's conception of her own power was not, like France's, based on a mathematical comparison between the manpower she could muster and that which a prospective enemy could marshal against her. She thought in terms of empire, wealth, trade returns, of all the resources on which she could draw rather than of the number of men she could put into the field. On the Continent she fought with allies whom she would help with men or material, by her exertions on the sea or in the air. As for her homeland, if it came to that, its defence depended less on masses than on skilful co-ordination of sea and land defences, while the development of air power tended to increase her reliance on a strategy that kept the enemy at arm's length rather than one that reckoned with the possibility of mass encounters at close quarters. Thus, until the present conflict, the 'demographic anxiety' felt by Continental nations conscious of their relative shortage of manpower in relation to that of a prospective enemy's was not a feature of the English national character. It could not be, for, traditionally, England had enjoyed over her foes an advantage comparable to that of a cat over a dog: in sheer brute strength the superiority of the dog is overwhelming and must eventually prevail, were it not that the cat can retire to a tree, make constant sorties, and harass the enemy by repeated swift thrusts, without ever exposing itself sufficiently to suffer a mortal hurt.

England's foreign policy in peace-time naturally reflected the nation's particular outlook. A country whose life is periodically menaced from the same direction has little freedom of choice in the conduct of its diplomacy; its primary aim is to seek prospective support from nations similarly threatened. A country that usually retains comparative freedom of action up to the last moment is less dependent on others, and the outside world offers it a variety of possibilities. It was in accordance with that traditional outlook and not with the new threat aimed at her that England continued to act in pre-war years. Her policy was not, as some would have it, undermined by a declining nationalism; on the contrary it corresponded to a national consciousness accustomed to deliberation, freedom of choice, leisure to make up one's mind, self-regulated participation in any conflict, 'staggered' contribution to any land fighting, heedlessness of the demographic factor, since this had not affected England's fate in the past. In 1938 I had a number of conversations with members of Parliament on the vexed question of conscription. They were usually surprised and sometimes annoyed that France should be so insistent on the enforcement of conscription in England. Even when I recalled that Germany's manpower was twice that of France, her industrial capacity three times greater in normal times and probably more under totalitarian rule, and that France might have to fight on three frontiers under conditions of fantastic inferiority, the staunchest friends would still smile sceptically, remind me of the Maginot line, of the advantages of defence over attack (assessed by Captain Liddell Hart as three to one), of the fact that this would be a technical war in which numbers would count for little and in which British sea, air and mechanical power would be of greater help to the French than divisions in the field.[1] They thought little of the German-Italian combination totalling 120 million people. Deeprooted in them was the age-old conviction that England's strength lay in the elasticity of her foreign policy, the looseness of her alliances, the flexibility of her war methods.[2] The recognition of a community of strategic interests between Britain and France was the sum total of their concessions to the need for concerted action and concentration of forces against the enemy.

What nobody reckoned with, either here or elsewhere, was a new historical fact: a nation's total will to war. When that will exists, spontaneously or otherwise, every ounce of energy in the nation is employed and brought to bear against the appointed enemy; when, furthermore, such total energy has been mobi-

[1] Technical superiority in the air coupled with sea power certainly saved England in 1940. Germany's victory over the French army was hastened by her technical superiority. Yet as others caught up with Germany in the technical field the manpower factor became once more predominant. *It was Soviet reserves that beat the Germans in the East,* and the U.S.S.R. for all its heroism had to lose more men than France could muster in all, before bloodletting began to tell on the invader.

[2] This may be true from a British point of view, provided the first enemy impact be withstood by Britain's Continental allies. Although this was not the case in the present war, the French campaign, brief though it was, gave her a short respite which she put to admirable use; and though she had the shining honour of resisting the coalition of the Central Powers for a whole year, who can say how long she could have held out if an Allied coalition on which she had reckoned, had not been formed and Germany had devoted to an English enterprise the millions she sacrificed in the East?

M

lized for several years, the advantage over other belligerents of
the nation thus prepared is overwhelming. Given such preparation in a nation thus mobilized, the demographic or manpower
factor carries full weight and, other factors being evenly
balanced, superiority in numbers becomes absolute superiority.[1]
Between the English and the German outlook, the contrast was
therefore more striking in every respect than that between the
outlook of Germany and that of any other nation. Against
German predetermination was set English freewill; against
Germany's total preparation was set England's tradition of a
gradual adaptation to the contingency of war; against Germany's mobilization of all industrial material and every moral
and human resource to the last fibre and sinew, was set the
English conception of elastic mobilization varying according
to circumstances. France was not prepared for total war either,
which is even more surprising, since it was her frontiers which
had to bear the brunt of the German hordes. But in her case
it was not her traditional outlook on war which was at fault;
apart from deficiencies in political and military leadership, and
a striking shortage in war material due to both, it was the very
rigidity of her conception of mass war. France was hyper-
conscious of the problem of numbers and aware of little else;
England practically ignored it.

The slow and apparently timid reaction to danger shown by
England from 1932 onwards was thus partly due to the underlying confidence of her citizens that history would repeat itself,
that England could adopt her own pace and yet display, in the
last resort, the great gifts of adaptation and improvisation which
had so often baffled and helped to defeat Continental despots.
The English people could not be aware that the circumstances
in which they had to think, act and, in the end, fight, had been
revolutionized; that the old rules of the game of war were turned
topsy-turvy and that, consequently, the diplomatic, political,
and physical preparations for that emergency must be revolutionized too. No experience of total will to war was recorded
by history, save perhaps in the case of Sparta, and to Germany's
enemies it meant little more than an expression signifying
German thoroughness. In 1914 the foreign and war policy of

---

[1] The 'other factors' comprise means of communication and other facili-
ties for the concentration of power, as well as initial capacity for production,
individual valour, etc.

England to be adequate for its task had only needed the adaptation of historical precedents to modern times. Not so in its preparation for the Second World War. What was required then was no adjustment but a revolution in the national outlook on Europe, on the implications of war, on the country's relative power in the twentieth century. Yet how could the English conceive that they would have to fight, not a despot relying on the allegiance of his people, but a people transformed into eighty million despots, that they would go into the field not in order to protect a so-called vital interest or serve a noble cause, but to save every body and every soul from total annihilation? Such a concept—difficult of apprehension even for Continental nations who still retained the memory of herd clashes, of struggles for partial extermination—would be completely alien to the English who had not known tribal warfare for nearly a thousand years. Thus the limitations imposed on the English outlook by their previous experiences on the Continent led this country to follow the path of tradition rather than to adapt itself to the resurgence of a herd menace. On the other hand the very broadness of the English outlook in other directions than Continental policy or Continental warfare had exactly the same effect, for when English interpretations of Continental affairs are inadequate it is often because English conceptions relate to the whole world and not to Europe alone.

What was England's viewpoint from 1932 to 1940? It was that of the head of a Commonwealth of Nations spread over the whole surface of the earth, linked by communications which it was the mother country's strategic duty to guard, bound by a common dynasty, common religious conceptions, a common language and a common legal tradition; that of the head of a progressive combination of states, suddenly faced with the prospect of a tribal war of extermination. Generation after generation, the trend of England's evolution had been towards a widening of the national field of vision, politically, strategically, and on the human plane. She was then suddenly brought back, without the transition experienced by Continental peoples, to the narrowest conception of man's struggles, the oldest species of conflict, that for the prevalence of one blood stock over another, the feud as in Kipling's tale between the Red dogs of the Dekkan and the Wolves of Seenonee, and this was emphasized rather than disguised by the mechanization of the pack or by the childish philosophies evolved for the vindication of barbarous instincts.

If the traditional English outlook was out of focus in regard to modern Europe, the plague that spread from the heart of Europe challenged more strangely yet the Commonwealth's conception of life. England, the Western anchor of the old Continent, had been tempted after the last war to forget that she was a European country and that she had derived from her European character the very sense and forward trend of her imperial pursuits. At Ottawa in 1932 she partly yielded to that temptation and might have yielded further had not Continental perils taken precedence over imperial hopes. Still, her national consciousness was neither purely insular nor purely European; nor was her foreign policy that of a free-lance among the nations of Europe. Both her policy and as an *ultima ratio*, her conceptions of warfare must take into account transoceanic routes and extra-European interests. Her freedom of action was greater in Europe, but less in the world as a whole, than that of other states. Her strategic contribution to European warfare was less because it had to be related to military responsibilities all over the world. This was both a burden and a safeguard: a burden because of the dispersal of English forces; a safeguard because others besides England were resolved that she should not perish and her enemies had to strike at many vital points in order to kill. As Proudhon foresaw eighty years ago, whatever the concentration of forces by a European power might be in the future, the interlocking of world interests from continent to continent, from ocean to ocean, would make it imperative for that power to strike not only at Paris, London, or Moscow. It must paralyse the Bosphorus, Suez, Singapore, Panama, Gibraltar, before it could achieve victory. It is the consciousness of that fact which forms part of the English outlook, clearly and consistently in the minds of statesmen, more confusedly in the thoughts of the nation at large. It is that imperial hand which from 1932 onwards added to the perplexities of Britain, faced as she was with dangers which the Commonwealth could not rightly gauge, though from 1939 onwards her imperial assets helped her both to fight the enemy and to remain the equal of her giant allies.

CHAPTER 16

IMPERIAL DILEMMAS

AS King George VI stood in the centre of the nave of Westminster Abbey on the glorious morning of 12 May 1937, the Archbishop of Canterbury, Primate of All England, tendered him the following oath in accordance with the Statute of Westminster: 'Will you solemnly promise and swear to govern the peoples of Great Britain, Ireland, Canada, Australia, New Zealand, and the Union of South Africa, of your Possessions and the other Territories to any of them belonging or pertaining, and of your Empire of India, according to their respective laws and customs?'

The King answered: 'I solemnly promise so to do.'

George VI was the first sovereign to take that oath in precisely those terms and thereby to consecrate, as between the nations of the Commonwealth, ties which thus assumed the nature of a covenant. From the dizzy heights of the triforium one had almost a bird's-eye view of the splendour below that seemed to unfurl in waves of colour from the transepts to the nave. The lofty vaulting which had just echoed the sound of the heralds' trumpets now lent to the two voices the depth and significance of time itself. The words were borne across the spaces of a world which had sent its rulers and ambassadors as silent witnesses of an English ritual; silent, though perhaps reflecting that the scarlet and gold of the ancient throne where the new king was presently to sit were almost the last in Christendom that had not withered. The ceremony of the Coronation went on. The only movement in the Abbey Church of St. Peter was the ripple of white, red, blue, gold and black that ran along the rows of court dresses, mantles, uniforms, ermine, tiaras, stretching in every direction down, across, along and upwards, filling its vast space with colour, above which only the grey stone vaulting sprang up in sheer nakedness:

'Will you to your power cause Law and Justice, in Mercy, to be executed in all your judgements?'

'I will.'

There was the King, isolated by the very performance of the

rite, yet surrounded by the Empire; linked to his land by age-old custom, yet no less bound to a broader present by a promise extended to numberless peoples. So also was England herself. I remembered Joseph Devlin's description of Lord Cecil of Chelwood as 'the man who has one foot in the Middle Ages and the other in the League of Nations', an epigram which made me smile but with a feeling very far from irony. For what would be anachronism elsewhere is real life in England, whose strength lies partly in her capacity to ignore or to reconcile contrasts of time, to span centuries and to add a fourth dimension to her natural existence. Here, in the Abbey, the weight of medieval words was brought into the young charter of a modern Commonwealth; the true spirit of an oath of chivalry informed the bonds of a twentieth-century League of Nations.

In the traditions and reminiscences associated with their monarchy the English show what in them is most withdrawn, self-centred, static and innately Western European; yet the monarchy helps to maintain an imperial community brought together by their outward ventures, sallies or flights away from their hearths and from the old Continent. A vast world system revolves round the local traditions of an island throne. The Commonwealth, a great composite body, also has 'one foot in the Middle Ages and the other in the League of Nations'. It partakes of both. In law, government, economics, its basic concept is that of a League of Nations. Its dynastic foundation, religious allegiance, and strategic intercourse derive from the feudal notion of an exchange of services for protection, of homage in token of a liege's duties, of recognition of a hierarchy at once temporal and spiritual.

Unique of its kind by reason of its dual inspiration, that structure in which past and present, perhaps past and future, are interlocked, has so far withstood every impact, while planned theoretical edifices crumbled to dust at the first test. It is true that there are between the nations of the Commonwealth bonds of a kind not to be found in a league of world or even European states. At the same time the dispersion of the British community leaves it at the mercy of powerful centrifugal forces that would not threaten a Continental group. Yet these forces have been successfully kept in check to this day, although the last ten or twelve years might have proved as perilous for the unity of the Empire as they were for the English nation.

Arbitrarily, one may divide the imperial problems which beset pre-war England into three general categories: the maintenance of close ties with states of the Commonwealth which, having already reached equal partnership with the motherland, follow a path of their own and might part company with her because of economic or political incompatibility—Canada, Australia, New Zealand and South Africa; the status to be given to nations of the Empire which claim but do not yet enjoy similar rights—particularly India; finally, the Irish question attended with the double difficulty of a territorial dispute and a threat of secession. This is by no means the sum total of the problems which confronted the central Power, but an outline of those which demanded its most urgent attention as bearing directly on the vital issue of imperial unity.

Of these questions, the Irish, which touched England's doorstep, was the least successfully handled. It was in fact the only imperial issue to be approached and treated in a manner fully illustrative of the National Government's shortcomings. In 1932 Fianna Fail, having defeated the Cosgrave party, came into power with a revisionist programme of which it made no mystery and which Mr. de Valera proceeded to implement by stages. Instead of either redressing Irish grievances or holding firmly to the Anglo-Irish Treaty, the National Government clung to its rights on paper but consistently gave the impression that its mind was not made up in practice. It rejected the Irish claim to secede, yet clearly showed that it would not implement that rejection by force. It grudged every concession in theory, but finally, after six years of skirmishing, conceded most of the points by an agreement so negotiated and framed as to persuade everyone that Mr. Malcolm MacDonald, the Dominions Secretary, was following in his own sphere the line of least resistance for which Neville Chamberlain's foreign policy had served as a pattern. It was certainly not interpreted as a deliberate act of good statesmanship. The agreement concluded in 1938 put an end to English control of naval bases in Eire at the only time perhaps when an otherwise questionable interference could be justified by the European emergency, yet it was too belated, half-hearted and timid in other respects to give England any tangible compensation in the shape of Irish friendship (assuming that any sign of friendship would otherwise have been forthcoming). Nobody knew, or appears to know to this day, whether Eire is a Dominion, a member of the Commonwealth in any capacity whatever, what her international status is, whether she is fish, flesh or fowl. The Irish 'settlement' was an unfortunate example of party compromise in a negative and not a constructive sense, a solution resulting not from positive contributions but from cumulative waverings. It looked like the outcome of a process of party exhaustion and was accepted rather than willed, on the then fashionable principle that a door is better left ajar than opened or closed. Those were the days when an agreement was hailed as an achievement in itself quite irrespective of what was put into it.

The Irish question has certainly diminished in importance and ceased to be a touchstone of England's imperial policy. What remains serious, however, indeed more serious than ever, is its strategic and territorial significance. The war has confirmed the obvious fact that England's relations with Eire have a direct bearing on this country's security. Few Englishmen nowadays would propose to employ coercion against Ireland so that she might be turned into a strategic appendage of England in war-time. Fewer still, on the other hand, would pay the true price which Eire actually sets upon her future friendship with England, namely the union of all Ireland. Yet a united Ireland is and will remain for the Irish the dominant national question, the answer to which conditions her future attitude towards England. It is quite clear that, from an Irish point of view, all the questions discussed with England up to the present date were hardly more than hors-d'oeuvres. As from 1932 Eamon de Valera understood that the era of British intervention was closed and that the Irish Government could nullify the 1922 treaty by a series of *faits-accomplis* without precipitating a serious crisis; that, in fact, nothing short of an attempt to annex Northern Ireland would drive England to resort to force against Eire. It is on that assumption that he acted and events proved his calculations correct. Ireland broke, one after another, her links with Great Britain until the state of things thereby created was, more or less reluctantly, endorsed by the British Government. Concessions on the part of England had not been made willingly; but they eventually fell like ripe fruit. The All-Irish union, on the other hand, was a totally different matter. Eire could not take the law into her own hands to settle such a grave territorial issue, for Northern Ireland would fight and so would England follow suit. Mr. De Valera recognized this to be a long-term problem; he had to wait, perhaps for one or two generations, perhaps for ever. But he has not given up, nor, apparently, have those who will carry on after him.

In February 1938 I spent a few days first in Dublin and then in Northern Ireland where the general election was being held. To speak of the contrast between North and South has become a worn out cliché. Suffice it to say that at the time both sides did everything in their power to stress the contrast between Orange and Catholic Ireland. The Southerners puzzled all outsiders and probably themselves by a lavish use of Gaelic on every public building (barring none). The Northerners proudly exhibited to visitors their brand new replica of the British Houses of Parliament each single interior detail of which had been minutely reproduced, but with so many mechanical improvements that everything save the Speaker's wig was worked by electric switches. That impressive edifice stands on Stormont Hill and, as a Cockney salesman on a busman's holiday remarked with reverence, 'must have cost 'em a tidy bit'. However, for all the differences between North and South familiar to all travellers, it is difficult to imagine anything more irreconcilable than the stubbornly opposed theses of the two parties as they were expounded to me by their respective Prime Ministers.

It seemed as though years of political feud had exaggerated the natural disposition and national outlook of both Mr. De Valera and Lord Craigavon, as though, indeed, the two opponents were deliberately overstressing what in each was most opposed to the other. The former was Irish with a vengeance, the latter so forcefully British as to make one feel that the Great Islanders on the other side of St. George's Channel were a meek, and inferior sub-class of the genuine species. Mr. De Valera, whom I had never met before, received me in his severe room at Government Buildings, a room that looks almost like an anchorite's cell. With unsmiling patience, indefatigable melancholy, with a sad, steady gaze looking far beyond me, Eamon de Valera demonstrated to me the arbitrariness of land annuities, of the maintenance of British garrisons in Irish ports, of the rights enjoyed by the British High Commissioner. Occasionally his tone would suddenly rise to a shrill, sharper note; then he would pause, as though slightly confused by his own outburst of vehemence, readjust the tone of his voice and resume his explanation at the former pace, the effect resembling that of an incantation in which the figures of past payments to Britain were invoked like magic spells. When it came to the subject of a United Ireland, his expression changed. Other problems only exercised his head; this one touched his heart. Something inexorable and final came into the big dark eyes curiously set into relief by the thick lenses of his steel-rimmed spectacles, and gave them not hardness but a deep determination that had both the forlornness and immutability of a dream. He said little on that question, yet enough to convince me that the Union was not only his life purpose but, in so far as he could command the future, his bequest to coming generations of patriotic Irishmen.

A few days later I found myself in the very 'English' drawing-room of Lord and Lady Craigavon at Stormont to hear an equally uncompromising case put with equally adamant determination, though in a more matter-of-fact, less didactic tone of voice. Lord Craigavon was a big, tall man, heavily built, with grey eyes dimmed a little by drooping, tired eyelids; he conveyed at once an impression of geniality and ruthlessness, suggesting adventurous days and unerring confidence in himself. His enemies in Belfast said that his Britishness went so far that he would even fight Great Britain if she compelled him to join with the Southern Irish. There certainly was in him, as in many Ulstermen, a touch of that naïve, unquestioning imperialism which had been both the strength and the limitation of some late English Victorians and which has lingered in Northern Ireland: a strong self-righteous nationalism blended with a serene belief in the moral force accruing from vested economic interests and with an admixture of touchy regionalism.

I asked Lord Craigavon whether his opposition to a United Ireland was final or would be qualified if either De Valera stayed within the Commonwealth or was replaced by a moderate pro-British leader. As I put the question, his answer was writing itself on his features. He took no time to consider it: 'Ulster's opposition is final,' he said. 'The Loyalists' sheet-anchor is the Government of Ireland Act. Under it we reluctantly accepted a separate parliament for Northern Ireland and to us that settlement of the Irish question was final. Our opinion will never change whatever De Valera may promise to Great

Britain. The people of Ulster,' he added ironically, 'know the reliance that can be placed on promises from Southern Irish politicians. Ulster is in the Empire and means to remain there.' As I raised the question of Catholic minorities in Northern Ireland, he went into a long explanation, the gist of which was that 'they were treated most generously' and that 'to do more would be unfair to the rest of the population'.[1]

On both sides the same adamant attitude strangely contrasted with the flexibility of English political thought, to which Northern Ireland no more conformed than did its Southern neighbour; and their recent success at the polls was not calculated to make the Orangemen more pliable. Nor was the fast deteriorating international situation, burdening England with new and pressing anxieties, likely to moderate Eire's vehement campaign for territorial revision. London's official line of policy was then: 'We will abide by Ulster's decision and back it.' Ulster's decision was in no doubt. The Loyalists were not ready to give up the privileges which they derived from their dual status. They had a parliament of their own and yet were represented in the Imperial Parliament at Westminster. They enjoyed fiscal and commercial independence and yet the economic benefits accruing from imperial tariff preference. Nor does the new Government in Northern Ireland show any sign of going back on its predecessor's policy.

The war has clearly illustrated both the drawbacks and the advantages of an ambiguous situation in Ireland. Ulster's loyalism has made it possible to turn Northern Ireland into a landing stage for men and supplies from America and a training centre, as well as an Atlantic outpost for the Admiralty and the Air Ministry. Eire's stern and at times dubious neutrality has made St. George's Channel a potentially hostile sea and Dublin an occasional resort for shady diplomatic dealings between Germans and pro-German elements, which of course the Irish Government could not prevent, while the abandonment of Irish

---

[1] This opinion T. E. Campbell, Catholic leader in Northern Ireland, vehemently contested, as would be expected, in his conversations with me. The Nationalists' chief complaint is that Catholic minorities in Northern Ireland have been prevented from forming regional 'blocs', by means of a skilful delimitation of constituencies which staggers their forces and which they describe as 'jerrymandering'. On the other hand their schools were given State grants whilst retaining their educational independence.

ports by Great Britain created during this war naval difficulties unknown in the last.

Indirectly, therefore, England has a territorial problem of her own. Although it is not so vital as those of Continental nations, her perpetuation of a national and strategic ambiguity remains a singularity of her historic outlook. Granted her submission that it is for the Irish to decide, and irrespective of the moral issues involved, the status of 'John Bull's Other Island' is characteristic of England's reluctance to compel solutions and force the hand of history. Her critics will say that her abstention is ungenerous if considered from an Irish point of view; it may with equal force be recalled that other nations would in this war have used coercion on the ground of vital interests. As it happened, the Irish policy of the National Government has had less serious effects than might have been anticipated and might well have been feared in the perilous days of 1940.

Between England and the other nations of the Commonwealth there existed no such legacy of national and religious distrust as burdened her relations with Ireland, and imperial policy was more successful on this broader field than it was at close range. Canada, Australia, and New Zealand enjoyed in 1932 their freshly acquired independence under the Statute of Westminster (1931) and nursed neither political nor constitutional grievances. In South Africa, rendered similarly independent, the memory of the Boer War might die hard among Nationalists; yet the burden of history was not so heavy as to overshadow South African life and the very distance separating her from England prevented her from suffering, like Ireland, from a sense of relative weakness and political inferiority. In respect of all these far-flung states the problems besetting the mother country were practical rather than historical: would their own national development remain consistent with their close membership of the Commonwealth, or would centrifugal forces prove stronger than the force of gravitation around the central Power?

While in the case of Eire geography and economics worked in favour of a close relationship with England which ethical factors tended to impede, the situation in the case of the other Dominions was almost exactly the reverse: geography, economics, and other practical factors might perhaps operate against imperial unity, whereas that unity was served by such moral links as the Crown, the law, and (with the exception of French Catholic Canada) religion. These were links that were not necessarily at the mercy of circumstances. And it is, incidentally, a singularity of the British Commonwealth that its permanent elements of cohesion should be primarily ethical, while the physical ties require constant revision and adjustment. This, again, is a factor which indicates the Western European inspiration of the British Commonwealth in contrast to any system conceivable to the Germans, in which the idea of physical power would be predominant.

This is not to say that practical considerations could or can be ignored. In the case of the British Commonwealth these might, according to policy and circumstances, strengthen or imperil the unity of the Empire. Thus economic interests might operate either as bonds or as disruptive forces; thus, strategic preoccupations might bind the states of the Commonwealth to England if she remained the keystone of a system of imperial security, or on the contrary encourage them to form other associations if she failed to ensure their protection. Thus the very predominance which England derived from her position in Europe might become a cause of disaffection if that position entailed the undertaking of commitments which the nations of the Commonwealth were unwilling to discharge. The conditions essential to the maintenance of imperial unity in practice as well as in principle were consequently definable as: putting an economic premium upon membership of the Empire so as to promote its economic cohesion; offering sufficient guarantees of military protection to ensure strategic interdependence; concerting foreign and general policy with the Dominions so closely and consistently as to eliminate all risks of divergent or contradictory action on any important issue. This is not all. For it must be said at once that any imperial policy followed by Whitehall towards Ottawa, Canberra, Pretoria or Wellington carries with it an indispensable corollary which concerns the Foreign Office, namely the preservation of a close friendship with the United States of America. America is the only world power which, by virtue of its economic standing, ethical kinship with Great Britain, and geographical position, might conceivably become an alternative centre of gravitation for the nations of the Commonwealth and which does in fact exercise upon them a measure of attraction. A war between England and

America would set insoluble problems to the members of the British community. One may therefore assert that the very maintenance of imperial unity is inseparable from that of happy relations between England and America. To the imperial prerequisites of that unity—namely economic, purely strategic and political co-operation within the Commonwealth—must therefore be added the maintenance of good relations with the United States, which has thus become, apart from other considerations, a cornerstone of British foreign policy.

Whatever its shortcomings may have been in other respects the National Government's conduct of imperial affairs was, on the whole, fortunate. The minimum conditions for the preservation of imperial cohesion, whether economic, strategic, political or diplomatic, were fulfilled. If one probes into the reasons for that fulfilment one may find that some are not altogether to the credit of the National administration considered as a truly national body. Thus, the tightening of economic links within the Commonwealth was due to the complete predominance of Conservative influence on this one point of policy; while the fact that the Dominions kept abreast of England in foreign policy was due to the very timidity of that policy on the Continent rather than to the National Government's boldness in the Empire. Strategic co-ordination was maintained thanks to the excellence of Britain's permanent services rather than to the dubious comprehensiveness of ministerial policy; and, finally, co-operation with America was rendered possible more by Mr. Roosevelt's accession to office than by the foresight of the National Government which on the question of war debts adopted an attitude which, though legally justified, was unimaginative *vis-à-vis* the United States.[1] However, the tangible results of the imperial policy followed from 1931 up to the war, were there in 1939 when the nations of the Commonwealth once more rallied to the cause of England, and, save for a brief hesitation on the part of South Africa, did so most determinedly. It may be worth recalling as particularly illustrative, some as-

[1] Mr. Chamberlain, as Chancellor of the Exchequer, was chiefly responsible for the drafting of the note which substituted a token payment for the repayment under the agreement previously negotiated by Stanley Baldwin. Legally the note was unimpeachable; politically it alienated an influential section of American opinion.

pects of the relations between England and the Dominions during that period.

In the early 'thirties, the need for adjusting the imperial economy was clear. Failing such an adjustment economic schism might set in. England had just introduced tariff protection into her national life, and, granted the *fait accompli* of protection, there was a powerful case for giving the Empire favourable treatment, if not, as some Conservatives advocated, for removing all impediments to trade within the Commonwealth. Moreover, even apart from the new fact of protection in Britain, the economic relations between the states of the Commonwealth were in any case ripe for revision at this period. So long as the Dominions had remained vast granaries, producers of foodstuffs, extractors of raw materials, the process of commercial exchange throughout the Empire had been relatively simple: England absorbed a large part of their exports and they imported her manufactures. Those days were now gone. Several factors had in recent years upset that balanced system: the continuous growth of home industries in the Dominions; the enormous rise in the world production of foodstuffs which, vastly exceeding the demand, caused both a glut of stocks in the Dominions and a sharp drop in world prices; the world monetary crisis, partly a consequence of overproduction,[1] which disturbed transactions between the Commonwealth and foreign markets;[2] and, finally, the incipient progress of England towards a more self-supporting economy, caused by a sense of international stress and a consequent tendency to insure herself against risks of blockade.

The Ottawa Conference which opened in July 1932, thus following closely on the return of England to trade protection after seventy-five years of Free Trade, unquestionably tightened the bonds between the mother country and the states of the Commonwealth. Its outstanding result was the enforcement of a comprehensive system of imperial trade preference in terms of both import duties and import quotas. That prefer-

[1] Overproduction in relation to existing demand and not to existing needs. The term is used, here, in its accepted and not its absolute sense.

[2] With such subsidiary complications for instance as the currency problem set to Canada. So long as no currency agreement was reached between Great Britain and the U.S.A. to fix a permanent rate of parity between sterling and dollar the Canadian economy, tied to both Great Britain and the U.S.A., remained especially disturbed as a result of that disparity.

ence fell somewhat short of the Dominions' most sanguine hopes, but it put a premium on their membership of the Commonwealth and one which could be increased in practice once the principle had been recognized and implemented. The conference, it must be emphasized, was a one-party affair, run as it was by the Conservatives with Stanley Baldwin to preside over it. Baldwin was too moderate to go as far as those fellow-members of his party who advocated Empire Free Trade, but he was enough of a Conservative to promote imperial preference even if it meant ruffling the susceptibilities or interests of some foreign nations.[1] Such as they were, the results of Ottawa fluttered several dovecots in England itself. Those in the Liberal and Labour parties who dreamt of world-embracing agreements criticized it as reactionary. Ramsay MacDonald, then in the process of conceiving his World Economic Conference, no doubt felt that the Conservatives were spoiling his wicket, which is exactly what they were doing. And considering his usual standard of achievement when he was put to the test, they may well have had some justification for narrowing the field of his future exertions. In terms of world economics a conference which sanctioned and enacted a policy of trade discrimination was open to criticism, though, since nobody anywhere showed the slightest readiness to act on world principles, such criticism was purely abstract. Judged on its imperial merits the Ottawa Conference was a wise move, failing which the economic structure of the Commonwealth would have been undermined. The imperial bird in the hand was worth more than two world ones in an abstract bush; that this should have been understood was a fortunate chance in days where that bush attracted uncommon attention. Trade preference, to be sure, did not solve all imperial problems, nor did it prevent the Dominions from looking elsewhere than to England for complementary markets, once they had made the most of the English outlet;[2] nor did they, on the other hand, check their own industrial development for the sake of absorbing more

[1] Although the Dominions complained with some reason that greater advantages could have been extended to them had it not been for the desire to protect the interests of the Argentine where there were considerable British investments.

[2] The increase in imperial trade which followed Ottawa did not exceed 6 to 10 per cent.

English manufactured goods; a fortunate thing, as it turned out, since the industrial capacity of Canada and even Australia has stood the Empire in good stead during the present conflict. But the privileges conferred on the members of the Commonwealth perpetuated bonds of common interest and maintained a common denominator between them all.

Ottawa and the economic policy followed thereafter in the same spirit were reactions of British self-defence in an economic world at war: the Empire collected itself for self-protection. Politically and strategically a similar development took place, though less conspicuously and more timidly. More timidly because it was for a long time an unwritten axiom of British foreign policy that England should not go further on the path of international commitments than the most hesitant of her Dominions would go. The effect of this was, on the one hand, to render Great Britain very shy of any contractual obligations with foreign countries and, on the other, to make concerted action with the Commonwealth slow and difficult whenever decisions on foreign issues had, after all, to be taken.

There is little doubt that the need to preserve imperial cohesion weighed heavily on British foreign policy in the years that preceded the war. England's waverings in those days cannot of course, be wholly explained by the Dominions' reluctance to accept new entanglements, nor can British indecision between various policies be attributed merely to the diversity of conceptions prevailing in the Commonwealth in respect of world and chiefly European affairs. These influences, however, played too great a part to be overlooked. The general problem which confronted pre-war England, caught as she was between her duty to the Empire and (in plain terms) the actual demands of a fast-deteriorating international situation, can be summed up as follows: Imperial unity could be secured only at the cost of boldness in foreign enterprise, imperial loyalty by excessive prudence in Europe, imperial power by its moderate use. In other words the full weight of the Empire would only be mustered in action if that action were not too far-reaching, and the Dominions Office, in order to succeed in its own sphere, had to clip the wings of the Foreign Office.

Obviously priority was, on the whole, given to Empire maintenance, and the attainment of that aim was thus a contributory factor to the dispersion of effort which characterized

N

British foreign policy for several years. Bold leadership on the part of England might perhaps have reconciled the dual needs of Empire support and international firmness, but as that leadership was lacking the first need was met at the sacrifice of the other. An illustration of the British dilemma and of the attempts to solve it was offered by the imperial consultations held at London in May 1935 on the occasion of the Royal Jubilee.

Inconspicuously beside the gorgeous display of regal pageantry, the statesmen of the Empire met discreetly and conferred. While the brilliant stage of the capital rang with cheers and glittered with lights, they quietly discussed world problems somewhere in the wings, confirming the saying of Nieztsche that what is truly momentous must take place away from the forum and its glory. The questions reviewed were obviously those which exercised all minds: the rise of Hitler and its inherent dangers; the recent Stresa Conference which had united for a fleeting moment England, France and Italy in an agreement to 'watch Germany', though, simultaneously, there was the already apparent threat of a breach of international law by Italy, then embarking on her Abyssinian venture;[1] the idea of a pact of assistance in the air intended to strengthen the Treaty of Locarno; the limitation of armaments (still academically considered); and, naturally, all the problems, economic, strategic or political, which had arisen within the Empire since the Ottawa Conference.

The great point at issue in May 1935 was this: for the last ten years, that is since the Treaty of Locarno, the attitude of England towards Europe had remained one of arbitration. She had not taken sides but had attempted to preserve, according to her lights, some sort of balance of power;[2] so that the very detachment of her foreign policy, almost that of *l'honnête courtier*, had made its endorsement by the Dominions a matter of course. Now things were different. Germany was stirring. England

[1] The question why British delegates at the Stresa Conference agreed with Italy on a common policy without openly raising the Abyssinian issue with Mussolini has remained to this day without a proper answer.

[2] A balance of power conceived on the wrong premise that, France being too strong and Germany too weak, the humble must be exalted and the proud curbed; only France was fast losing the technical superiority which made up for her crushing inferiority in numbers and in industrial power, whilst Germany was growing to inordinate strength in all these respects.

might have to take sides, though for purely defensive purposes. She had to reinforce the Treaty of Locarno which guaranteed the Rhine frontier, in other words tighten her links with France. Did the Dominions agree that 'England's frontier was on the Rhine' and that, consequently, this principle might have to be implemented by strategic precautions? Did they agree that England was right to adopt a line of policy common to herself, France and Italy at the Stresa Conference? Did they agree that a pact of mutual assistance in the air between the three countries would provide the best weapon wherewith to put substance into the Locarno Treaty? Should Germany be intimidated by stern warnings or placated by the concession of a right to moderate rearmament? Should France be backed in her policy of intransigeance towards Hitlerite Germany, or would such support encourage her to become provocative?

Such were the questions that English statesmen would no doubt put in those days to the representatives of the Dominions, partly because the Dominions' answers had to be heeded, partly because England herself had not made up her mind as to the answers. What the precise advice of each government in the Commonwealth may have been on all these points can only be surmised. No doubt there was a variety of counsel among them. But the consensus of opinion can be gauged and its effects on British policy assessed from circumstantial evidence. The Commonwealth, to be sure, agreed with Great Britain that isolation was no longer possible, and acknowledged the fact that England's frontier was on the Rhine—as Mr. Baldwin had declared in the House a year before—for these were matters of common sense. Yet when it came to positive action common sense did not suffice. What was wanted was a penetrating vision of European facts. From their distant observation posts, looking out as citizens of the world, the nations of the Commonwealth did not see the map of Europe in proper perspective. They could hardly fail to underrate the German menace which, for European peoples, darkened the map of the Continent. They were inclined to consider European problems in terms either of morality or of practical business. Morally, why not give Germany a chance instead of repressing her? Practically, why not make concessions to her and show her that fair and straightforward dealing would pay? If precautions had, temporarily, to be taken against her, why not make up for this act of unfriendliness in some other way such as a greater readiness to limit armaments all round? Germany was a totalitarian state, but so was Italy. Why fear the former and not the latter? And as for France, it would not pay to countenance her uncompromising attitude towards Germany and her refusal to grant Germany equality of armaments. France might go too far and drag England into troubled waters. The more England felt that her strategic frontier lay on the Rhine, the more advisable it was to prevent British interests from being gambled away by French rashness. Such were the comments heard in those days, and they had all the more effect on English minds since they were an amplified echo of English thoughts. Such as they were, they contributed to the contradictions and diffusion of British policy. The Foreign Office thought of an air pact to reinforce Locarno but, as a counterpart, the old scheme of a convention to limit air armaments was exhumed from dusty files. The 'frontier on the Rhine' became a watchword, but on 18 June England sanctioned German naval rearmament by an agreement which was supposed to cure her inferiority complex, and incidentally allowed the Reich to build the submarine pens which have since cost so much blood and tears; the German menace was recognized but, apart from the decision to rearm, Great Britain was in fact prevented from taking effective steps to counter it.

Shortly afterwards the Abyssinian crisis broke out and diverted general attention from the German to the Italian threat, jeopardizing incidentally what little was left of an Anglo-French entente after the naval treaty with Germany. But the Abyssinian affair did not take a serious turn before August, and between May and August the vacillations of British policy had probably been increased by England's desire to take the Dominions' point of view into account. She went on doing so throughout the following years in the Abyssinian, the Spanish, the Rhineland, the Austrian and the Czechoslovak crises, and the Commonwealth's growing influence on British policy must certainly be counted as a new and important feature in recent British history. It is indisputable that the necessity of maintaining active unity within the Empire handicapped British policy. It is equally indisputable that for England to impair that unity would have been sheer folly, whatever advantages she might otherwise have gained from it. Indeed, the only sound conclusion which experience seems to warrant is that closer, not looser, contacts should be kept up between the nations of the Commonwealth. Had imperial consultations been a long-standing practice, the Dominions' grasp of European problems in pre-war days would have been firmer and concerted action less hesitant. This conclusion applies with even greater force to strategy. Strategic co-ordination within the Empire was good in so far as the permanent services were concerned and had the means to make it effective. Those means, however, were limited in this as in other respects. Despite the setting up and operation of the Committee of Imperial Defence, whose task it was to plan ahead and assess general requirements, the events of December 1941 and the early months of 1942 have since shown that such planning fell far short of the requirements of such a gigantic task as the protection of a world-wide system. To that extent past lessons indicate the need for an organization not merely relying on existing machinery but also capable of securing from the Executive and from Parliament means commensurate with the magnitude of the task.

Although the great structure of the British Commonwealth has so far proved stronger and more resilient than political systems based on theory, although it has thriven by reason of the very empirical nature of its development, there is neverthe-less a case for rational planning in relation to certain aspects at least of its life. This would seem to apply chiefly to the two branches of its communal activity which come under the head-ing of power: namely, economics and strategy. In both, British policy has chiefly concerned itself so far with bestowing on the associated nations such privileges as render membership desir-able. The memory of great and recent dangers suggests the need for broader conceptions so that the physical ties between the states of the Commonwealth may assume as permanent a value as the ethical, in a world where the factor of power is likely to play a dominant part for a long time to come.

The third order of truly capital problems confronting imperial statesmanship in pre-war days concerned the raising of peoples who did not yet enjoy home rule to the status of 'equal partners'. By far the most important of these lies in India. While a discus-sion of the Indian question would be out of place here, no refer-ence to British imperial policy can omit some mention of the British outlook on the subject. For eighty-six years—that is, since the rights of the East India Company were vested in the Crown by the Act of 1858—world opinion has regarded India as the symbol of British overseas power. Her huge resources have contributed to England's greatness and, conversely, her protection as a reservoir of riches and a link on the road to the Pacific has long burdened and even governed British strategy. Her man-power is a source of strength, her openness to multifarious influences a liability. Finally the world has assessed Great Britain's colonial activities on her Indian record, while her critics have found an inexhaustible wealth of argument in India's social, racial, religious, political, and economic conflicts; for the Indian touchstone was equally applied by friend and by foe, for better and for worse.

No one who has not devoted a lifetime to the study of the Indian question can without presumption return a proper verdict on it. What however strikes a dispassionate observer is the levity, the nebulous irrelevance, of many attacks upon British rule in India. Faults which are clearly part of the Indian scheme of things are reckoned as shortcomings of the British administration. Critics complain in the same breath of excessive interference on the part of Great Britain and of her unwillingness to solve the countless problems set by the complex nature of Indian social and religious history. Home rule for the Indians, whether good or not in itself, is advocated in the name of such Western notions as democracy or 'progress' which, in India, have just so much currency as is needed for external propaganda. The fact that India, left to herself, might and would become a playground of predatory powers or return to feuds in which the so-called 'progressive' elements would be crushed, is generally passed over in silence by 'progressive' critics. Nor has it yet been found how, save with external help, an elementary basis for some future national unity could truly emerge from a variegated community with dozens of races, with some 225 languages (excluding dialects), twelve full-dress religions and hundreds of secondary faiths, with over two thousand castes within the Hindu community alone and ruthless prejudices among them all, with each race, caste, and religion breeding and maintaining feuds and distinctions more deeply set and entrenched than national differences ever are in Europe, even in the midst of a fierce struggle. Has the word 'democracy' any meaning common to both a Brahmin and an Untouchable; the term 'religious tolerance' any significance acceptable to both a Sikh and a Mohammedan; the word 'self-govern-ment' the same meaning for a politician of the All Indian Congress and the Ruler of an Indian State? To be sure, the value and import of these words also vary from man to man and group to group in our own countries. But such basic concepts as national identity, the state, the rights of the human person independently of the group, religion, race, sect, caste, class, have at least a common currency. During the conferences which preceded the passing by the British Parliament of the new Federal Constitution for India, the great problem set to legislators was far less to determine the degree of control that was to be left to the British Crown than to reconcile the infinite diversity of views and prejudices between states and provinces, religious communities, racial and national groups and castes. A student of the question without being so naïve as to believe that Great Britain had no axe to grind in India, was bound to be convinced of one thing by any contact at the time with the parties concerned: even a completely disinterested power attempting to solve the Indian problem solely on its merits and to find the common denominator of its conflicting elements would have needed years to reach the beginning of a settlement and would have had to employ coercion on all sides to enforce it.

The Constitution of 1935 certainly went as far as was possible in those days to strike a political balance, within the new Federa-tion, between Indian states and Indian provinces, and within the provinces between the various races and communities. In England the Constitution was attacked from the Right by Conservatives who thought it put too much control in the hands of the Indians and from the Left by Labour, who did not con-sider it progressive enough. As to the former, they seemed to underestimate the force of political claims even in a backward country and the consequences which might attend any refusal to make concessions, while the latter forgot the Indian poli-ticians' habit of drawing the attention of Westerners to political grievances because they have a high 'box-office' value in Europe, and of thus diverting attention from the most deadly and least reconcilable Indian feuds, which are not political at all but arise from religious, racial and caste issues in the face of which Western influence is virtually helpless and for which Western rule obviously cannot be held responsible.

British policy in India cannot become one of total aloofness or total absention. Politically it seems to have struck a reasonable balance between conservatism and Utopianism. The 'middle course' invariably favoured by Great Britain, which may produce shocking results when issues of war and peace are at stake, has far better effects in imperial policy where the time factor is less imperative, or, rather, where hasty clear-cut attitudes may prove destructive rather than constructive. Where progress undoubtedly appears desirable is in two fields of action in which, unlike many others, there is room for improvement by the protecting power or under its influence: one is economics and the other education. The standard of living remains very low in India, perhaps not so much owing to 'vested interests', as a facile school of thought would have it, as because of a weak system of communications and distribution. The standard of education is also low with, according to the census of 1931, 327 millions of illiterates out of a population of 353 millions. In both respects the British record here is probably more open to criticism than it is in other directions.

Apart from its intrinsic merits, the Indian question throws light on an important aspect of the political development of England: the growing tendency of public opinion to exert pressure on issues which by their very nature are inaccessible to investigation by the layman. Public common sense can only be of value when directed to questions to which the ordinary man can apply his own standards of judgement. Given such a problem as India, such standards are not applicable. To take a simple example, there is nothing in common, especially in the emotional realm, between the English sense of values and the Indian: an Englishman rates his dog a thousand times higher than a high-caste Indian an untouchable. When the British have had to intervene on behalf of what in England would have been the elementary protection of the underdog, humane public opinion in the country has often protested against that intervention in the name of what it regarded as 'democracy'. The fact is that in order to defend democracy or even elementary humane principles in India, England would normally have to act autocratically. How is public opinion to comprehend that? And yet it is more and more inclined to pass judgement on such governmental action. What then is to be the outcome of those great problems which have for many years been left to a specialized *élite* in England, but on which public opinion and collective emotion, in accordance with prevailing tendencies and Western standards, now increasingly brings pressure to bear? The question, to be sure, may be asked in the case of other countries also. But history and geography have it that England, of all nations, is confronted with overseas problems of infinitely greater complexity than most states. And the fact is that in no nation, perhaps, is the breach between past and present so clear as it is in England in this precise respect: that foreign and imperial issues have passed from the hands of an educated minority to those of the general public which, albeit intermittently and spasmodically, suddenly focuses its attention, sentiments, and prejudices upon them. This may well be one of those inconspicuous revolutions characteristic of English history. Arising first in connexion with India, a paramount problem, the change may register itself with equal force in connexion with all British imperial problems.

No nation has a better record of technical competence in handling imperial questions. Yet in no other centre of a great empire is public opinion so profoundly ignorant of them. In this contrast lie the elements of a serious dilemma in the future. It is idle to pretend that the 'enlightenment of the people provides a solution'. A subject which a conscientious student may need several years to grasp cannot be fully explained to forty-eight million people in the course of a general election, or by newspaper headlines. That is demagogy, not democracy. The growing tendency of all men to share in the discussion of the most intricate problems is certainly a feature of our times, and probably a wholesome one. To oppose that tendency leads to autocracy; but to yield to it wholly leads to chaos. In England itself the matter is serious enough, though not more so than in other countries; but in relation to the British Empire it is very serious indeed and still remains to be solved. The status of India was temporarily fixed in 1935 under the impact of agitation from the forum in every direction, or in spite of it. In the post-war world other problems will have to be tackled, and it may be wondered what formula will be found in order to preserve the popular control which is essential in democracy and yet to allow considered action on the part of those who, alone, have the means of forming a judgement.

VII. THE CHURCH

CHAPTER 17

RELIGION AND POLITICS

My kingdom is not of this world,
ST. JOHN xviii, 36

We must reform our banking system.
DR. TEMPLE, Archbishop of Canterbury

THE title of the present chapter imposes its own strict limitations. It does not attempt to cover the broad and complex subject of religion in England but concerns itself solely with the part that religion plays in the social and political life of this country. Despite the unquestionable weakening of religious faith in contemporary England, that part remained in pre-war days one of the distinctive features of the English community where, constitutionally and practically, directly or indirectly, religion still influenced politics more than in most European nations.

To the eyes of an outside observer almost all English churches, the Established and the non-Established, have many characteristics in common whereby they all differ from any non-English church in Europe. Their chief purpose seems to be moral rather than spiritual, and social rather than individual. Their action aims at, and bears on, the temporal evolution of this world in a fashion markedly political, and not solely on account of a causal relationship, accepted by religious ethics, between life in this world and life in the next. Indeed, one sometimes feels that religious principles are often valued here because of the service which they perform in the enforcement of social order, if not absolutely in proportion to it. Social behaviour and social discipline seem to be a more immediate object than the stirring of individual consciences; or, to express it in another way, the English Church appears to act on the assumption that the improvement of man can be effected through the spreading of social morality better than through a spiritual approach to the individual by such direct means as, for instance, sacramental confession in the Roman Catholic

Church. Thus the churches have probably put more heart into the long struggle for the maintenance of 'The English Sunday', than into any attempt to confirm the belief of their own members in particular articles of faith. Being almost wholly unmystical, religion in England lays stress on conduct rather than convictions and strives to maintain or expand social discipline rather than to enhance the sense and quality of worship.

Within the Church of England alone, the long controversy on the Prayer Book, and the protracted discussions of the Church Assembly on points of Protestant dogma have shown the extreme diversity of views on fundamental doctrines prevailing among members of the same denomination. Typical examples were the differences expressed in the Assembly on such points as the significance of the Trinity or the nature of the Eucharist. No unanimous decision could be reached or precise guidance given on the question whether the Eucharist was a permanent reality or a symbol. Dogmatically there is nothing rigid about the Established Church. One of the most original features of its history is therefore the contrast between the flexibility of its religious dogma and the rigour of its demands in the temporal world. The Church traditionally seems to make up for its tolerance in spiritual matters by an equal degree of intransigeance in moral and social issues, and it expects from the community a formalism which it does not display in its own ritual.

In this particular respect things have changed so much in England during the last century and, especially during the last twenty years, that it may not be impertinent to recall what Stendhal wrote on the English sabbath in 1826, always remembering that though not an atheist he was a bitter anti-clerical. 'The unfortunate workers, the toiling peasants [in England] have nothing which they can call their own save their Sunday. But the religion of the English forbids them any kind of pleasure on Sunday, and it has contrived to turn that day into the gloomiest thing in the whole world. No greater evil could conceivably be inflicted by any religion on a people crushed under work on every other day of the week. Apart from their fifty-two Sundays, the English have three holidays in the year; this adds up to fifty-five days, which is nearly two months, in other words almost the sixth part of their existence. The religion of the English, coming to the aid of a melancholy climate, thus turns

into the deepest gloom the sixth part of the lives of those who
follow it. Even the Jesuits are very far from doing so much harm
to the most obtuse Papists who share their superstition.'[1]

This severe judgement completely ignores the credit side of
the balance sheet and is, moreover, incomplete and biased.
But what gives interest to the quotation is the line of attack
chosen by Stendhal. What struck and shocked him in England
was the extreme interference of the Church not with conscience
but with society and its imposition of severe regulations on the
temporal life of the people. Himself a scathing censor of ethical
intolerance on the part of the Church of Rome, he took to task
the social intransigeance of the Church of England.[2] Though
with considerable qualifications, any Continental observer
would probably have made the same sort of remark some twelve
or fifteen years ago. Since then, however, a marked change has
come over the relation between religion and social life in England and, especially, there has been a transformation in the
influence of the Church on the nation.

Among the English it is, of course, common knowledge that
their own acceptance of Church or Chapel interference with
their way of living rests largely on their conviction that the
Protestant religion was, in England, a powerful instrument of
emancipation and therefore, in exchange for services rendered,
it attempted and largely contrived to impose its codes of living
on society and to dictate written or unwritten laws by parliamentary, parochial, local or direct action. Although the true
heirs to the fighting Puritans are not the Established clergy but
such dissenters as the Methodists and the Baptists, the Church
of England also has its Puritan streak and shares much of the
Puritan tendency to regulate temporal as well as spiritual conduct. Moreover, as an Established institution it is partly a temporal as well as a spiritual power. As for the English people in
general, they have been trained by history to accept a considerable measure of religious control (in the broadest sense) over
the community's pursuits whether out of habit, where the
Church of England is concerned, or through the true Puritan
tradition in the Free Churches. Such an acceptance has in
many cases become a formal social habit or a social duty for the

---

[1] *Mélange de Littérature* ('Lettre sur l'Angleterre'). My own translation.

[2] Whilst acknowledging, later, that 'Puritanism had given England her
freedom'.

upper classes; in others it is still a matter of real conviction. In either case, though the contemporary Englishman is not very religious in a spiritual sense, he does not openly refuse observance of regulations or conventions of religious origin.

Until the first World War, the Church of England displayed, along with a degree of severity on social ethics, a strong bias towards political and social conformity.[1] It was, on the whole, conservative, politically and socially, and left reformism in both these realms to the Free Churches. The new development in the evolution of the Church of England, and more generally in the national life of the country, is the strong tendency of the Church to extend its range of action to almost every kind of social and political pursuit or interest and to follow a reformist, almost a revolutionary, path in these matters.

It is one of man's most deeprooted traits to bring God into every human quarrel, and in any international or other conflict for each protagonist to nail the flag of Divine Providence to his own mast. In this we do not differ from the pagans save that they were more logical than we: having a variety of gods who took an active part on either side in every affray, the believers, if defeated, could find explanations of their plight derogatory neither to themselves nor to their gods. It is obvious that no church can or should refuse to bless or comfort combatants who may be about to die, without regard to the merits of their cause. In fact the more a Church remains within its own realm as a spiritual force, the more it behoves it to ignore political antagonisms and to render its services to believers in full independence of temporal issues or prejudices. That no Church in the past has drawn the line at that wholesome form of abstention and that all Churches have constantly brought their spiritual weight to bear on political issues both in war and peace is indisputable and accounts in recent years for a degree of disaffection among believers in many countries.

Yet it is also in recent years, when the state increasingly invades the realm of personal behaviour, that the question whether the Church should 'take sides' has become so difficult to answer, even by those who in the past clung to the idea of a purely spiritual Church. Should religion, on the ground that it

[1] As distinct from the Roman Catholic attitude of 'resignation' to political conditions, which proceeds from the will to confine Church action to the spiritual realm.

must remain above parties, stand aloof from the growing social problems which divide the world, rend consciences and often take precedence in human minds and consciences over the gravest personal issues? Should it ignore the fierce ideological conflicts of our day for fear of losing its serene impartiality and its value as an ultimate refuge, or should it step into the arena to give practical guidance lest men should cease to take religion into account as a source of moral help?[1] In other words should the Church, when choosing between two contrasting symbols offered by the Scriptures, stand by the principle that its Master's Kingdom was not of this world, or help to drive the money-changers from the precincts of the Temple. The dilemma, to be sure, is more vital for the Roman Catholic than for any Protestant Church, since the former broadly accepts the notion of resignation to the established order and non-interference in temporal matters[2] and cannot easily depart from that principle, while the history of the latter is bound up with memories of political and social intervention.

Faced with that alternative the Church of England and of course, to an even greater degree, the Free Churches have resolutely, though with varying degrees of circumspection, chosen to follow the path of action and cracked the whip not only at the money-changers but at many other tangible enemies. In a recent speech, Sir Stafford Cripps uttered words which would certainly be countenanced by every one of the clergy: 'Remember that you can never arrive at a sound judgement on any of these [social and political] matters, unless you have some firm basis by which you can judge right from wrong, justice from injustice. Our religion supplies us with the means of judging aright and so we must use our religion in all our social and political judgements.' Sir Stafford Cripps, a politician, thus wants to bring religion to bear on temporal issues; and the speeches or sermons delivered by the High and Low Church ecclesiastics from the benches of the Upper House or from the pulpit certainly bear witness to the fact that such a view is completely shared by most representatives of the Church. As for

[1] These questions are distinct from that which has caused many great historic controversies (and chiefly those on the question of the Establishment) namely: Should Religion be a force in the State as such or only touch the nation through the individuals who compose it?

[2] Save by the Vatican as a State.

the Free Churches their views on the matter were never in doubt.

With regard to the Church of England, we may go further and say that it now tends to resume in the midst of twentieth-century struggles the policy of revolutionary intervention of the seventeenth-century Roundheads. The Puritans had risen against regal absolutism and assailed the moral laxity of the society; the modern Church, though in a milder and more prudent fashion, attacks Capitalist absolutism and denounces social inequality as immoral. The Leftward progress of the Church of England has probably been facilitated, if not stimulated, by its gradual impoverishment; so has its departure from strict social conformity. And the fact is that to-day many of its members seem, on matters of social reform, to steal a march on the Free Churches who, by tradition, were as non-conformist politically and socially as doctrinally.

What again, is a common trait of all English Churches is their disposition, or in some cases determination, to associate the temporal evils against which they now take arms with the influence of the Church of Rome. They readily identify the religious with the political crusade. A recent address by Dr. Townsend, Moderator of the Free Church Council, shows that tendency to be even more vehement among the non-established Churches. Dr. Townsend, speaking at the fourth annual Congress of the Council said *inter alia:* 'The policy of the Roman Catholic Church in four European nations (Italy, Spain, Greece, France) has brought damaging blows, one after the other, to the Christian religion. The Vatican is involved in the rise of Fascism. . . .' That contention has been in recent years a dominant theme in Free Church discussion of the international situation and also, though expressed in more diplomatic terms, among the members of the Church of England. In this, as well as in its increasing tendency to challenge the existing order, English Protestantism follows the seventeenth-century pattern.

The comparison however must not be carried too far, for between the two epochs there are very important contrasts. The Puritans were then a determined minority fighting to enforce a certain way of living as well as a new political régime. The Church of England, to-day, is an official body which has lost a good deal of its hold on the people and naturally strives to regain it. Socially and politically it tries, in fact, to catch up with a popular development which tends to escape, outdistance or ignore its influence. That development took place independently of religious considerations. The enormous pressure of social and ideological problems on the human mind, particularly after the first World War, threatened to take precedence over that of religious rule or beliefs and consequently to render Church action academic and religious guidance unheeded by millions of communicants. By tackling the problems which were foremost in the minds of the people, the Church[1] is therefore resorting to temporal action in order to regain its hold, and by adopting 'advanced' views on social and political problems, it is revolutionary or reformist after the event and not, in true Roundhead style, *motu proprio*.

The distinction is capital, for it means that the social and political conformity of the Church has simply shifted from the past to the present: England, like most countries, moves towards the Left, irrespective of the labels or state of parties according to parliamentary terminology. It is to that development that the Church conforms itself, in some instances showing signs of overtaking it. This is clearly different from the spirit of Puritanism, which went right against not only the existing order but all species of conformity, and acted on sheer convictions irrespective of their popularity. The distinction is also important for another reason: the Church in England has long derived its moral strength from its constant readiness to challenge facile impulses and compel discipline. Conformist *vis-à-vis* the régime, it was not so *vis-à-vis* human nature. In that respect it retained its Puritan inspiration, and English education, which laid the stress on moral character, bore in this the hallmark of religious influence. To-day, the Church, whilst still bringing pressure to bear on society on behalf of moral discipline, is less strict on this point than in the past and is formally punctilious rather than ethically exacting. Politically the Church of England follows its people onto their own ground, that of economic and class preoccupations, and assumes their own orientation. It stoops to conquer, perhaps to retain its conquests; or in other words, it falls into step with prevalent opinion in the hope of

[1] The position of the Roman Catholic Church in England is not discussed here because, however powerful its influence in the past or its potential influence in the future, it does not at present penetrate the social consciousness or act upon the national way of life.

persuading on the way. This is different from the old fighting spirit of the Puritans. Indeed the Church shows 'realism', not only in adapting its outlook to that of the majority, but also in the methods whereby it tries to increase its following. Church publicity is a new departure in religious history and although it does not always go to the length of imitating a West London parish which proclaimed on large posters: 'The Church of so-and-so is a jolly good church and the Rev. So-and-So a jolly good preacher,' it certainly tends more and more to make religion permissible matter for advertisement.

However, what remains or resurges is the will to act in a broad field, to extend the range of action, and the intention to give, albeit by diplomatic and popular appeals instead of by forceful militancy, a political currency to moral principles. What remains also is the characteristically English conviction that the value of religion, given the right spirit, is increased, not depreciated, by descending into the political arena. Few epochs of history, of course, have afforded such tempting opportunities for Church intervention. Times like the present—when the borderline between economic and ideological problems is completely blurred, when every conceivable issue serves as a pretext for a conflict of ideas—are particularly propitious to an intervention of the spiritual power in the temporal world. Never could the Church claim with more justification that circumstances warranted its traditional mission to offer guidance; never, on the other hand, was the risk of a confusion of duties greater for any Church, since it has become more and more difficult to draw the line between true moral inspiration and an inevitable tendency to act in a partisan spirit on doctrinal grounds. A case in point was the Abyssinian crisis. Morally, the Church of England and the Free Churches were justified in condemning Italian aggression. There is little doubt, however, that their anti-Italian campaign might have been less forceful if, behind Italian Fascism, they had not been aiming, as they thought, at the Church of Rome and Papism. And events have proved that all English churches showed greater leniency towards semi-Protestant Germany, despite Germany's appalling moral record, than towards Catholic Italy. Both Germany and Italy were involved in the Spanish War, and though the Germans[1] behaved

---

[1] The Italians were the more numerous but the Germans, while taking smaller risks, were the more ruthless.

more barbarously than the Italians, ecclesiastical vehemence, whether in church or chapel, was chiefly directed against the Catholic nation. At the time there was ample evidence of this bias, not only in Church quarters but among church and chapel goers, especially in the west and north of England, where 'Papism' was then identified by its critics with political and religious intolerance at the very moment when it might have justified charges of excessive toleration.

The Abyssinian quarrel marked the height of Church intervention in ideological conflicts. In the Spanish War, ecclesiastical action was slower and, at first, more hesitant, on account of the anti-clerical policy of the Spanish Republicans and of their partial association with Communism. It was the support given by Rome to Franco which turned the scale and practically determined the English Churches to take sides; this of course is a further illustration of the influence exercised by religion in ideological matters. In other words, it was the very insularity of the Churches in religious matters which rendered them actively 'European' in political directions. During pre-war years they became very 'European' if one means by that term that they shared, more than for a long time previously, in the conflicts which divided the Continent. While it is true that the Church of England and the Free Churches took their share in this on Christian principles, they also took it on anti-Papist principles.

On internal, racial and economic issues, the swing towards the Left has been remarkable and was perhaps hastened by those ideological considerations which prompted the Churches to back the Left régimes in the international field. For the Nonconformists to be politically in opposition was no new departure; for the Established Church it is, of course, a novelty. And it is a fact that the Church of England has become, particularly during the war, one of the most vocal advocates of social and economic reform. There is little that happens or is discussed in this country on which the higher clergy have not an opinion to express, and their range of interest is truly universal, since it ranges from such questions as bombing from the air, on which religious comment is inevitable, to improvements in the banking system, on which clerical guidance is less to be expected. It is an interesting question whether the deliberate broadening of Church action and its adaptation to prevalent social tendencies have in fact achieved tangible results and improved Church attendance or, to speak more generally, stimulated a more widespread interest in religion.

If one judges merely on the statistics of churchgoing in this country, there is little evidence of an increase in Church influence. The number of churchgoers in Great Britain is estimated as, on the average, between four and five millions, more than half being Roman Catholics. Leaving aside the Roman Catholics, among whom the percentage of communicants is very high, this means that in Protestant Great Britain less than a twentieth of the population goes to church regularly. It is true that if few Englishmen are anti-religious, or even completely indifferent to religion, the proportion of those who practise is, at all times, small. Indeed the limited influence exercised by worship may well be one of its permanent incentives which lead the Churches to extend their activity to other fields and to work through other means. But it is a fact that, even in war-time, churchgoing statistics do not in themselves support the view that religion has become more popular.

Church attendance, however, is not the sole evidence on which a judgement may be formed. The English do not like ritual behaviour for its own sake, and the number of Protestant churchgoers who merely practise for the sake of doing 'the right thing' is therefore probably smaller than among Roman Catholics; while, conversely, there may be a large number of tentatively religious people who do not feel sufficiently convinced to attend a church, and many others who consider active worship as a definite commitment on which they hesitate to embark. I am told that in camps and military establishments much interest is shown if not in religion as such at least in the application of religious solutions to contemporary problems and that the percentage of listeners to the B.B.C. religious talks and services and sermons is surprisingly high. This confirms the striking impression that religion in England tends to be more and more a mental interest and less and less a spiritual one; or, if we may thus far generalize, that England remains a Christian country chiefly in an ethical sense. The effect of the war, which has thrown into the melting pot most of the political values on which Europe lived, and the general loss of a sense of direction which characterizes our period, would naturally incline those who honestly try to find a sound basis for thought and behaviour to look for it outside the chaotic field of social and political controversy. To that extent the tendency of the Churches to offer guidance on a growing number of lay questions may be said to meet half-way a fairly popular demand.

It is now a moot point whether the Churches can gratify such a demand or run the risk of adding to human perplexities. Church views on many subjects must, with the best intentions, remain amateurish. Furthermore, the very diversity of persuasions in this country involves another danger: that of a wealth of conflicting advice which would add to the confusion of thought instead of clarifying it. Nobody can dispute the fact that the people of modern Europe need moral support not only now in their present struggle but infinitely more so when it is over and has left behind it a chaos, both material and metaphysical, such as the Continent has probably not known for ten centuries. No sane man, religious or not, can deny that Christian ethics taken in the broadest sense do still offer solid values to which to cling, perhaps the only ones which may safely be accepted. This does not mean that any Christian persuasion can solve all problems, but seems, on the contrary, to suggest that its upholders should limit their range of action; for the dragging of religion into every political, social, economic, or financial pursuit would only cheapen its currency, and by associating it with particular ideologies or popular tendencies in fashion at a given time, discredit religion when the fashion changes.

It is a great problem for all Churches, and the more so for English Churches whose past services in the cause of political freedom induce them to ride every political storm in the hope of controlling it. English storms they have controlled. In recent years they have followed rather than led a widespread movement of English political forces towards intervention in ideological feuds on the European scale. And yet, whilst so acting they have unwittingly added to European divergences because they have introduced religious resentment against another Christian persuasion into their well-intentioned crusade on behalf of international law and behaviour. As a continent torn by war, divided or depressed in spirit, with lawlessness and disbelief in all human values prevailing everywhere, Europe cannot afford division in what is left of Christian influence. Nor could the island churches hope to play by themselves the part of the moral rebuilder. If the great gap left by the Reformation between Protestant and Catholic doctrine cannot

by its nature be bridged, it must at least be hoped that in days
when all Churches do (and perhaps must) enter upon temporal
ground and offer guidance to a bewildered continent, they will
not, as in the past, present the spectacle of ancient feuds at a
time when the supreme task of the spiritual power, as well as
that of every temporal power, should be the preservation and
rehabilitation of whatever remains of true humanity in Europe.

FROM MUNICH TO THE BATTLE OF BRITAIN

And David put his hand in his bag and took thence a stone, and slang it, and smote the Philistine in his forehead, that the stone sunk into his forehead; and he fell upon his face to the earth.

So David prevailed over the Philistine with a sling and with a stone, and smote the Philistine and slew him; but there was no sword in the hand of David. I SAMUEL xvii, 49, 50.

FUTURE historians may reckon the two years between September 1938 and September 1940 as both the most crucial and the most baffling in modern times. In exactly two years, the peace of the world was threatened, illusively restored and believed to be saved, twice challenged again and then lost; civilization was gambled away, defended, brought to the verge of total destruction, and then saved or at least preserved by a stroke far more unexpected, incredible and momentous than that which smote Goliath and stopped the Philistines.

Whether these historians will share our concept of civilization is a different matter. They may argue that in resisting German imperialism Europe opposed an inevitable process of unification and that her struggle was prompted by principles and convictions which proved ephemeral. Yet only by such gestures of resistance has she hitherto preserved the diversity which is both the source and the mark of her genius. Nor is it certain that conquest and coercion must eventually be redeemed by progress, and temporary setbacks of human culture made good by the supposed virtues of systematic unification. The fall of Ancient Greece, the stamping out of the Alexandrine civilization, the destruction of the Incas' Empire, or, in modern times, the recurrent eclipses of Poland and the Prussianization of Austria, have all, in varying degrees, been cultural catastrophes and sheer losses. To question the urgency of the call to arms against Germany in 1939 future historians must of necessity have a conception of the world based on gregarious uniformity and not on diversity or individual values—which, alas, they may well have. Otherwise they must admit that a German victory would have dealt an appalling blow not only to our present way of life but to civilization absolutely, and that in opposing Germany single-handed from June 1940 to June 1941 England did during that year prevent the destruction of European civilization. One cannot yet say 'saved', since its survival, even after Germany's defeat, is no foregone conclusion. On the other hand, they may well consider that during the previous year both England and France were chiefly responsible for allowing Europe to be brought to the verge of annihilation and that from 1919 to 1939 British policy or lack of policy in Europe largely contributed to frame the context of events in which a total German victory became possible and seemed, for a time, inevitable.[1]

It is a singularity of England's modern history that in peace she should so often fail in her European duties and yet afterwards stand as Europe's champion at the eleventh hour; that she should by turns help loosen the European fabric and decisively contribute to save it *in extremis*. Her European sense lies more deeply buried in her national consciousness than that of Continental nations, and though that sense is as much a determining factor for her as for any other country of Europe, it is less easily aroused.

Till September 1939, she was only half-heartedly European. Save for the Abyssinian crisis, in which she was directly involved, her function in European affairs was comparable to that of a catalyzer in chemistry, that is, of a body which provokes chemical reactions between other bodies without sharing in those reactions. She had after the last war encouraged collective security as a prerequisite to disarmament but refused to accept the responsibilities inherent in its proper working.[2] She encouraged France to disarm in order to remove a German grievance, yet would go no further than Locarno in her guarantees of Continental stability. She often countenanced the claims of the defeated nations for territorial revision yet would enter into no undertakings with those at whose expense revision would be achieved, in the event of such a process provoking international

[1] This book being only concerned with England stresses English responsibilities only. This does not mean that those of other nations are ignored or comparatively underrated.

[2] Even in 1935 Britain, whilst ready to operate such a system in the specific case in point, Italy, still refused to generalize it and to commit herself to its operation against Germany should the need occur.

disturbances. Whilst from 1931 to 1935, she had under Labour guidance sought to reduce the weapons wherewith the Continent might have restrained Germany, from 1936 to 1939 under Conservative auspices she actively contributed to weaken the system of alliances which was another barrier to German expansion. From 1919 to 1939, failing an all-embracing scheme of effective security, any Continental system of protection against a German or Totalitarian threat would in practice have had to be buttressed either by France or by Russia or by both. Acting on the mistaken beliefs that a balance of power demanded a comparative weakening of France's strength, that Germany could best be rendered innocuous by concessions, and that entanglements in central and eastern Europe antagonized Germany without helping the Western Powers, she helped to disrupt a Continental order which offered at least some resistance to German expansion. By deserting Czeckoslovakia at Munich and allowing her piecemeal dismemberment—an inevitable result—for the first time in twenty years, France accepted western isolation, while England put the final touch to a policy which, wittingly or not, with motives varying from idealistic promptings to shortsighted realism, she had in fact pursued almost consistently since 1919. And yet the term 'final touch' is not quite accurate. One step remained, to render the context of the war-to-be as unfavourable to the Western Powers and as favourable to their enemy as policy could conceivably make it; and during the eleven months which elapsed between Munich and the German aggression against Poland this last step was taken. Hardly had Neville Chamberlain had time to prophesy 'Peace in our time' when the carving up and occupation of Czechoslovakia began and in March 1939 Germany attained her long-awaited aim in Central Europe. The Western Powers were then, at last, roused to the point of guaranteeing the security of Poland, the next state on the German list, and even of considering negotiations with the U.S.S.R.

Judgement on the responsibilities of each state for the failure of these vital negotiations which began in April and ended in August must be deferred until such time as complete evidence is available. It will be remembered that the Russian claim to control the Baltic States and to post garrisons in Poland was the main bone of contention, and that the refusal of the Western Powers to grant these demands led Russia to take the startling course of concluding a treaty of non-aggression with Germany; but irrespective of the moral merits of the case, the fact remains that the chance of confronting Germany with the certainty of a long war on two fronts was then lost. By 24 August, not only was war certain but its context was exactly what the Germans wanted. In September 1939 and in June 1940 England was confronted with Continental forces which, however unintentionally, she had helped to unloose, and with a Continental pattern which she had helped to devise. Thus she fought against odds which her own policy had itself increased. Such a judgement may sound severe to English ears. But no Englishman will clearly understand post-war Europe and her reactions to his own country unless he is aware of the dual feeling towards England which is common to the overwhelming majority of Continentals: a profound gratitude for her act of faith and her lonely struggle after June 1940 and at the same time a deep-rooted conviction that British foreign policy had been an important contributory factor in the rise of Germany and especially in the weakening of most Continental means of resistance to the German onslaught.

When Poland was attacked, Great Britain at once reacted like a European power; she found her true European self. There was no wavering in her declaration of war which, indeed, was only delayed for forty-eight hours because that of France was delayed by an absurd requirement of constitutional procedure. Her determination to honour her pledges did not, however, either redress her moral and physical unpreparedness for the sort of conflict which the Germans were soon to wage. Whilst France had done very little to utilize the costly respite secured at Munich and prolonged by eight months of 'phoney war', England for her part prepared for total war with the slow deliberation of one who has the choice of day, place and weapons. She acted on the assumption absurdly accepted by General Gamelin, that thirty-two divisions in a year or so would represent the sum total of her contribution to land warfare while her lists of reserved occupations in the early months of the war baffled her friends and succeeded in imparting some wit even to German cartoonists. She was doing her duty according to the letter but was not yet conscious of preparing physically and mentally to meet the greatest armed threat ever aimed at European civilization.

Even the Norwegian campaign during which the Allies had their first sample of German warfare did not sound the alarm. France and England wrote Norway off as a case of strategic mismanagement not to be repeated. English newspapers began to spread the consoling axiom that 'man for man' Allied fighters were a match for any Germans—a very dangerous saying, since, as an English journalist[1] excellently put it, 'the Germans have developed the unfortunate habit of never fighting man to man'.

And then the crash came. Within a few weeks after the 10th May, when German columns crossed the Belgian and Dutch frontiers, the German hordes were lining the western seaboard of Europe from the Pyrenees to Tromsoe. Holland, Belgium and finally France had collapsed. Every single state of continental Europe was either occupied by Germany, subservient to her will, or powerless before her. What to Continental peoples had been a short interlude in the midst of the tragedy, the period between the evacuation of Dunkirk and the German offensive on the Somme, had meanwhile brought home to the people of Great Britain the full import of the disaster in the shape of ten haggard and disarmed divisions: almost the sum total of the army wherewith England was now to face the most powerful war machine in man's history. By the 18th June German staff officers in Calais could direct their field glasses towards the cliffs of Dover and discuss the most favourable spots for a landing. French troops fought in the Maginot line until the 24th, but the Continental campaign was over.

All nations have their peculiar weaknesses, faults, even permanent deficiencies inherent in their geography, temperament, historical heritage, as well as their periods of lowered vitality. The distinctive feature of great nations is not their ability to behave well or righteously at all times, which is impossible and, even if it were possible, would probably be a sign of mere spineless mediocrity. What singles them out is their capacity to produce greatness at a vital moment and, by an act of supreme greatness, so to redeem their own failings and so to shape history as to strengthen their own fabric for a long period to come. On 19 June 1940 England redeemed all her past failings. Germany had planned to cast history 'for a thousand years'[2] in

[1] Nathaniel Gubbins, who so often *castigat ridendo mores*.
[2] Hitler *dixit*.

a mould of her own. Britain broke that mould and thus set
history free. On that day Winston Churchill said that, come
what might, generations to be would at least proclaim: 'This
was their most shining hour.' It was, and will be so recorded.

Those who analyse the causes and motives of a gesture which
then saved Europe, the decision of Britain to fight on, may well
ascribe it to considerations in which the promptings of national
greatness were not the sole inspiration. They may say that no
other course was open to her, or that the people who thus challenged a formidable coalition were not fully conscious of the odds
against them. But a great action is precisely that. It consists
precisely in setting oneself a task far above one's normal
strength, in an act of faith transcending the normal calculation
of probabilities. The argument that no other course was left is,
in any case, invalid. In exactly similar circumstances Italy, for
instance, *would* have found another course simply because she
has not yet acquired a true sense of national greatness capable
of lifting her above her own self. As to the part played by an
underrating of the true odds against Britain, it would be difficult
to maintain that the man who for twenty years had followed
every symptom of the European disease and consistently warned
his countrymen against Germany failed to realize the full extent
of German might or, on that very 19 June 1940, failed to paint
the most realistic picture of the situation. All those who were
witnesses of the English people's conduct during those fateful
days know it for a fact that the nation then showed a supreme
sense of its own greatness and a full readiness to pay the crushing price which that greatness might exact.

When the national spirit is thus roused to deeds far beyond
the normal demands of duty, the national outlook is also
broadened. The sense of sacrifice eclipses, for a time, what
usually is self-centred and introvert in a nation's mind. England
in June 1940 and until the end of the Battle of Britain was more
European than she ever was before or afterwards, in that she
identified her own defence with the liberation of Europe and
found a powerful stimulus to her exertions in the thought that
she stood as a champion for all the peoples who lived in shackles
beyond the dark coastline of the Continent. There was a sense
of dramatization—of epic stardom—in the heart of most
Englishmen, as there was in the heart of the fighter pilots who
fought the Luftwaffe above their heads, and as there always is

in those whose life and death, usually humble and unnoticed, suddenly assume a fateful meaning for a large section of mankind. That feeling is naturally far less acute now after years of war when other spectacular forces have come into play. In those days it pervaded Englishmen in the discharge of their simplest duties. They did not fight or toil only as men who defend their own land. They were the Horatii whose struggle would decide far more than their own destiny, the Horatii with Europe as their Rome. Even the elderly milkman would deliver his bottles with an underlying sense of playing the hand of fate and, joke as he would, every bus conductor obscurely felt that he was serving the needs of mankind.

The end of the Battle of Britain, which roused boundless hopes in occupied Europe and wrecked from the start all German plans for a new order acceptable to the subjugated peoples, also marked the end of that phase of the war which might be described as that of the Act of Faith. From that time onwards the continuation of the struggle, hard and fierce though it might be, heavy though the odds remained, became a practical proposition. The struggle was indeed to be hard, for the German failure to break the R.A.F. and thus open the way to an invasion was followed by eight months of night bombing. This, from the German point of view, was the continuation of the Battle of Britain by other and less costly means. During that period England not only stood the test but survived other and perhaps greater, though less conspicuous, perils. Such was the desperate shortage of destroyers which, if it had not been made good, would probably have meant the success of the German blockade. Bombing from the air did not break the English morale but it altered the British outlook on the war. Englishmen were still conscious of the fact that the world was watching, wondering how they would stand their ordeal. They still knew that they were purchasing with their lives and possessions the honour of playing the leading part in a world drama. But their thoughts took an inward turn. To resist bombing and not only to resist it but to do it with good grace was the business of the day. The barber who in July or August extended to the whole of Europe his exalted sense of crusading was now concerned not only to dodge the bombs during the night but to show increased elegance the next morning behind a broken shop window. England took pride in devoting attention to little things with even greater care than usual: that was her challenge to the Hun. To display in the morning well-parted hair and uncrumpled cuffs became for every man a challenge—until such time as Wavell's 30,000 in the Libyan desert could be turned into millions on the Continent. Mixed with these feelings was, at least during the early raids, a grudge against Continental states, and chiefly against France, for having, albeit unwittingly, supplied Germany with advanced bases for air attacks against this country. This sentiment, which was natural enough, did not last. And although the ordeal of night bombing inevitably rendered England more self-centred and less conscious of Europe, thus narrowing her field of emotions, if not of vision, the twelve months or so during which Britain stood alone were not only glorious pages in her history: they will remain as an epoch of her life when her people were at their best not only in those qualities which history chooses to exalt, but in those human dispositions without which history would be little more than an absurd record of meaningless battles, pompous declarations and tiresome treaties. For it is those dispositions, far more than the vague and changing definitions of war or peace aims, which testify to the existence of a civilization to fight for. That in their darkest hour this people should have remained quietly human in their daily life, that they retained their tolerance and good humour at home when they had to show Spartan defiance to a hostile world—this is the real proof that their cause was good, their defence justified, and that their championship of Europe, conscious or not, was not an empty word.

No nation can remain for long at its highest pitch. The years which followed could not reproduce the atmosphere and the reactions that were England's in those days. But for those who had the privilege of sharing the life and preoccupations of her people at a time when no one else stood in the way of the barbarian, a few memories, easy to recapture, bear witness to the fact that greatness, when and where it appears, springs from humanity and not, as the Germans will have it, from its destruction or perversion.

CHAPTER 19

WAR STRATEGY AND WAR POLICY

IN July 1940 and for some time after, a section of the Vichy press made a point of publishing war news under the headline 'The Anglo-German Conflict'. This revealed a desire to present the war as something which had ceased to affect France and thus to support the absurd claim that the Armistice had given the French blissful peace and lasting neutrality. But it also betrayed the genuine illusion that, save for a limited contribution from the United States, the war would remain confined to a straight fight between Germany and England which could not last very long.

Such a narrow view, rejected of course by non-Vichyites, was never accepted in England. Consciously with statesmen, more confusedly among the people, the conviction prevailed here that British resistance would bring about a coalition almost certain to include the United States. In this hope England was fortified by historic precedents. In her conception of the inevitable spread of the war she was naturally trained by her world-wide outlook as an imperial power. Such an outlook had somewhat diffused her vision of Europe in peace-time, but it now gave scope and foresight to her assessment of future possibilities. There were indeed several other elements of her national and imperial make-up which had previously been liabilities in her Continental policy, but which now turned into tangible assets. Such were her geographic detachment, the precedence she had often given to global rather than Continental considerations, the economic links between the Commonwealth and the United States, the dispersion of the Empire, and, in a different realm, the religious and moral insularity which sustained her in temporary isolation.

None of the belligerents finally involved can boast of having planned or foreseen, even partially, the development of a war which took so many unexpected turns. Least of all could England, in her desperate predicament in June 1940, have done much more in the way of planning than parry the worst blows and work full speed ahead on her armaments. Nevertheless, making full allowance for the tremendous margin of uncertainty and the existence of countless unknown quantities, there was a stubborn and fairly consistent undercurrent of British thought and purpose running below the shifting and swelling waters. Despite weaknesses, errors, blunders and occasional disasters there was more continuity in British strategy than any of the other belligerents could show. This was largely because England had no preconceived plan and kept an open mind. But what she did possess was a very strong tradition of maritime warfare, and to this she clung, adapting it to modern requirements. Thus eventually she imposed on friend and foe alike a strategy and pace of action which suited her own mood and requirements. That strategy lacks the scientific precision of the German nor does it necessarily require the breeding and schooling of generations of military theoreticians: it springs from the very nature of British maritime power, from the dispersion of its components, and its keynote is space rather than order and cohesion.

Broadly speaking the six months from June to December 1940 covered what might be described from an English point of view as the 'save-your-skin' period of the war, when Britain's problem boiled down to a plain and deadly issue: how to parry the lethal thrusts. For in those days she might have lost the war as a result of either invasion, bombing from the air, blockade or defeat in the Mediterranean.[1] Yet during the same six months every one of these threats, which all materialized, was successfully met. The Axis' failure, in a period so vital that it was to set the future course of history, was chiefly due to the following factors: German miscalculations, the R.A.F., the Royal Navy, the British wage-earners, Winston Churchill and General Wavell.

Four at least of the German mistakes were blatant. Mystically bent on their *Drang nach Paris* the Germans did not follow the British after Dunkirk but completed the campaign of France thus allowing England a brief but decisive respite. They gave up their attempt to break the R.A.F. at a time when Fighter Command was beginning to be sadly depleted, because they did not dare to incur losses vastly inferior to those which a year

[1] England could have lost Egypt and Gibraltar and yet have fought on, but the strain on the Western front and on communications would then have become unbearable.

later they suffered on their wild goose chase in Russia. Their bombing of England was irrational and its concentration on London tactically and psychologically absurd. Finally, they lost the Mediterranean for ever by relying on Italy to clear it for them when they could easily have afforded to do it themselves. Each one of these mistakes was more serious than their coming adventure in Russia which the conqueror could delay but not avoid and which might have succeeded had they previously broken the English power.

Germany's miscalculations however are but the negative side of the picture. On the positive side the achievements of the R.A.F. and the Navy must, by all reckonings, come first. As for the resistance of the people to air bombardment the chief credit must go to the wage-earners whose ordeal was incomparably harder than that of people who could fall back on a country house or a safe hotel, or, at worst, could relax during the week-end.

The shaping of events in the Mediterranean from June to December 1940, was the hinge between two phases of the war: that of pure 'back-to-the-wall' self-defence and that in which England began, though on the smallest of scales, to bring her own pressure and strategic initiative to bear upon the course of the conflict. In June England's paramount need was to protect her own island, her heart, since a wound there would have been mortal. The Mediterranean, vital though it was, only came second. Prudence counselled her not to divert troops from the homeland until a surplus was available beyond the requirements for home defence. Yet if this course were followed the Mediterranean might be lost before England had mustered sufficient resources to man her outposts there as well as her own coastline. Such was the dilemma. Winston Churchill did not hesitate. He at once took the bold decision of sending part of his scanty forces to Egypt, a master stroke which completely transformed the whole pattern of the war. Considered after the event the first and clear advantage gained was, of course, that Egypt was saved and, since Germany never invaded, saved without sacrifice to the homeland. The daring decision was typical of the outlook of a maritime power. By carrying the war to Africa, England was not only protecting an outpost of vital importance. She was extending the scope of the conflict, when the enemy preferred to localize it. She was instinctively resorting to a strategy of dispersion when Germany had everything to gain by concentration on the single Western track. At a time when the world was wondering if England had enough soldiers and rifles to repel even a small-scale invasion, in the very midst of the 'save-your-skin' period, with the enemy thinking in terms of days and miles on the other side of the Straits of Dover, England acted in terms of years and world-wide operations. There is little doubt that Churchill's bold move at such a time not only impressed the enemy but decisively contributed to lure Germany's strategy to the path of deliberation and diffusion which invariably tempts her sense of grandeur and now once more proved fatal to her ambitions.

This decision may well have been the turning point of the war. For it displaced the centre of gravity of the conflict and began to put a premium on mobility and agility which are at all times the main assets of a maritime power, the only ones that Britain could then command. It is not, of course, suggested that the fact of garrisoning vital links on the Empire routes and of using the fleet as a vehicle was in itself an act of farseeing statesmanship. British strategy in this respect is dictated by such facts as her insular situation, her Navy and the existence of remote nerve centres, the protection of which is elementary. Geography itself forms the A.B.C. of Empire strategy. But the great act of statesmanship was to think and act in terms of long-term Empire strategy at a time when, to the whole world, the problem of British defence seemed circumscribed for months to come by the necessities of the problematic protection of Britain herself against an enemy far superior in actual and potential striking power, thus relieving the congestion of the Western front and preparing the way for the future by broadening at once the field of thought and action. Shortly afterwards, on the same principle, similar dispositions were taken in respect of Palestine with a view to the defence of Syria and Iraq. In German eyes, such a policy, presupposed greater means than Britain actually possessed. And in fine the failure to inflict a lethal wound on an elusive enemy certainly hastened Hitler's attack in the East in the hope that one mighty stroke would suffice to dispose of Russia and smash the back axle of British power in the Middle East. Had Churchill taken any other line, it is clear that the Mediterranean would have become an Axis lake and that the issue of the war would indeed have narrowed down to a bare fight across the Dover Straits.

P

Thus long before the conflict extended to Russia it had, under British initiative, lost its limited European character and become potentially a world war. As things turned out, Wavell not only stood his ground in Egypt but before the end of December 1940 struck deep into enemy territory, west, east, and south of Egypt. The fall of the Italian Empire had begun and there were released immediate possibilities for the further spreading of British intervention in the Middle East, realized during the early months of 1941. In 1941 and 1942, to be sure, the war in Africa underwent varying fortunes. Yet these temporary setbacks never cancelled the initial advantages gained at a vital moment by an achievement of far-reaching strategy. As early as the summer of 1940 England had once more succeeded in luring a Continental power on to the uneasy path of scattered amphibian strategy where its numerical, technical and operational superiority could not fully assert itself.

While England naturally adapted her strategic outlook to a new age by adding the air factor to the sea factor, she still followed the traditional line of a 'non-land power'; so too Germany, a Continental power, haunted by world-wide aspirations, re-enacted her whole mystical strategy of a *drang nach osten* aimed at the Middle East, the Anglo-Russian hinge which was also an Anglo-Russian bone of contention, and in so doing, reconciled the two states and prepared her own downfall. From the early months of 1941 her efforts began to dissipate themselves over the diverse map of British interests in the Mediterranean and the Middle East. She failed in Egypt, in Syria, in Iraq; and all over the scattered Eurasian front, and yet she conceived and partly attempted to accomplish, first in 1941 and again in 1942, a gigantic pincer movement through the Caucasus from the north, and Suez from the south. Meanwhile she was throwing submarine crews into the battle of the Atlantic, thus assuming at once the crushing burdens of a great sea power and of a vast land power. In this strategy she displayed and exhausted all the resources of her warlike genius and, as ever, came very near to success. But near to success in such an undertaking is near enough to catastrophe. Whatever the relative contribution of each power to Germany's defeat will ultimately prove to be, certain it is that England's old strategic instincts, had, long before the coalition was formed, caused a stronger and better war-equipped enemy to tread a path which would lead to his undoing.

In turn, the U.S.S.R. and the United States were brought into the war, both as a result of aggression and in self-defence, at first with unfortunate results. British help which in the early months of the Russian campaign played a decisive part in the defence of the U.S.S.R. put a new strain on England's sea power at a time when the German menace was growing in the Mediterranean. The Japanese aggression could only be inadequately met and resulted not only in the disaster at Singapore in February 1942 but, indirectly, in the depletion of the African front with consequent setbacks. From December 1941 to July 1942 was in fact the gloomiest period in the whole war for Britain. She lacked the heroic stimulus of 1940. She was defeated in the Far East and in Libya. Her American ally had suffered appalling reverses. Her Russian ally seemed during the early summer to yield before the second German onslaught. With the entry into the arena of another formidable maritime power which had evolved a deadly technique of amphibian *blitzkrieg*, the broadening of the field of war was now proving too much for her. Furthermore, she seemed for a time to have lost her grip. There were waverings in the distribution of her forces over the numerous theatres of war, indecision in her strategy and even in the use of sea power which Germany had snubbed by moving the *Scharnhorst* and the *Gneisenau* from Brest through the very straits of Dover; and all the while the vital Battle of the Atlantic was causing increasing concern. The tables were turned in the autumn of 1942 when the weight of the coalition began to tell on the enemy, with the victorious offensive of the Eighth Army, the victorious Russian offensive from the Caucasus, and the successful American-Australian counter-offensive in the Pacific.

Thus Britain succeeded in holding out and often taking the initiative without engaging her main forces, until both what she considered the decisive phase in Europe had been reached and her Western ally had achieved the concentration of its own forces on a similar scale. In other words she delayed the principal and most costly action of the war until that action should have a maximum and probably a decisive effect. From the point of view of national preservation this was a striking achievement since next to avoiding destruction the paramount need of a country at war is to win without incurring losses that will enduringly, perhaps finally, cripple her.

In the past England succeeded in waging her wars at a considerably lower cost than Continental nations. The protection of a sea frontier demands less men than a land frontier so that, with skill in both policy and strategy, an island nation can postpone large-scale slaughter until she strikes her final blow, instead of shedding most of her blood in mere defensive action. Traditionally England's policy and strategy made good use of her natural advantages; her policy, in the choice and timing of alliances, her strategy, in delaying the main action until the occasion was propitious and allied support adequate, and meanwhile, in engaging limited forces on selected points where the enemy could not bring his numerical superiority to bear. The classical example is the choice of Torres Vedras by Wellington and, more generally, the whole British strategy during the Peninsular War. In the last war this path, successfully pursued for centuries, could not at first be adhered to. The long Western Front had to be guarded and England was, for the first time since the Hundred Years War, engaged in land warfare the extent of which was determined not by herself but by the enemy's impact.

It is therefore all the more remarkable that in this war she should have been able ultimately to resume her traditional course as a maritime power, that of delayed action and economy of forces. Egypt, Libya, Tunisia, Italy, have been the 'Torres Vedras' of this war, all points of contact with the enemy, where he could not bring up and deploy his superior numbers or even maintain superiority in manœuvre, until Britain could face him with her main forces almost intact and with her Allies' forces equally concentrated and ready to strike at the enemy's heart.

It is a far cry now from the days when her very national existence hung in the balance, when even the stoutest optimists believed that her survival could only be purchased, if at all, at the price of an appalling holocaust. There seemed no question, then, of classical maritime strategy, dependent for its success on the formation of a coalition around her. But that coalition did take shape and, after June 1941, Soviet Russia, as a land power bore the main brunt of the land fighting. It is therefore sometimes said that Britain could not have conducted the war at a relatively low cost had it not been for Russia's massive contribution to the attrition of German power; and it is often inferred from this that she had the corresponding duty of incurring heavy sacrifices in order to lighten Russia's burden. The assessment of the Soviet contribution is just; the inference is questionable. Soviet Russia was attacked by Germany and thus drawn into a war which Britain and France on the contrary, had freely accepted. Until the spring of 1944 the Soviet Union's primary objective was the liberation of her own territory. These facts no whit detract from the Russian people's heroism nor from its decisive effect on events, but they indicate that there would have been nothing morally objectionable in delaying a British offensive in the West until Soviet Russia had passed from the stage of territorial reclamation to that of truly offensive warfare against enemy territory. Had the Western offensive been wilfully deferred while the means of action were available, the chief moral objection would have been its disregard of the sufferings in occupied countries whose vitality was steadily ebbing and whose morale could not, like the Russian, be sustained by the knowledge that their own armies were still fighting on their national soil. But that policy was not, in fact, followed. To delay the main action does not mean to postpone it until others have fought the war out but to time it according to expediency, that is, to engage it when it becomes both practicable and effective. The date and circumstances of a mass landing in the West or the number of Allied troops to be used were not for Britain discretionary points. Conditions had to be fulfilled without which any attempted offensive could only have ended in a fiasco. Taking into account the world-wide military commitments of British forces and the vast requirements of a sea and air power in men for productive and operational purposes, it is most doubtful whether Britain alone could at any time have mustered strength enough in the West to hold a broad land front against Greater Germany. Nor would the temporary diversion of a number of German divisions have affected decisively the turn of events in the east so long as the Germans were still deep in Soviet territory. Finally, an abortive operation in Western Europe might have had disastrous effects on the morale of the occupied nations and have prejudiced the results of later and more successful attempts on the Continent. Whether Allied preparations could have been hastened, other theatres of war found, and the pace of events forced by greater exertions on the part of the Western powers: these were the truly relevant questions which exercised the anxious minds of occupied peoples. But to none of them can adequate answers be given until complete data are available. What at the present juncture already seems unwarranted is the assertion that a more 'costly' British strategy would have earlier defeated an enemy whose tactical excellence, other factors being equal, has yet to be disproved.

Last but not least, the striking contrast between the enormous losses borne by Soviet Russia and the relatively moderate casualties incurred by the British Commonwealth up to that time is not only a contrast between Eastern and Western Europe. This is an aspect of the war problem which must be faced squarely and frankly, apart from its emotional context, unless we are to shirk an issue which dominates the development of Europe.

The Western nations of Europe, great and small, are old states. However high their degree of health respectively, their powers of biological recuperation in terms of re-population is not comparable to that of the countries of Eastern Europe like Russia, or even Poland; they are less physically resilient and their national existence is affected by war casualties more lastingly and deeply. Being highly individualistic with a conservative conception of the family, they maintain a population level relatively static. In varying degrees all Western nations have, in the twentieth century, become conscious of the demographic problem. They have undergone a mental and political process which can only be defined as a growing demographic psychosis: it is both an inferiority complex in terms of numbers, as compared with the vast ethnical groups of Central and Eastern Europe or Asia and an acute awareness of the value of human life. This is, of course, encouraged by individualistic standards of morality which have less currency in nations where either collectivity or the state takes precedence over individual values.

Like most phenomena of social evolution, this was first felt in France where 'demographic consciousness' assumed an almost pathological character and profoundly influenced international and external policy. But more generally that growing consciousness has engendered in Western Europe a more or less acute, and direct, species of 'defeatism'—if one may use the term in a non-depreciatory sense—a reluctance to purchase national prestige or interest at the cost of over-weakening the national body. In England demographic consciousness is as yet no more than dawning, largely, perhaps because it has not been an object of public discussion, since the biological effects of war have been less oppressive and because the numerical factor counts in the defence of an island for less than it does in the case of a Continental nation. Even so, the Singapore disaster revealed, apart from other contributory causes, a psychological reaction against sacrifices of lives which, for equal stakes, would have been more lightly accepted in the last war. Furthermore the frequent references now made in the press to the birthrate curve also indicate a new awareness of the demographic issue. Even in highly populated America, that issue has influenced war policy and the conduct of operations.

Britain's gesture in 1940 and the heavy odds which she then accepted showed her able to rise far above considerations of demographic economy. The will to fight overrode all other considerations. Nevertheless, her stand thus taken, any war strategy which did not take into account the need for sparing the nation's blood at least during the defensive and pre-offensive phase of the war, would have been unwise and dangerous. Conscious or not, the fear of unlimited losses potentially exists in Britain as in every Western nation and, if not taken into account before it became a matter of public concern, might have made deep inroads into the national resolution. In preventing this, wittingly or not, her 'classical strategy' took account of the existence of a problem which for emotional reasons the 'Open the Second Front Now' campaign failed to appreciate. It is naïve to ask whether this motive can be described as 'selfish'. All states do obey 'selfish' considerations, even though they can rise above them when stirred to great actions. The determination of a nation to survive has, in turn, two contradictory effects: one is to key her up to acts of heroism beyond her apparent power, the other to make her thrifty of her physical reserves. The storms of 1940 produced the first of these effects, British strategy, the second.

Now the most serious point arising out of that strategy, was that of its repercussions on Europe, a continent whose very survival is an immediate issue: for the date of Europe's liberation raised a biological problem of the first magnitude. First, it should be put on record that those European peoples who, at the greatest cost, remained faithful to the

Allied cause readily understood any delay in action because of
the overriding need of ensuring victory. But considering the
deadly threat of national extinction under which every occupied
nation was living, considering their lowered vitality, a far more
serious evil than the heaviest losses incurred by any belligerent,
they would certainly have resented such a delay, and would
have remembered it long after the war, if it were proved that
the policy of Britain and the United States was to reduce their
own casualties, either by delays or by protracted bombing, at
the expense of a wounded continent. The occupied peoples of
Western Europe regard themselves as partners of the first hour
with Britain. They have been able to live and endure much
from the enemy and the leaders thrust upon them because they
believed in an unwritten bond of solidarity with the British
people. They think it natural to help the common cause by
untold sacrifices and they have borne the ordeal of a very heavy
Allied bombing as a war necessity. On the other hand they
place on Great Britain a corresponding obligation, that of a
comrade-at-arms who, in their cause, does not shirk sacrifices.
This is a point to be borne in mind, for it affects future relations
between this country and a liberated Continent. It is on her
regard for Continental salvation as well as on her shining behaviour in 1940 that England's Europeanism will be judged.

That Europeanism which shone in 1940 has been less convin-
cingly displayed in the conduct of British war policy, as distinct
from strategy, which, it must be frankly recognized, has hitherto
chiefly been based on non-European conceptions. The very
broadness of British strategy in a world war may account for a
comparative neglect of the Continental factor. Relying first on
the Commonwealth, then on Russia, America and China,
Britain instinctively adjusted her policy to the needs of her
strategy and her primary care was for her relations with her
major allies. The problems raised by a militarily disabled Contin-
nent were treated as secondary considerations—a matter of
greater or lesser success in propaganda among the occupied
peoples. The 'Four Powers' strategy based on the British Empire,
the Soviet Union, the United States and China, has produced a
'Four Powers' policy proclaimed by many official statements.
British policy in Europe has, save for her relations with the
Soviet Union, depended on expedients, on day-to-day impressions or reactions to events. It has not rested on a broad and

firm conception of Britain's permanent relations with European states but on administrative convenience in dealing with a few statesmen or persons representing each state: and even within that limited field it has not always shown consistency. While expediency justified or explained the emphasis laid on global, at the expense of European, considerations, Britain's future remains closely bound up with Europe and especially Western Europe. Weakened as a Western European power, as she would be if her Continental policy were either too high-handed or too lax, Britain would be correspondingly weakened as a world power. Politically, as well as strategically, that great issue may well be decided with the ending of the war.

CHAPTER 20

BEHIND THE OLD WOODEN WALLS

AS I write this chapter, huge tanks lumber by along a once peaceful country lane and past a very old man who stands back against the hedge gazing at them, his shears in his hands. The tanks are probably on their last lap before they cross the sea, carrying in their venture no less than the fate of an ancient continent. The old man who clips the wild grass on the roadside does what he can to preserve some of the traditional trimness of an English by-way. Or, as he himself puts it when he feels like grumbling: 'Ts' all wurry wull winning warrs [he uses the poetic plural as lending point to his argument] in all 'em foncy spots, an' Assams and Toonises and woot nots, an' I bain't sayin' naught agin it, an' they would'n listen to me nowise if I did anyways, but watt will urr youngsters say, anon, when they be back from licking all the foul lot, an' they're home and can't recognize their auwn blessed land ne'er more?'

They will, I think, recognize their own land, literally and figuratively—unless the crop of Portal houses is unduly large and obtrusive. For, although the war has sown the seeds of many future changes, England at present still stands in many of the old ways. Englishmen themselves are naturally conscious, above all, of what transformations the conflict has brought about. What, on the other hand, chiefly strikes a Continental observer is the extent to which England has succeeded in preserving her own true self, physically and morally.

The war, for almost every Continental country, has meant a decisive, all-embracing revolution, whether that revolution was a prelude to war, as with Germany, or a consequence of war independent of the will of men, as with France and most occupied countries. England has gone to war and stood the impact of war very much as her own permanent self: a diverse, heterogeneous nation whose self-defence embraced the protection of her right to remain composite, diverse, multifarious in every sense, constitutional, political, social, economic, religious and racial. Her claim to uphold that right and continue to exercise it under the pressure of war was perhaps the boldest article of her audacious challenge to an enemy who had mustered his colossal might by the very process of casting eighty million bodies and souls into a single mould, and by eliminating from the national compound every conceivable element of difference and diversity, every principle of heterodoxy. Between Great Britain and Germany the struggle was indeed that of human variety against standardized power.

This quality of diversity is one which the Germans despise so much that their modern history is a succession of attempts to exorcize it from their own national body. In 1940 they held England's effort to preserve it to be a sure guarantee of her early downfall.[1] Yet this quality is the very mainspring of British resilience and staying power. Indeed the greatest advantage of insular defence is perhaps the time-lag which it allows for a gradual adaptation of the national life to an emergency which Continental states can successfully meet only by a brutal transformation of their national structure, often with lasting and revolutionary consequences. That England should have retained her national integrity in previous instances was perhaps not surprising. But that she should have largely succeeded in protecting it this time, when, of all the threats aimed at her, the ideological was the most serious, is a considerable achievement.

It is true that, bracing herself for the supreme endeavour in 1940 and 1941, she did take a number of steps which encroached on individual, local, or group liberties, and which entailed an extraordinary use of the State's authority. The much debated Regulation 18b, the round-up of aliens, the restrictions on the rights of organized labour, the expanding range of State action at the expense of parliamentary or local privileges: all these obviously run counter to English political tradition. Yet what is chiefly remarkable about such a measure as, say, 18b, is not the vesting of discretionary powers in the Home Secretary in time of war: it is both the moderation with which they have been used and the close, constant supervision, of their exercise by Parliament and public opinion. This it is which fundamentally distinguishes the outlook of a democratically alert community from that of nations politically dulled and numbed. As to the range of State action, it remains to be seen whether its increase

[1] One of the main themes of German propaganda at the time was that England's congenital disability to 'totalitarianize' her ways of living made her incapable of withstanding the impact of total war.

will be temporary, or whether the prevalence of socialist views will make it a permanent feature of English life. In any case the ultimate decision lies with the electorate. Meanwhile the spectacle of England at war, and very efficiently at war, strikes an absolute contrast with every totalitarian notion, and one which Englishmen themselves are occasionally apt to forget when a new restriction causes some grumbling here and there. Let us for a moment look at England through the eyes of a denizen of totalitarian Germany and imagine a few entries made in his note-book.

They would probably read very much like this: 'The majority of people here persist in regarding policemen as men whose job is to direct traffic and arrest common criminals so that their police force remains unaccountably popular. The detention of persons on political grounds causes unbelievable rows everywhere, even in the House of Lords, whose members are not directly affected by the locking-up of a few common individuals. English judges occasionally show class prejudices but the Government does not follow the usual practice of telling them whom to condemn, so that there is little co-ordination of effort between Executive and Judiciary in the repression of political agitation. On the other hand a Fascist leader, named Oswald Mosley, no doubt a very distinguished personality, who had been previously arrested, was released a few months ago; and the extraordinary thing was that the order to release him was given not, as would be expected, by people of his own persuasion but by the Home Secretary who is a notorious anti-fascist. I have not been able to ascertain the practical advantage that the State or Party drew from that decision. It must be, therefore, something to do with the Intelligence Service.'

'Recently the English have had a few labour strikes. Though they make occasional arrests, they refrain from the classical practice of shooting down a few leaders at random as an example to others; the strikes are usually broken by a well-known labour leader called Ernest Bevin, who is in the Government, and not by the Conservatives, who affect to stand back so that the putting down of the strike may not be described as class warfare. They increase the men's wages! I suppose the increase is later duly recovered from the men and sent to the Party Fund.'

'Politically and constitutionally the situation is difficult to explain in terms intelligible to us. For instance, they have made what they called a party truce, and this has been, on the whole, respected. Yet when a woman member of the Liberal Party (they still have a Liberal Party) decided to break the truce by standing for Parliament, when she should not have done so, not only did she remain at large, not only was she not even sent back to her kitchen, but it really looked as though the whole might of the State could not prevail over her feminine whim. This may be an instance of democratic degeneracy, though I have not been able to ascertain that she stood in high personal favour with the English Führer. Apart from this truce, they have made no political or constitutional revolution, which is not surprising among an unimaginative people. Parliament still functions, except that parliamentary week-ends are much longer than in peace-time. The assembly often has to give way to the Executive but I have a feeling that if it came to a real show-down the Executive might not get the better of Parliament.'

'They call the war a people's war, but it is led by a descendant of Marlborough, and, unless I am much mistaken, he loves to find precedents in tradition and history, for I observed that his speeches, particularly in 1940, were strongly reminiscent of those of the Earl of Chatham. The extraordinary thing is that he allows people and newspapers to tell him that he may not be their leader for life and that the whole question must be reconsidered when the war is won. (They still pretend to believe this possible.) There are, of course, many striking contradictions in their way of living, although the English themselves do not seem to bother about them. For instance they still observe such medieval customs as introducing peers into the House of Lords according to an ancient ritual, and they have their Lord Mayor's show in the City of London as an assertion of local City rights. Yet they go to such modern extremes as to appoint women to state offices and to organize collective life in factories and hostels in order to achieve greater concentration of their industrial power. And all the while in the same House of Lords, peers discuss the best means of protecting individual freedom, as though it could matter to them anyhow! In general, Englishmen always seem to go on arguing about rights, privileges, liberties and such like, and in this respect their Führer, although he occasionally bullies them, seems to be as foolish as any. Perhaps these discussions amount to no more than an hypocritical way of screening their war effort by pretending to think of something else.'

'Many people here debate what they call socialism, and millions of them seem to consider it quite natural to preach it and yet to defend their monarchic system all the same. Indeed, their monarchy seems to be the only thing which English people do not argue about, save for a few men on the extreme Left who look to me as though they would feel very embarrassed if the régime they advocate came to pass. As to the role of the monarchy in war-time, this is the most baffling feature of a baffling country. You would have expected the English King to take advantage of the war and claim his right to Führership. Yet he seems content with watching others exercise power! Some people at home might put this down to lack of a proper political education, while the English, with their habitual self-complacency, call it respect for the Constitution. I, for one, suspect that he must be a very wily man and that there is some trick behind it all, for who has ever heard of a man who would not seize power if he could get it (and he had all the trumps in his hands) or of a people who show such devotion to a man and yet would not follow him blindly? And how some of them can talk of socialism on such terms would be incomprehensible, if one did not know that there are subtle and far-reaching arrangements behind these apparent contradictions and complexities. The clue is probably to be found in a book which the English affect to treat as a children's tale but which is obviously a disguised handbook for prospective Führers. It is called *Chronicles of Pantouflia* and has been written by a Scottish Machiavelli named Andrew Lang. I shall merely quote the last sentences in the first part ('Prince Prigio') to prove my point: "Then he said aloud: 'I wish to seem no cleverer than other people!' Then he ran downstairs and the Princess noticed a great difference in him (though of course there was really none at all) and so did everyone. For the Prince remained as clever as ever he had been; but as nobody observed it, he became the most popular prince and finally the best beloved king who had ever sat on the throne of Pantouflia." I remembered this the other day when listening to their Chancellor of the Exchequer. He was comparing figures of expenses and receipts and spoke with well feigned candour as though he really was foolish enough to believe that his budget could ever be balanced. He knew it could not, of course, but made it appear he was not clever enough to see through his own statement of accounts. And nobody dared to say anything really damaging because he appeared to act under such honest self-delusion. We know, of course, that England will never be able to pay for the war on the basis of a non-totalitarian economy. She has done so by a trick so far but somebody will have to pay. I *do* wonder who it will be?'

This fanciful picture claims to do no more than set in relief some of the contrasts between the tendencies and features of England at war: social innovations, yet the preservation of ancient customs; centralization of power, yet regard for local privileges; far-reaching mobilization combined with tolerance; overburdened economy without abandonment of fiscal ortho-doxy; medieval attachments and bold projects of reform; unity of effort and political differences: all these are permitted and co-exist at the present time here and nowhere else in Europe.

Given the factors which determined Great Britain's defiant gesture in 1940 and made a successful struggle possible, and given the capital fact of the Channel barrier, I would set the maintenance of constitutional, social and political diversity as next in importance among the great causes contributory to the British success. First, the impact of war, at its worst, did not produce either a cleavage of opinion or a breach in the nation's morale, because the régime, whatever faults Englishmen find with it in detail, remained elastic and 'liveable'; because its diversity and flexibility prevented it from being, like the French, strained to the utmost limit even before the supreme test. Second, this constitutional flexibility has practical, as well as moral and psychological, advantages: it allows the Executive to be strong and to act strongly, for the very reason that citizens enjoy enough safeguards against abuse of power to allow that power to be used if needed. One of the most important results of executive strength or stability[1] is the good quality of the permanent services[2] which in this war have been a decisive

---

[1] The pre-war Executive was weak but stable, with the result that the permanent fighting services worked unimpeded.

[2] This involves a danger, as I tried to show in Chapter X. With regard to the fighting services, the latitude they enjoyed happened to be a godsend considering the shortcomings of the political Executive and the, then, weakness of Parliament.

factor in British defence. Before the war the permanent services
of the Air Ministry and the Admiralty largely atoned for their
quantitative unpreparedness—the fault of the government—by
their technical foresight and managing ability. In particular
the creation, within a very few years and against political odds,
not only of an air fleet highly efficient in technique and staff but
of an air tradition which rivalled the centuries-old naval tradition and gave the Old Wooden Walls their modern counterpart,
must be acknowledged as a startling feat. Its decisive effect can,
again, be judged in comparison with France, which also
possessed highly skilled technicians and designers of aircraft
but suffered from an air policy deeply vitiated by governmental
instability.

Taking all these points into account, one may well say that
the institutional flexibility and the consequent stability which
Britain still enjoyed at the time of her hardest ordeal have been
the foremost factors in her success; and these, as witness other
nations' vicissitudes, can only flourish in a diverse and heterogeneous context.

However, the fact that these assets stood Britain in good stead
by preparing her to 'shock-absorb' the impact, does not imply
that they have remained altogether unimpaired by the war or
that they must in any case survive it. All conflicts, and the
present one more than any before, cause a hardening of the
country's institutional life, a kind of arterio-sclerosis of its institutions, which all converge towards the same end and, as a
result, lose much of their versatility. Parliament, Law, local
government, trade unions, parties, economic and financial organization, all tend to become cogs in the war machine instead
of living organs with different functions and distinct identities.
That process has gone much less far in England than elsewhere,
for each institution has been able to live, so to speak, on its
reserves and to go on striving for its rights as well as contributing
to the prosecution of the war. But reserves are not inexhaustible,
and any people at war, even the constitutionally sensitive
British people, show greater care for victory than for the safeguarding of their national customs or characteristics. They may
demand that Parliament should exercise a vigilant control of
affairs, but they will expect Parliament to give up that right
if it clashes with the superior advantage of, say, military secrecy.
They will wish the Law to uphold justice, but they would

question the decision of any judge who set a point of professional integrity above the immediate interest of the community. They accepted the release of a Mosley presumed guilty, in the belief that he probably could not do much harm, but they might well resent the release of another Mosley presumably innocent if, though legally unimpeachable, he were harmful in fact. Labour still stands for various rights but does not allow them to trespass on the field of war requirements. In other words, the guardianship of the rights of the Constitution and of society, however singularly alive the English may be to it, cannot, in war-time, be more than a secondary object. The sacrifices of their rights, and even of their identity, which institutions are thus obliged to make to the conduct of the war, inevitably alter the balance of the nation's life by impairing the relative value and character of each institution. Diversity of functions tends to give way to uniformity, multifariousness to one-way traffic.

This in itself may be of little consequence if the process ends with the conflict. Where this development is of more serious import is when it happens to coincide, as it does at present, with a European tendency towards social uniformity and constitutional simplification chiefly on the bureaucratic basis. Mechanical efficiency has come to be rated higher than freedom, refrigerators to be more desirable than independence of thought. Régimes capable of achieving the maximum efficiency and of producing the greatest number of refrigerators per family, may well become as popular when peace has returned as in war-time were those which turned out war equipment the fastest. In that respect régimes of great social and political diversity may well be under a severe handicap as compared with powerfully centralized systems able to throw every single value into the melting pot in the supreme quest of efficiency. Whether English opinion will follow this line of political development remains to be seen.

I, for one, am inclined to think that whatever attraction such a conception of life may at present exercise on a good many English minds is but a passing mood.[1] As John Buchan observes

[1] It would be interesting to find out to what extent the 'Love-in-a-luxury-flat' type of cheaper American films has affected the English public. Very markedly no doubt, and it is a theme worth more than a passing reference. It is however reassuring to note that at the time when the United States entered the war, there was a wholesome American reaction against that dangerous species of drug.

in his *Montrose*, 'Human nature, and expecially English human nature, invincibly tends towards a duality'; and that deep-rooted 'doubleness' of the English temperament still constitutes a safeguard against any drive towards uniformity—that very uniformity against which, consciously or not, Great Britain has taken arms and already fought for five years.

The problem is worth considering from another angle, that of the country's social and political evolution during the war.

CHAPTER 21

THE PEOPLE AND THE FUTURE

IF the story of the Sleeping Beauty were retold in contemporary idiom, the most interesting part would be the description of the awakening castle. What would be the reactions of a whole cross-section of society overtaken by time and how would it behave in a century of which it knew nothing? In many countries, one effect of total war has been to put all sorts of thoughts, pursuits and occupations to sleep for years and thus to postpone certain processes of development until they can be resumed in another age—for war years travel fast and unexpectedly. What may then be their subsequent course is, in many respects, as conjectural as the behaviour of the awakened inmates of the Sleeping Castle. This applies to most European countries, many of whose national pursuits were interrupted by the will of their leaders or by the accidents of fate. England, on the other hand, thanks both to geography and to political wisdom, was able to save her people from the prick of the fatal spindle. England at war lived as England. The 'agitation, the din', which Jules Maurel described as characteristic of England during the Napoleonic wars, when repression deferred development everywhere else, are still noticeable in this war. They are manifestations of life within a nation which allows itself a modicum of freedom and latitude. The effect of this traditional practice is to make post-war revolutions improbable, since revolutions are chiefly due to the forcible repression of tendencies which must eventually find outlets in extreme thinking and violent action. With the possible exceptions of Sweden and Switzerland, England is very nearly the sole European country whose natural development has not been crippled by the fact of war; she is the only European belligerent who has *fait 'la part du feu'* socially and politically. So that despite many inevitable restrictions and limitations upon freedom, the trend of evolution here remains in general an open, though a somewhat confused, book.

Of that book perhaps the most significant feature lies in the conflict of tendencies bearing on post-war issues. It is not easy

to define the terms of the conflict, nor even to draw a clear line
between the antagonists. The bone of contention is, broadly
speaking, the sense of the word 'progress' or, as many would
call it, of the word 'Left' in social and political life. This in itself
is not unique in twentieth-century 'democracies'. What we are
concerned with, however, is its English aspect and this we may
approach by way of the story of David Low's camel and afterwards of the incident of Aneurin Bevan.[1]

The camel in one of Low's cartoons, was the British Parliament, loaded with a huge burden of piled up legislation. The
intended inference was clear. Parliament cannot carry the
control of everything but should discharge part of the weight
onto Specialists. These specialists are the bureaucracy, eager to
help the camel—at a price: the price of their own expansion
and increased power. The Bevan incident, irrespective of Mr.
Bevan's own merits or ideas, illustrates an aspect of the problem,
different yet related to the first, namely: what is to be meant by
the Opposition? Is this to be a well marshalled, thoroughly disciplined regiment, an officialdom in temporary opposition, a
provisionally non-conformist conformity? Or an active, variegated combination of men each entitled to individual thinking,
even to the point of dissenting from the main body? Now what
is the connexion between Mr. Bevan and Low's camel? It is
this: that both those who wanted a light-travelling camel and
Mr. Bevan's would-be expellers were acting on the same underlying belief in the simplification of institutions, the same conviction that the infinite complexity of modern problems can
best be solved by the process of simplifying the means of dealing
with these problems. Compel Mr. Bevan to toe the party line
and you have simplified the Labour Party by total discipline.
Unload the Parliamentary camel by generalizing state-control
and bureaucracy and you will have simplified the constitutional
problem until the range of state action is so comprehensive that
Parliament is reduced to a debating society and there is no
problem at all. On the other hand the course of disciplining a
particular Mr. Bevan shirks instead of solving the issue raised
by the existence of many thinking Bevans, whether their think-

[1] Mr. Aneurin Bevan was accused of repeatedly violating Labour Party
discipline and the question of his retention within the party gave rise to a
long controversy, in the early months of 1943, involving both his own position and a grave issue of principle.

ing be right or wrong; and the fact of unloading the camel does not dispose of the load but entrusts it to an anonymous body which may run away with it or bury it. For Low's cartoon is not, as the melancholy look of the pictured beast intended to suggest a Case for the Camel, but a Case Against the Camel. The true case for the Camel is better illustrated by a fable of, I believe, Indian origin, in which a tortoise overburdened with her cumbersome shell is persuaded to sell it to a grass snake for whatever is the local equivalent of a lettuce, with the immediate result that a ravenous vulture swoops on her unprotected body and devours it. The burden of Parliamentary duties is not only a weight but a shield, for the volume of transactions is the measure of Parliament's effective control over the nation's affairs and, vicariously, the measure of popular control. A characteristically English reaction to Low's cartoon would be to get a stronger camel, a larger Parliament which through its various committees could deal with an increased range of problems, rather than to dump the load where nobody can check its contents and its disposal. A characteristically English reaction to Mr. Bevan's dissidence would be to take his views as a fact, palatable or not, but a fact that coercion might harden and not eliminate. In that light the first vote on the maintenance of Mr. Bevan within the party was undoubtedly wise. The escape, however, was narrow and neither on the issue of principle then involved nor on the question of the camel's future has the final word been said.

All periods of moral and political uncertainty produce dogmatic attitudes, for dogmas provide positive (though arbitrary) values to which men can cling. They also produce a consequent intolerance. The present period is no exception. A strong current of dogmatism and a degree of intolerance are equally apparent in the English 'Left'. The main dogmatic tenet is the belief in the value of State Control as a remedy for capitalistic excesses and for social inequality generally. Its corollary is an inordinate faith (inordinate for Englishmen) in the virtues of comprehensive, all embracing Planning with a capital P. The effect of this doctrinal outlook is to brand all opposition either to State Control or to Planning as something in the nature of Reactionary Heresy in the eyes of those of the True Faith. They are inclined to lump all opponents into the category of Cigar-Gold-Chain-Top-Hat-Supercapitalists who form the stock-in-trade of overworked cartoonists. They are equally intransigeant in their views on foreign problems and towards foreign men or groups who do not make use of a similar vocabulary. Against this dogmatic trend there is now apparent among the Lefts a counter-current which runs closer to the traditional English outlook of freedom and doctrinal flexibility. The line of demarcation between the two sides is not fixed, nor does it correspond to a lesser or greater degree of 'Leftism'. To invoke an historic parallel, I would suggest the existence among the Left of a more English distinction than that between more or less 'advanced' views. Democracy, as understood by the Left, has its Puritans and its Cavaliers: the former intent on their State Creed as the Covenanters on their Gospel of Salvation and, consequently, on sharp dogmatic distinctions between parties; the latter have, like the Cavaliers, a more flexible conception of life, and admit in modern party politics an elasticity which to them is the charter of true democratic legitimacy. Will that duality eventually resolve itself into a compromise, the Dogmatists shedding their wildest theories, the Traditionalists their worst encumbrances? Or will England suffer the familiar evils attending a profound division of the Left? Or, again, will the war cause a reshuffling of parties, a sequel suggested both by the Leftward trend of many Conservatives, and by the reluctance of a part of the Left to champion undiluted Socialism? The answer will emerge in a post-war environment yet to be shaped, in which such capital facts as the duration of the conflict and the length of the casualty lists will count decisively.

The practical effects of the war itself are diverse and contradictory, and there is nothing to prove that party guidance or party programmes either reflect or determine the popular trend of thought on social and political problems. To take a few instances of that diversity and these contradictions: Parliament in war-time tends to be submissive to the Executive for reasons of national discipline; but on the other hand the very necessity for discipline creates, at least in England, a deep yearning for freedom of action, for the right to dissent from officialdom or from the party line. Again, industrial concentration has enlarged the scope of collective life by setting up huge workmen's hostels, but the very experience of communal existence provokes a reaction in favour of individual or family life which is also stimulated by the war-time encouragement of rural pursuits.

Likewise, conscription produced a merger of classes, yet the hierarchy of the army—gradually evolved according to social, educational or technical status—is not conducive to equality and social levelling. Class-consciousness, in the same way, was at first strengthened by the conflict, inasmuch as equality of sacrifice in blood breeds resentment against inequality of social and economic position; but, conversely, the war puts a premium on technical skill and tends to create an aristocracy of the working class which may make a deep inroad into working-class solidarity.[1] Finally, to take account of an important external factor, Russia's marked departure from orthodox Marxism may well alter, if not altogether cancel, the sort of ideological influence which she exercised on the English working class by virtue of her brilliant fighting record.

In trying to distinguish what is temporary or superficial from what may be lasting, in the trends of thought of England at war, one important fact must be borne in mind. The English people have a strong sense of contract as between the government and the governed, and of its right to ensure that its sacrifices shall be both justified and rewarded. That sense is not dulled by war, but sharpened. Other nations engaged may be exclusively concerned with the degree of enemy penetration into their territory. The English fight too, but they also want to know the positive as well as the negative, or defensive, aim of the conflict. What are they fighting for? What is to be done after the war? On what terms of contract between rulers and ruled are they toiling and struggling? Those questions exercise English more forcefully than Continental minds. Though such preoccupations were temporarily eclipsed by the events of June 1940, they resumed their hold on the people as soon as the worst peril had receded. When questions like these are asked and no ready answer is available, the inclination of governments may well be to improvise answers in order to placate popular feeling and avoid demoralization, while politicians or self-appointed Tribunes of the People are tempted to raise further questions and to stir up popular demands for yet more comprehensive details. In the present war and in the state of sharp ideological awareness in

[1] There is a strong current in England towards enhancing the social status of skilled workmen and bringing them to social parity with 'white-collar workmen', a tendency naturally encouraged by Conservative thinkers as counteracting the class-against-class ideology.

Europe, to tell the English people that they were fighting for their skins did not prove an adequate reply. 'For our civilization' might have filled the bill, if that civilization and the threat to it had been clearly defined. No convincing definition was however given, and the result was to turn the question of war aims, both as regards its internal and its external implications, into a running controversy. Broad and somewhat vague programmes, often improvised in haste, cropped up from official and non-official Brains Trusts, ranging from sound plans for the rebuilding of London to less sound recipes for the rebuilding of the world according to regional spheres, continental or trans-oceanic circles, and other geometrical figures. Voices were heard at the microphone, in the press and even on the stage, preaching revolutionary ideals, proclaiming the indisputable right of heroes to enter the gate of the City of the Future, but unfortunately refraining from revealing where lay its key. The familiar voices were heard hawking elusive ideals which, like drink to Macbeth's porter, 'provoke the desire but take away the performance'. In such discussions of post-war aims, it is not easy to distinguish the deep current from the mere froth on agitated waters. A strong English demand is often wrapped in temporary ideologies knitted together by amateur reformers. Better standards of education and health, a greater participation of the people in the management of its economy, security for the young and the aged: these no doubt are solid and purposeful claims rightly strengthened by the war. Full State control, comprehensive planning from Brighton to John o' Groats and from cradle to grave: to what extent do these represent more than a sectional tendency or passing desire for totally organized life in contrast to the total uncertainty of the fighting man's existence? To strike at the sort of conservatism which, disguised as traditionalism, is, in fact, a sordid attachment to financial interests, is to strike to good purpose; yet the war-time tendency to hit out at random at anything that offends the eye of full-blooded social levellers is an idle and purely demagogic gesture. A sound community eventually finds its feet in the world of ideas as in the world of action. Fighting England did it as from July 1940. Thinking England is beginning to do it in the fifth and sixth years of hostilities. Ideological growths in a war-time hot-house, and awkward graftings from the branches of alien dogmas, are now beginning to wither. The lively scepticism which keeps a check on occasional flights of political imagination is already helping to sort out sound practical possibilities from shoddy demagogic fancy ware.

As usual, the English national pattern is less likely to be influenced by theorists than by hard facts and recorded experience. Behind emotional controversies experiments are made and Parliamentary work done which will probably be of far greater consequence than the hazy schemes conjured up by the Universal Planners. In industry the system of Joint Production Committees and Regional Councils set up for the purpose of ensuring running efficiency suggests a new basis for economic control: that of industrial parliaments ranging from the factory to the regional unit, in which all interested parties, workmen, employers and unions would be represented, provided always this does not detract from the rights of labour and the unions. On a broadened basis and with a larger scope of action this system might be a flexible, parliamentary, method of economic control as an alternative to the tentacular growth of State bureaucracy. On the other hand the State control of war industries may well have come to stay, for the case against it seems to be very weak. The present encouragement, under pressure of war needs, of farming and rural pursuits should certainly become a fixed feature of the national life in a country whose urban development is excessive. In the field of education, initiatives taken for war purposes, such as the Army Education Corps, ABCA, the organization of lectures and plays for workers' communities, have all evoked a popular interest which is the best justification for a general reform of education. The development of health services, also prompted by the war, has established the need for wide reforms in that field also. Many features of the Beveridge Plan are likely to take root. Whether the whole Plan will prevail depends not only on votes cast for or against it but on the strength of a post-war Exchequer which, in its turn, depends on the duration of the conflict and the extent of the consequent mortgage on the national revenue. In general, future organization and legislation are likely to embody lessons from experience in every branch of social activity, rather than articles in programmes laid down on dogmatic lines. To take a case in point, dogmatic reformers would strike equally hard at mining royalties and at the system of tenant farming on the ground that both are anti-socialist. Yet, while experience indicates that the former is a burdensome abuse, the latter is considered by many farmers and landworkers (who, after all, are primarily concerned) as preferable to either State ownership or excessive sub-division of the land. This is where usage would draw the line between reforms of proven value and mere dogmatic importunity.

However, speculation, even if sound, as to what may emerge from present experiences, undertakings and projects probably does not lead very far. What will shape post-war England is the sum total of individual experiences and trends of thought. These may change and vary before the conflict is over, but there are already simmering thoughts, emotions, and interests which are very inadequately expressed by pronouncements from the platform, the microphone, the stage, the screen. For all these offer, and probably must offer, stereotypes rather than realities. Present-day England is sharper, more vehement, less conformist, more acutely aware, more demanding, less resigned, far less attached to conventions, more moody socially and morally than pre-war England. Discounting what is purely temporary and, even more generally, what is part of a war atmosphere, some of these tendencies may well manifest themselves in post-war generations, if not among those whose habits were already crystallized at the outbreak of the conflict. The younger English men and women are more tolerant or more inquisitive in their personal and emotional lives; less tolerant, more critical, less 'live and let live' in their social-political outlook. Intellectually their interests, though more intermittent, perhaps more temperamental, are often well ahead of what chance interpreters of a people at war seem to think. Granted that the return to peace will settle each separate existence in its social pigeonhole, much of the English social and moral conformity, with its credit and debit side, will have gone. Certainly the still powerful Puritan framework has been shaken, were it only by the impact on it of so many years of social and sexual promiscuity. The general yearning for constructive action and new knowledge must have contradictory effects: intellectually it may cause an indiscriminate absorption of superficial rubbish as well as of sound learning; politically it may produce gullibility in the face of demagogic clichés as well as a keen desire to build; socially it may encourage the discarding of good traditions as well as of lumber. But the yearning is there and will somehow have to be gratified. That is the task of the *élite*. It is one that recurrently presents itself after a war, and the past teaches that when a nation does not find within itself an *élite* capable of discharging its duty, it is tempted to fall back on the State as dispenser of political, social, moral and intellectual instruction and amenities. In regard to matters of life and government, the post-war Englishman is likely to show less resignation, passive or good humoured, than his predecessor, largely, perhaps because he will have less philosophy and may, for a time, expect more from the outside world and be less self-secluded. His non-accepting bent may be brought to bear alike on the casual and on the essential problems of life: on the tyranny of hotel managements who treat him like an inmate in a reformatory, on the fabulous cost of medical treatment and legal proceedings, on the inadequacy of old-age pensions, as well as on such larger matters as foreign policy in Iraq; and without doubt the attitude of Englishmen on such a point as licensing hours may reveal significantly their social attitude of mind, an attitude more questioning, more critical, less benevolent than it was—which does not mean either less human or less generous—about things in general.

What will emerge from all this? A diverse, resilient, lively society, if that potential energy finds proper outlets; a sense of frustration which inclines a people to remit its interests and responsibilities to the State, if that energy remains unspent. This, then, is the inevitable conclusion: the answer is with the *élite*, with the post-war *élite* which may come home from Italy, Syria, the Western front, as well as from the heart of England. The answer will lie with members of Parliament, with the nature of its opposition as well as of its leadership, with lawyers, doctors, writers, playwrights, cinema producers; it will depend on what they do and say and write; on whether their contribution is diverse, conscientious, calculated to keep a society alive and moving, or merely facile and mass-minded, turning society into a State-regulated community, sterile and inhuman.

Perhaps the paramount fact of English post-war evolution will be this: that, for several years, no currents of thought have traversed the European continent. For some time, therefore, England will have to be wholly creative and self-reliant in the shaping of her own intellectual and moral features. This is a situation seldom found in the history of any European nation.

There is much mental activity in occupied countries, but its fruit may take long before it is, if not obvious, at least assimilable. And meanwhile England alone in Western Europe has been able to experiment, to think freely, to live freely. From the tortured experience of other nations she may, later, have much to learn. What, however, she, alone in Western Europe, does or can retain, is a sense of continuity, of the continuity of Western society, of the diverse pattern of life. That is what she has protected and can show. Any Totalitarian country could display—even though posthumously—a brilliant record of State-regulated life. The English nation can show her record of life preserved and war conducted by human diversity. When her people return to internal pursuits, her leaders and her *élite* must at the same time turn towards the outside world. And at that moment her fate, what she makes of her own life and institutions, may well be as vital to Europe as was her gesture of defiance in June 1940.

CHAPTER 22

WHAT is to be England's way once the German enemy has been overcome? What will her name stand for, what will be her part in a liberated Europe? That largely depends on her. To say that isolation is no longer possible is not enough. To say that she is ready to participate in the operation of some system of collective security is only begging the question: on what understanding and to what purpose will she co-operate? Even now the old British dilemma between a European and a non-European destiny reappears in the very speeches of her statesmen. Is Europe to be England's primary concern? Does she conceive herself as a European power with world-wide interests or as a world power interested in Europe only as a secondary concern? We hear at one and the same time that the salvation and reconstruction of Europe are the conditions precedent to the establishment of any world order and, on the other hand, that European and world interests together are to be entrusted to the United States, the British Empire, the U.S.S.R. and China. Let there be no misunderstanding about this: the two notions are absolutely incompatible in practice. Whatever assurances may be given that a Big Four policy in no way means a directorate of the four powers, it is as such that it will be interpreted and rejected by the European continent. The England of 1940 entered the European family as England never had in the past. Strategically England was alone for a year. Morally and sentimentally she had never been closer to the heart and reality that is Europe.

What is now at stake and may be imperilled by the Big Four policy is the European prestige which that gesture earned her. And what is at stake too is the permanence of Europe as her diversified self: for the Old Continent has suffered so much that, failing a British contribution and a whole-hearted one, it will seek another solution which will be self-centred, which will impair her many-sided character. That Europe was able to survive was largely due to the survival of England. That England's fight was successful was largely due to the fact that

Europe rejected the German heresy and refused to form an unbreakable unit around Germany. Never before in history had the European reality asserted itself with such force as in this struggle of unarmed men against an all-powerful enemy. Never before had England's struggle more closely coincided with, and belonged to, the historic resistance of Europe against uniformity. Now that Great Britain's fight has been backed, and successfully backed, by extra-European and partly European powers, her policy tends to stress her world-wide pursuits and associations rather than her European reality, save perhaps in so far as operational necessities on the Continent turn the thoughts of a statesman towards this or that nation of Europe. It is understandable that post-war problems should be particularly complex. For the allegiance of the British nation is divided between European and extra-European interests, between her vision of extra-European strength and the temporary spectacle of weakness in the European framework. There is no question, of course, of an imperial power whose world pattern presents a unique example of international government abandoning its worldwide pursuits. But England must know where her centre of gravity truly lies. Her policy and aims will become clearer to herself only as she achieves a clear consciousness of her own nature and of her significance. Never has the old motto, γνῶθι σεαυτόν—Know Thyself—carried a more urgent message. No English war or peace aim can be of permanent value or even make sense unless England knows what she is, to what she belongs, and what is most essential in her own destiny.

It often happens that a country tentatively frames a policy on temporary wishes and slogans, but her permanent policy is shaped according to her own instincts and national determination. Many of the peace aims recently discussed or contemplated amount to little more than a projection on the future of passing ideas and changing moods. Some of these ideas may materialize; some of these moods may last. Yet most of them are as yet no more than a shapeless vision, attractive perhaps, but subject to variations. Take the two following facts: on the one hand the profound will of the English nation to fight on in June 1940 and on the other those world conceptions evolved thereafter, such as the notion of the Big Four. Which is the stronger of the two? Certainly the former. In June 1940 England fought as her own self as a civilized Western nation. That fact carries more weight than any conception of the future contingent on what may happen hereafter. That is the truly firm ground, indeed, the bedrock. She fought for what she was, as herself and as part of a European scheme of life and thought. Let us try to describe what this was and also against what kind of menace England fought: for the character of the danger is certainly relevant to the nature and purpose of the struggle.

However she may differ in habits, moods, or superficial ways of living from most European countries, England accepts like them and more than most of them, these tenets:

That the individual is not merely the subject of the State Executive but is an object in himself.

That the State must not be stronger than the society which it represents and must not turn that society into a regulated machine.

That, whether by law or consensus of opinion, the rule of the majority must be tempered by the protection of the rights and convictions of the minority.

That every man is entitled to hold and profess his own moral, political and religious beliefs, irrespective of the prevailing policy of the Executive, provided that he does not attempt to force them upon others.

That the object of the State is to serve and not to coerce the community, and that, consequently, persecution or discrimination between citizens on racial or religious grounds is not permissible, nor justifiable by reasons of state; and that socially, politically, internationally, the weak have equal rights, if not equal means, with the strong.

It is in the nature of man that such principles should often be violated in practice. Yet these convictions have become axiomatic in the West. They are part of our living atmosphere, of the air we breathe, and, perhaps, for that reason, we sometimes become unconscious of our vital need of them. In London, Paris, Athens, Oslo, The Hague, men will fight and die for their defence. Whether we are Catholics or Protestants, whether we use the decimal or duo-decimal system, whether we are Monarchists or Republicans, whether we cut our potatoes with a knife or with a fork, drink tea or coffee in the morning, drive on the right or on the left-hand side of the road, our reactions are identical when these tenets are seriously transgressed or threatened. In Germany, on the other hand, a man may accept the supreme sacrifice for many reasons, including some which would make an Englishman or a Frenchman smile. He may fight for his land, more often, alas, for that of others, for his wages, his farm, or his party, but he is not likely to fight for these principles nor even to bother much about their maintenance. He only cares about their violation when the eventual result happens to be the kind of fate which now awaits the German nation.

It is imperative to recall these things, for Englishmen have often been more aware of the striking contrasts between themselves and, say, the French, in manners, habits or practices, than of the fundamental contrasts between themselves and the Germans, which lie deep beneath a few apparent similarities. The same Frenchman whose habits may superficially be so alien to an Englishman, will give his life for the same motive and like him sacrifice it in a forlorn venture where neither national nor individual interests are at stake. Like him too, irrespective of religious beliefs or particular codes of conduct, he appreciates and respects individual life and thought which is above race, herd, sect, nation or dogma. Insularity may often blind Englishmen to the strong ethical links that bind them to other nations of Western Europe or the Mediterranean seaboard, nor, in the norma course of events, would the average Englishman attach any importance to those links. He would be more likely to grumble at the lack of telephone boxes in the streets of Paris than to be attracted by the French love of individual liberty. On this inconspicuous but overriding community of profound beliefs and inspirations, a European block has however been formed in the last tragic years of European history. It has been formed against Germany and not in support of Germany as would have happened if only the daily interests and superficial habits of men had been at stake and if Europe had only thought in terms of physical and social advantages. It is because of the ethical revolt of Europe that Germany suffered her first defeat not only in the Battle of Britain but in the failure of her New Order. Nor would the assistance of Russia and America, powerful though it was, have broken Germany if Europe had surrendered her soul.

England both shares and enriches the Western way of living

and thinking, by what in her political and social outlook is specifically hers, belonging to her own historic development, as an island of Western Europe. Apart from her generally Western features, she has her own singular ones. She lays more emphasis than the Continent on some aspects of tradition, and on the value of traditional as against orthodox institutions. Her life and, to some extent, her policy, has long been guided by an *élite*, partly aristocratic, more than by the State. She vests greater power in society and less in the State. She had a simpler party system, one that allows for successive party governments rather than for composite ones. Finally and above all, she has hitherto relied more than any other European nation on unwritten social codes and less on imposed regulations. To take an example borrowed from everyday life, any passenger in England—even in war-time—may buy a cup of tea in Salisbury, carry it into his compartment, and leave the cup there at Barnstaple. He can drink his tea at leisure instead of gulping it on the platform because whoever owns the crockery trusts to the social sense of the passengers. The result is an economy of controlling personnel. Extend the principle to matters of greater moment (if any matter may be of greater moment to Englishmen than tea drinking) and you have the difference between a community regulated to the last dot and overburdened with written rules, and one which is self-regulated by sheer respect of the social contract and which saves its energies for more creative or enjoyable activities than the control of citizens by other citizens. This principle of self-regulation which demands not only a code but a tradition is a characteristically English contribution to progress. It is one which does not defeat its own purpose as does a comprehensive control of life which, by making the performance of duty compulsory, divests it of all moral or social value and thus destroys the very basis of human progress.

What England stood for in June 1940, she did not have to define precisely because it was real and deeprooted. It was what was essentially Western in her, whether or not in a specifically English way. What she fought for was not a social or political state of things open to criticism like any other, but her right to alter that state of things in her own way, according to her own conception of development. It is stupid to say that because as late as 1939 a good many people were still destitute and a

R

greater number on the dole, the régime was not worth defending; or that alternatively England was only worth defending in so far as a remedy for all social and economic evils was guaranteed by the government. Social and economic injustice is shocking, but it is not everything and it is not only for a régime that civilized men fight. It was one of the enemy's cleverest strokes of propaganda in Allied countries to place the problem of war and peace on the social plane, as though a civilized nation only existed in terms of an index of prices and wages. To exploit the social differences of our time was all the shrewder on the part of Germany since she herself had been in a virtual state of war since 1933, and thus, by the simple process of mobilizing everybody for war purposes appeared to have solved her own social problem. (She hoped to solve it later at our expense by the even simpler process of turning Europe into a two-class community with Germans for aristocracy and the rest for Plebs.) For Western Europe the social question, although it did in fact rankle and make inroads into public morale, was not the sole issue at stake in 1939. Individual, political, daily liberties, ethical values, the elasticity of the régime, the right to change, revise, reform, complain, dissent, all these were at stake. An English worker may be on the dole, and hate his fate and the powers that be on account of it. Yet there is nothing inexorable in that fate. A German worker on the contrary buys a temporary security at the price of all these other values, and he can only enjoy it in as long as he remains compliant. National Socialist Germany never understood that anybody in Europe could wish more than to be fed and drilled daily, physically and mentally. Still less did she expect men to fight for régimes socially and economically inequitable. Yet what Western Europe fought for, and went on fighting for despite military defeats, was not a social and economic state of affairs existing at a given moment, but a permanent way of living, thinking, grumbling, discussing, which transcends the social and economic state of affairs at any particular time. The Western struggle was chiefly ethical and England, socially the most inegalitarian of all Western states, remained the most adamant before German propaganda precisely because she was defending her values, traditions and diversity rather than a rigid social and economic order.

Those values, traditions and that diversity, were above all

the real object of Germany's attack. Her threat was aimed at
the Western world and all that it stood for. It was not so much
England's wealth that Germany wanted to destroy. It was
England's value to the West. France and the Low Countries
and part of Scandinavia once overcome, Italy and Spain disguised in their respective shirts, the defence of this diversity,
identified with the Western world, and which in the past Germany has repeatedly tried to destroy, was left to England alone,
since through England's defeat the German dream of uniformity would have been fulfilled. Western civilization, Western
individualism, Western spiritual strength would have gone.
Germany was to have the run of Europe, turned into a parade
ground for her armies of pseudo-philosophers, for her intellectual and moral goose-stepping. Germany's target was the West,
far more than Russia, whose territories she may have coveted,
but whose collective outlook she considered adaptable to her
own.[1]

It was this profound antagonism, the German herd conception
of the world opposed to the English championship of diversity,
which, despite new and confusing elements, gave and still gives
its true character to the present conflict. To misread that character would involve losing the benefits of victory, nullifying the
sacrifices borne by millions of men and would perhaps lead to
a third world war. The English struggle was clearly, whether
intentionally or not, the defence of the West and of England's
Western self. The German struggle was for the annihilation of
the West. These facts are apt to be confused or eclipsed by
ideological notions which in the course of the conflict have been
superimposed on the fundamental issue and which must be
clarified.

It is often said that the present struggle is 'a revolution', or that
the war is a revolutionary war. Nobody, however, has seriously
attempted to elucidate that statement, one that, according to its
meaning is either self-evident or unfounded. If it means that the
war did and will bring great changes in its wake, it applies in
varying degrees to all wars. If on the other hand the term 'revolutionary' suggests, as it properly should, that this war has been
waged for the purpose of defending or enforcing a revolutionary

[1] An inadequate view, no doubt, for Russian collectivism does not exclude
recognition and protection of diversity in fields other than the social and
economic.

state of things, that is an equivocation. The only country which entered the war with a revolutionary programme was Germany. Her internal programme was revolutionary inasmuch as she used revolutionary methods to ensure her ethical as well as her physical preparation for war; her revolution was in fact a new and unprecedentedly thorough form of mobilization. Her external programme was revolutionary in that it planned the absorption of Europe and its subsequent division into a racial hierarchy with the *Herrenvolk* at the head, a division by castes ranging from the Mastermen to the Untouchables. Italy's revolution was completed in 1923 and her only revolutionary aim in the war was to grab some land in the wake of the German armies. There is nothing new or revolutionary in that. As to the Allies, which of them was defending a revolutionary order or avowedly aiming at one? War-time demands for reforms do not constitute a revolutionary objective, and the very difficulty which all the Allied powers have experienced in defining any political aims beyond the acceleration of reforms already discussed before the war eloquently demonstrates that no premeditated revolutionary plan was afoot or had a bearing on their decision to fight. The war, by interrupting processes of development in many countries and demanding popular sacrifices in all, has rendered the necessity of social reforms more apparent and social claims more imperative. All this does not make the conflict revolutionary.

Another assertion, related to the first and equally familiar, deserves more attention. It is the common allegation that this war differs from previous ones in that it is ideological rather than national. Unquestionably it did break out in a Europe seething with ideological controversies and feuds. But the thesis that the war is ideological is, again, ambiguous and, unless explained and qualified, can only serve to confuse post-war issues.

An ideological war is a war waged by a nation, groups of nations or parties within a nation, for the purpose of compelling the adherence of others to a creed, or alternatively, of defending that creed against its assailants. A national war is one waged with the object of acquiring further dominions, more territory, sovereignty over other nations, or, alternatively, for the protection of the threatened territory or of independence. Of course, in so far as most nations have beliefs, institutions, principles, and habits of living which constitute their ideological atmosphere, any national war is also ideological since it implies the defence, or the enforcement on others, of such beliefs and ideas as are part of a people's patrimony. Only a conflict the object of which would be the seizure of a point of vantage could be described as purely national. Conversely, only those conflicts the sole object of which would be the change of persuasion of the vanquished could strictly be described as ideological. There have, in point of fact, been very few wars in the past in which ideological aims did not screen national ambitions or in which national purposes were not furthered by ideological weapons. Even the Crusaders were tempted by temporal acquisitions. Charles V of Habsburg, in his wars against France, used the religious weapon along with the Spanish phalanx just as Hitler softened enemy resistance to his armoured divisions by ideological propaganda. Prussia in the eighteenth century owed her rise to the birth of the Prussian state through the ideological League of Augsburg. England's defence of freedom during the Napoleonic wars allowed her to make incidental profits, while Napoleon bore on his banners the mottoes of that very freedom which he had virtually suppressed in revolutionary France.

What is revolutionary in the present conflict is the extent of physical and moral destruction which it has caused and which will compel many nations to make a fresh start, not because of revolutionary ideals but from sheer necessity. Its ideological aspect comes from the fact that the belligerents had radically antagonistic ways of living. But so have Russia and England. Yet this did not prevent their alliance, and from 1941 onwards their differences were forgotten in their common cause. The enemy, on the other hand, accentuated these same differences. It was by placing the conflict on the social ideological plane that he compelled the Allies to try and make an ideological case in their turn. The result could only be unsatisfactory on their side, since the very nature of the West is to be less systematically ideological and to be ethically heterogeneous. Germany's war was not ideological in its final aim. Her purpose was not to convert Poland or France or any other nation to a creed but to acquire territories the snatching of which she would then have justified by the ideological assertion that Europe must be united, that a social revolution would serve unity, and that Germany alone held the key to the future. Ideology entered only as a war-stimulant, as part of the war-machine and as an instrument for the consolidation of war conquests. To suggest that Germany's war was ideological in purpose because she used ideology in that way is like saying that because the German army used tanks to defeat its enemies its aim was to generalize the use of tanks in Europe. National Socialism, as 'philosophically' expounded by Germany, is not even new: it amounts to little more than a combination of racial notions borrowed from Gobineau, anti-individualistic theories blending together bits of Marxism and Teutonic herd-instincts and party rule borrowed from Lenin. Only in Germany could such a patch-work be called philosophy.

On the other hand the Powers who fight Germany have their own diverse views on community life and progress, views differing very widely from Washington to Moscow, and it is in fact chiefly on notions called 'ideological' that they differ most. For each nation the truly ideological element was the mere fact that each was defending its own way of life and the right of its allies to their respective ways of life. Each was protecting, not its perfection, which exists nowhere, but its right to remain perfectible according to its own lights.

It is the sum total of these diverse outlooks, of these variegated régimes, all with their faults, but all capable of improvement, which represents civilization. And it is the will to impose uniformity or human subservience which represents barbarism. Abstract ideas do not rest on a void; their fate is linked with that of physical civilizations capable of harbouring, defending and promoting them; their richness depends on many contributions. The German conception is even more idiotic than brutal, for a world dominated by a single nation, itself dominated by a single brain, is in the long run sheer abstract nonsense. In June 1940 that was not very far from coming to pass in Europe. It might not have stood for long but its achievement followed by the disruption of the German order would have meant the wrecking of European civilization. What would have been left of our ideologies if the Battle of Britain had been lost? And who can therefore oppose it to the allegedly 'inferior' pursuit of national salvation and the allegedly 'superior' prosecution of an ideological war? Nor can it be said that the stimulus to England's struggle then was ideological. She defended herself as she was, championed the Europe that then was; she was saved by her permanent naval tradition, her new-found air tradition, her stubborn traditional determination not to be bullied, and her Conservative Prime Minister. She was not saved by a belief in revolutionary war aims or in any ideology save a hatred of Nazi Germany which would probably have been as effective had Germany been Imperial, Bismarckian, Communist, Republican, or ruled by an Anglican divine unexpectedly adopted by the Germans. The capital lesson to be learnt is the fact, proved by the temporary success of German propaganda, that social injustice in a nation renders it vulnerable in time of war, because social preoccupations are in the foreground in the twentieth century, as were national preoccupations in the nineteenth and religious in the sixteenth and seventeenth. But they are part of the human problem and not, as gregarious communities would have it, the whole problem. It is not for these that Europe has fought. Ideologically and otherwise we know what we fight against. We are not all agreed, save in vague terms, on what we are fighting for. So the division between purely ideological camps, though tempting, is hard to clarify, while the division between nations according to a greater or lesser tendency to aggression or their traditional habits and ways of life is comparatively clear.

The real difference between this war and practically all wars recorded in history is the unprecedented extent of the German national menace. And it is the fact that the German example has shown the world the appalling concentration of power which a single highly populated nation can muster by the process of destroying all individual resistance and thought within itself and turning its whole people into a war machine. Germany had achieved this through National Socialism. But once diversity of judgement and all individual opposition were destroyed within her frontiers any political creed would have produced the same result. In Germany Communism might have had the same effect. A people that is capable of rising and following its führer blindly on an anti-Bolshevist slogan, then of accepting an alliance with a Communist state, and then of attacking it without notice and without even questioning the motives of its leader, is a public danger, whatever creed produces that condition of somnambulism. Given such a people and such a power, the Hitlerite menace was more far-reaching than any previous threat in history. It was not aimed at certain territories, or at certain people but at all territories and all people. And the threat differed from others not only in magnitude but also in kind. It was in the absolute sense of the word a threat of extermination. The Western Powers in 1939 were fighting on unequal terms not only because they lacked planes and tanks but because the full extent and import of the German war aims could not be conceived by civilized minds. Indeed not even the German victories in Poland and in the West brought about that realization. It was only the Russian campaign that truly revealed the colossal proportions of the German machine and its ruthless purpose of extermination.

And because the main German weapons and sources of strength were the ability to enforce subservience, because the success of Germany depended on popular readiness to accept herd philosophies, the West in the broadest sense, individualistic and ungregarious, was the first to react, however inadequately, against the menace, and was undoubtedly Germany's chief enemy.

War and peace aims must be based primarily on the lessons of the past and on the underlying realities of the situation, and broadly speaking, Europe's aims are her own reorganization and her own protection. In both England has an immense part to play, but she can only do so if she knows what she wants to be as clearly as what she wants to do. In the past she has followed by various means a policy of balance of power. She followed this policy even up to the last war, though under another name, which sounded better morally, calling herself an arbitrator. This has now become impossible, first, because the post-war situation of Europe and the world will not allow for uncertain policies hesitating between one course and another, but, above all, because if England pursues a policy of balance of power or arbitration, she will lose the allegiance and friendship of those nations whom her lonely struggle has brought nearer to her. From the Continental point of view, England must choose between being European and not being European. 'To be or not to be,' that is the crucial question. To be European half-heartedly, and then to withdraw from European responsibilities or associations when other pursuits take precedence over Continental ones, will be the surest way to alienate the Continent. The result will be that all those nations of the Continent who need English help, as England needs theirs, in order to create a Europe free from German or other mass domination, will be weakened in their struggle for the maintenance of a diverse and truly Western civilization. The Big Four policy is but another and more distasteful version of the policy of arbitration, of a policy which has given point to the arguments of German propagandists, namely, that England only took from Europe what suited her book. Continental nations expect much of her. It is for her to give an answer of the same kind and quality as that which she gave in June 1940. Once that answer is given, once it is clear that she lives truly in Europe, her words and her deeds will carry their full weight. That is the first prerequisite of her contribution to the rebuilding of Europe.

In the second place, if civilization is to be saved, and its salvation is by no means a foregone conclusion even when victory is won, we must first defend that civilization where it exists and in those countries whence it can best be spread. Western civilization is not geographically confined to the west of Europe. In Scandinavia, in Switzerland, in Greece, in Czechoslovakia, the principles we have tried to defend were accepted and practised before the war. It is through the countries which preserve these principles as a reality that continuity must be asserted; it is from their firm platforms that we can start rebuilding. If we wish to defend what in the West we call democracy, it is where democracy is first workable that it must be protected; and protected not by the nauseating propaganda which is one of the curses of our age, but by native culture on the one hand and political support on the other. There are small nations of Europe who had evolved a finely democratic way of living but who have since been abandoned to the mercy of the conqueror. There are others where democracy could ultimately have succeeded, but which were left to despair and eventually yielded to German pressure and turned totalitarian because we could not back them. Many people seem chiefly concerned with the future status of Germany and the greater or lesser degree of generosity with which she should be treated. They seem less interested in the fate of Norway, Denmark, Czechoslovakia, Greece, Poland, Yugoslavia, Holland and Belgium—all of which, in varying degrees, could have served to bring about the kind of Europe we wanted if we had helped them to do so, and if before the war there had been a European ethos as there has been one struggling to be born under German occupation; if we had tried to protect free conceptions where they existed, instead of believing that they could miraculously spread in places where they had no foundations and no roots.

As to the protection of Europe, there, again, the lesson must be drawn from experience rather than imagined by the process of wishful thinking. Europe must be protected first against Germany, against Germany with her proved tendency to aggression. She must be protected in particular against Germany as the most favourable playground for ideologies of uniformity and for dogmatic mobilization, and in general against the kind of danger which though it first appeared in Germany may re-emerge anywhere in Europe or Asia: that of a nation entirely devoted to and subjugated by a dogma which turns a people into a herd marshalled for ideological war by any would-be dictator. For this war, on our side, is not ideological but, if it is anything more than a war of self-defence, it is an anti-ideological war fought against the exploitation and abuse of ideas by mass propaganda. In many countries, indeed in many of the countries which are genuinely democratic and liberal in outlook, the anti-ideological war may yet have to be fought again after victory has been won in the field, for 'the evil that men do lives after them'. Alone of the main Western powers of Europe, England has retained the continuity of her institutions and ways of life and is still on her feet, ethically as well as physically. Her first task is to decide whether she will follow the European path, and follow it decidedly. Her second should be to remain her diverse self in the midst of the chaos of ideas which will follow the European war. For it is as such that she can offer the greatest contribution to the moral and cultural defence of Europe.

Her foreign policy has yet to be framed. It is now little more than a projection of her war strategy, one that lays stress on her relations with foreign nations according to their respective strength and usefulness as partners in the war, whether in Europe or in the Far East. To consolidate these relations after the war is no doubt an essential aim of British policy. But such things as her allegiance to the West and her future relations with France go far deeper than what is called foreign policy. They are part of the very 'raison d'être' of England in that civilized world which she has so well served. They are facts of nature, of a nature which is not merely geographical and physical, but also moral and traditional. What she strove to protect may be as imperilled a few years hence as it was in 1940. For England to lie hesitatingly at anchor on the edge of Europe would mean that she was relaxing in her struggle at the very moment when she was most needed, and when she herself needed most. The way of life which she succeeded in retaining, when kindred nations were overcome, forms part of the flare path of the Western Europe of to-morrow. Her own lights must not be put out just when these kindred nations are beginning to light theirs after years of darkness, for the path is still full of perils.

INDEX

DATE DUE

SEP 29 '69			
OCT 19 '72			
FEB 29 '73			
MR 23 '77			
F			
SE 18 '80			
GAYLORD			PRINTED IN U.S.A.